p. 156.

WOMEN OF ISRAEL
BY
GRACE AGUILAR.
D. APPLETON AND COMPANY

THE

WOMEN OF ISRAEL.

BY

GRACE AGUILAR,

AUTHOR OF "WOMAN'S FRIENDSHIP," "MOTHER'S RECOMPENSE." "VALE OF CEDARS," ETC.

VOL. I.

NEW YORK:
D. APPLETON AND COMPANY,
549 & 551 BROADWAY.
1872.

CONTENTS OF VOLUME I.

THE

WOMEN OF ISRAEL.

INTRODUCTION.

Among the many valuable works relative to woman's capabilities, influence, and mission, which in the present age are so continually appearing, one still seems wanting. The field has, indeed, been entered; detached notices of the women of Israel the female biography of Scripture, have often formed interesting portions of those works, where woman is the subject; but all the fruit has not been gathered: much yet remains, which, thrown together, would form a history as instructive as interesting, as full of warning as example, and tending to lead our female youth to the sacred volume, not only as their guide to duty, their support in toil, their comfort in affliction, but as a true and perfect mirror of themselves.

To desert the Bible for its commentators; never to peruse its pages without notes of explanation: to regard it as a work which of itself is incomprehensible, is, indeed, a practice as hurtful as injudicious. Sent as a message of love to our own souls, as written and addressed, not to nations alone, but as the voice of God to individuals—whispering to each of us that which we most need; thus it is we should first regard and venerate it. This accomplished, works tending to elucidate its glorious and consoling truths, to make manifest its simple lessons of character, as well as precept; to bring yet closer to the youthful and aspiring heart, the poetry, the beauty, the eloquence, the appealing tenderness of its sacred pages, may prove of essential service. In this hope, to bring clearly before the women of Israel all that they owe to the word of God, all that it may still be to them, the present task is undertaken.

We are far from asserting that this has not been attempted, and for the larger portion of the sex, accomplished before. Religion is the foundation and mainspring of every work which has been written for the use and improvement of woman. Female biographers of scripture have, we believe, often appeared; though the characters of the Old Testament are so briefly and imperfectly sketched, compared to those of the New, that but little pleasure or improvement could be derived from their perusal. Yet still, with the writings of Sandford, Ellis, and Hamilton before us, each exhibiting its authoress so earnest, so eloquent in her cause, with "woman's mission" marked so simply, yet so forcibly, in the little volume of that name, has not woman of every race, and every creed, all sufficient to teach her her duty and herself?

We would say she had; yet for the women of Israel something still more is needed. The authors above mentioned are Christians themselves, and write for the Christian world. Education and nationality compel them to believe that "Christianity is the sole source of female excellence." To Christianity alone they owe their present station in the world: their influence, their equality with man, their spiritual provision in this life, and hopes of immortality in the next. Nay more, that the value and dignity of woman's character would never have been known, but for the religion of Jesus; that pure, loving, self-denying doctrines, were unknown to woman; she knew not even her relation to the Eternal; dared not look upon Him as her Father, Consoler, and Saviour, till the advent of Christianity. We grant that the Gentiles knew it not, till the Bible became more generally known, till the Eternal, in His infinite mercy, permitted a partial knowledge of Himself to spread over the world—alike to prepare the Gentile for that day, when we shall all know Him as He is, and to render the trial of His people's faith and constancy yet more terribly severe. We feel neither anger nor uncharitableness towards those who would thus deny to Israel those very privileges which were ours, ages before they became theirs; and which, in fact, have descended from us to them. Yet we cannot pass such assertion unanswered, lest from the very worth and popularity of those works in which it is promulgated, the young and thoughtless daughter of Israel may believe it really has foundation, and look no further than the page she reads.

How or whence originated the charge that the law of Moses

sank the Hebrew female to the lowest state of degradation, placed her on a level with slaves or heathens, and denied her all mental and spiritual enjoyment, we know not: yet certain it is that this most extraordinary and unfounded idea obtains credence even in this enlightened age. The word of God at once proves its falsity; for it is impossible to read the Mosaic law without the true and touching conviction, that the female Hebrew was even more an object of the tender and soothing care of the Eternal than the male. The thanksgiving in the Israelite morning prayer, on which so much stress is laid, as a proof how little woman is regarded, is but a false and foolish reasoning on the subject; almost, in truth, too trivial for regard.

The very first consequence of woman's sin was to render her in physical and mental strength, inferior to man; to expose her to suffering more continued, and more acute; to prevent her obtaining those honors and emoluments of which man thinks so much; to restrain her path to a more lowly and domestic, though not a less hallowed sphere; and, all this considered, neither scorn towards the sex, nor too much haughtiness for themselves, actuate the thanksgiving which by our opponents is brought forward against us. It was but one of those blessings in which the pious Israelite thanks God for all things, demanding neither notice nor reproof.

To the Gentile assertion that the Talmud has originated the above-mentioned blessing, and commanded or inculcated the moral and mental degradation of woman, we reply that even if it do, which we do not believe it does, its commands are wholly disregarded, and its abolishment is not needed to raise the Hebrew female to that station assigned her in the word of God, and which through many centuries she has been permitted, without reproof or question, to enjoy. The Eternal's provision for her temporal and spiritual happiness is proved in His unalterable word; and therefore no Hebrew can believe that He would issue another law for her degradation and abasement. If, indeed, there are such laws, they must have been compiled at a time when persecution had so brutalized and lowered the intellect of man that he partook the savage barbarity of the nations around him, and of the age in which he lived; when the law of his God had, as a natural consequence, become obscured, and the Hebrew female shared the same rude and savage treatment which was the lot of all the lower classes of women in the feudal ages. The protection, the glory, the civilizing influence of chivalry extended, in its first establishment, but to the baronial classes. We see no proofs of the humanizing and elevating influence of Christianity, either on man or woman, till the reformation opened the BIBLE, the whole BIBLE, to the nations at large; when civilization gradually followed. If, then, the situation of even Christian women was so uncertain, and but too often so degraded, for nearly fourteen centuries after the advent of Jesus, who his followers declare was the first to teach them their real position—was it very remarkable that the vilified and persecuted Hebrew should have in a degree forgotten his nationality, his immortal and glorious heritage, and shared in the barbarity around him? Granting for the moment that such was the case (but we by no means believe it was), if the degradation, mentally and morally, of the Hebrew female, ever did become part of the Jewish law, it was when man was equally degraded, and the blessed word of God hid from him.

The situation of many of the Hebrews at the present day proves this. In but too many parts of the world the Israelites are still the subjects of scorn, hatred, and persecution: and their condition is, in consequence, the lowest and most awfully degraded in the scale of man. But it is not to woman that degradation and slavery are confined; as, were it a portion of the law of Moses, would inevitably be the case. It is the consequence of cruelty, of abasement in social treatment; yet even here, when mind, principle, honor, all seem overthrown from such brutalizing influence, the affections retain their power.

Whatever of spiritual hope, of human privileges, the word of God bestows on man, and to which the mind, darkened and despairing from the horrors of persecution, may yet be open, are shared by the Hebrew wife, and imparted by the Hebrew mother.

Were it a portion of the law of Moses to enslave and degrade us, how is it that we do not see this law adhered to and obeyed, as well as others claiming the same divine origin? Neither Christianity nor civilization would alter or improve our condition, were it indeed such as it has been represented. The Hebrew ever loves, protects, and reverences his female relative; and if, indeed, he do not—if he deny her all share in immortality, and, in consequence, thinks she has no need of religion now, nor hope hereafter, it is because the remnants of barbarism, ignorance, and superstition remain, to have blinded both his spiritual and mental eye; yet whatever he may be accused of believing, his acts deny the belief. Why is he so anxious that his wife and daughters should adhere to every law, attend to every precept which he believes the law of God? If they have no soul, no portion in the world to come, it surely cannot signify how they act, or what they believe in this? Why are they blotted from the minds and hearts of their relatives, if, as it may sometimes happen, they intermarry with the stranger? If they have no spiritual responsibility, no claim, no part in the law of God, why should they be blamed and shunned, if they desert it for another? But it is idle to follow the argument further. The charge is either altogether false, or based on such contradictory and groundless report, as to render it of little consequence, save as it affects us in the eyes of those who uphold, that till Christianity was promulgated woman knew not her own station either towards God or man.

Simply to deny this assertion, to affirm, that instead of degrading and enslaving, the Jewish law exalted, protected, and provided for woman, teaching her to look up to God, not as a severe master and awful judge, but as her Father, her Defender, her Deliverer when oppressed, her Witness in times of false accusation, her Consoler and Protector when fatherless, widowed—aye, as the tender and loving Sovereign, who spared the young bride the anguish of separation from her beloved: merely to affirm, that with such laws woman was equally a subject of divine love as she is now, would not avail us much. The women of Israel must themselves arise, and prove the truth of what we urge—by their own conduct, their own belief, their own ever-acting and ever-influencing religion, prove without doubt or question that we need not Christianity to teach us our mission—prove that our duties, our privileges, were assigned us from the very beginning of the world, confirmed by that law to which we still adhere, and will adhere for ever, and manifested by the whole history of the Bible.

A new era is dawning for us. Persecution and intolerance have in so many lands ceased to predominate, that Israel may once more breathe in freedom; the law need no longer be preached in darkness, and obeyed in secret; the voice of man need no longer be the vehicle of instruction from father to son, mingling with it unconsciously human opinions, till those opinions could scarcely be severed from the word of God, and by degrees so dimmed its lustre, as to render its comprehension an obscure and painful task. This need no longer be. The Bible may be perused in freedom; the law may be publicly explained and preached to all who will attend. A spirit of inquiry, of patriotism, of earnestness in seeking to know the Lord, and obey Him according to His word, is springing up in lieu of the stagnating darkness, the appalling indifference, which had reigned so long. Persecution never decreased our numbers. As the bush which burned without consuming, so was Israel in those blood-red ages of intolerance and butchery. In the very heart of the most catholic kingdom—amongst her senate, her warriors, her artisans—aye, even her monks and clergy—Judaism lurked unconsumed by the fires ever burning round. The spirit was ever awake and active, ready to endure martyrdom, but not to forswear that God whose witnesses they were. Persecution was a crisis in our History; prosperity the reaction; and from that reaction the natural consequence was the gradual rise, growth, and influence of indifference. Indifference, however, has but its appointed time: and Israel is springing up once more the stronger, nobler, more spiritually enlightened, from his long and waveless sleep. Free to assert their right as immortal children of the living God, let not the women of Israel be backward in proving they, too, have a Rock of Strength, a Refuge of Love; that they, too, have a station to uphold, and a "mission" to perform, not alone as daughters, wives, and mothers, but as witnesses of that faith which first raised, cherished, and defended them—witnesses of that God who has called them His, and who has so repeatedly sanctified the emotions peculiar to their sex, by graciously comparing the love he bears us, as yet deeper than a mother's for her child, a wife's for her husband, having compassion for his people, as on a "woman forsaken and grieved in spirit." "Can a woman forget her sucking child, that she should not have compassion on the son of her travail; yea, she may forget, yet will I not forget thee." "As a mother comforteth her children, so will I comfort thee."

Were not these relations holy and sanctified in the sight of the Lord, would He use them as figurative of His long suffering love? Many terms, similar to those above quoted, prove, without a shadow of doubt, the tender compassion with which He regarded woman long before He used such terms to figure His compassionating love towards Israel, when sinfulness called forth His long averted wrath.

Let us then endeavor to convince the nations of the high privileges we enjoy, in common with our fathers, brothers, and husbands, as the first-born of the Lord, by the peculiar sanctity, spirituality, and inexpressible consolation of our belief. Let us not, as women of Israel, be content with the mere performance of domestic, social, and individual duties, but vivify and lighten them by the rays of eternal love and immortal hope, which beam upon us from the pages of the Bible. A religion of love is indeed necessary to woman, yet more so than to man. Even in her happiest lot there must be a void in her heart, which ever-acting piety alone can fill; and to her whose portion is to suffer, whose lot is lonely, O what misery must be hers, unless she can lean upon her God, and draw from His word the blessed conviction that His love, His tenderness, are hers, far beyond the feeble conception of earth; and that whatever she may endure, however unknown to or scorned by man, it is known to Him who smites but in love, and has mercy even while He smites.

To realize this blessed conviction, the Bible must become indeed the book of life to the female descendants of that nation whose earliest history it so vividly records; and be regarded, not as a merely political or religious history, but as the voice of God speaking to each individual, giving strength to the weak, encouragement to the desponding, endurance to the patient, justice to the wronged, and consolation unspeakable as unmeasurable to the afflicted and the mourner. Do we need love? We shall find innumerable verses telling us, that the Lord Himself proclaimed His attribute as "merciful and gracious, long-suffering, abundant in goodness and truth, keeping mercy for thousands, forgiving iniquity and sin;" that "as far as the Heaven is above the earth so great is His mercy, extending from everlasting to everlasting." We have but to read those appeals of the Eternal to Israel, alike in Jeremiah and Isaiah, and many of the minor prophets—and if our hearts be not stone, they must melt before such compassionating love, such appealing tenderness, and feel we cannot be lonely, cannot be unloved, while such deep changeless love is ours. Do we need sympathy? Shall we not find it in words similar to these, "In all their afflictions He was afflicted, and the angel of His presence saved them? In His love and in

His pity He redeemed them, and He bare them, and carried them all the days of old." Do we need patience and strength? Shall we not exercise it, when we have the precious promise, "*Wait* on the Lord, be of good courage, and He shall strengthen thine heart?" Shall we droop and grieve beneath the wrongs and false judgments of short-sighted man, when we are told the ways of God are not those of man—that He knoweth our frame, and readeth our thoughts—that not a bodily or mental pang is ours which He does not know and compassionate—aye, and in His own good time will heal!

To throw together all those verses which confirm and prove the loving-tenderness borne towards us by the Eternal, would be an endless and a useless task. We can but point to that ever-flowing fount of healing waters, and assure those who have once really tasted, and will persevere in the heavenly draught, that it will never fail them, never change its properties, but each year sink deeper and deeper into their souls, till at length it becomes indeed all they need; and they themselves will cling to it, despite of occasional doubt and darkness, inseparable from our souls while denizens of earth.

Nor is it only the verses containing such gracious promises, which will yield us comfort and assistance. We may glean the glad tidings of Eternal Love from the biographies and narratives with which the sacred book abounds—there may be some meek and lowly spirits amongst the female youth of Israel, who would gladly clasp the strength and guidance which we proffer them from the Bible, could they believe that God, the great, the almighty, the tremendous and awful Being (as which they have perhaps been accustomed to regard Him), can have love and pity for themselves, or give comfort and aid to trials, which appear even too trivial to ask, or to excite the sympathy of man. We would lead them to look earnestly and believingly into the history of every woman in the Bible, and trace there the influence of God's holy and compassionating love. We are not indeed placed as the women of Israel before their dispersion, or as the wives of the patriarchs before the law was given; yet their God is our God. It was not to a race so perfect, so gifted, so hallowed, as to be free from all the present faults and failings of the sex that the Lord vouchsafed His love. No, it was to woman, even as she is now. The women of the Bible are but mirrors of ourselves. And if the Eternal, in His infinite mercy, extended love, compassion, forbearance, and forgiveness unto them, we may believe He extends them equally unto us, and draw comfort, and encouragement, and faith from the biographies we read.

In a work entitled "The Women of Israel," some apology, perhaps, is necessary for commencing with the wives of the patriarchs, who may not lay claim to such holy appellation. Yet, as the chosen and beloved partners of those favored of God, from whom Israel traces his descent, and for the sake of whose faith and righteousness we were selected and chosen as a peculiar people, and the law given to be our guide through earth to heaven, we cannot consider our history complete without them; more particularly as their lives are so intimately blended with their husbands; and that in them, even yet more vividly than at a later period, we may trace the Lord's dealings with His female children, and derive from them alike warning and support.

Eve, indeed, may not have such national claim, but if we believe that her history, as every other part of Genesis, was penned by the same inspired law-giver—that Moses recorded only that which had been—we shall find much, indeed, to repay us for lingering a while on her character and life. To the scepticism, the cavils, the doubts, and (but too often unhappily) the direct unbelief in the Mosaic account of the first disobedience of man, we give no heed whatever. We must either believe in the Pentateuch or deny it. There can be no intermediate path. The whole must be true or none. It is not because much may appear obscure, or even contradictory in the sacred narrative, that we are to pronounce it false, or mystify and poetize it as an allegory.

We are simply to believe, and endeavor to act on that belief. So much is there ever passing around us that we cannot solve; our thoughts, in their furthest flight, are so soon checked, can penetrate so little into the wonders of man and nature, that it appears extraordinary how man can doubt and deny, because he cannot understand. In this case, however—the history of Eve—truth is so simple and clear, that we know not how it can supply such an endless fund of argument and doubt. To remove this groundless disbelief, to endeavor to render the narrative clear and simple to the female youth of Israel, and, even through Eve's sad yet consoling history, to prove to them the deep love borne towards us from the very first of our creation by our gracious God, must be our apology, if apology be needed, for commencing a work entitled "The Women of Israel," with our general mother.

Beginning, then, from the very beginning, some degree of order is requisite in the arrangement of our subject. Our aim being to evince to the nations and to our own hearts, the privileges, alike temporal and eternal, which were ours from the very commencement—to prove that we have no need of Christianity, or the examples of the females in the Gospel, to raise us to an equality with man—to demonstrate our duties and secure us consolation here or salvation hereafter—the word of God must be alike our ground-work and our guide. From the past history which that unerring guide presents, our present duties and responsibilities, and our future destiny, will alike be revealed. In a simple biography each life is a sufficient division; but, with the exception of the wives of the patriarchs and one or two more, we have scarcely sufficient notice of individuals to illustrate our design by regarding them separately. There appear, therefore, seven periods in the history of the women of Israel, which demand our attention.

First Period—the Wives of the Patriarchs, including Eve, Sarah, Rebecca, Leah, and Rachel.

Second Period—the Exodus, and the Law considered as affecting the condition and establishing the privileges of women.

Third Period—Women of Israel between the establishment of the Law and the authority of the Kings, comprising sketches of Miriam, Deborah, the wife of Manoah, Naomi, and Hannah.

Fourth Period—Women of Israel during the continuation of the Kingdom, comprising, amongst other sketches, Michal, Abigail, the Shunammite, and Huldah.

Fifth Period—Babylonish Captivity, including the life of Esther.

Sixth Period—the War and Dispersion, and their effects on the condition and privileges of women in Israel.

Seventh Period—Women of Israel in the Present time, as influenced by the history of the Past.

For five of these periods, then, we perceive the word of God can be our only guide, and this at once marks our history as sacred, not profane. If, therefore, there should be parts which resemble more a religious essay than female biography, we reply, that to inculcate religion, the vital spirit of religion, is the sole intention of these pages.

We wish to infuse the spirit of truth and patriotism, of nationality, and yet of universal love, in the hearts of the young daughters of Israel; and we know of no means more likely, under the divine blessing, to accomplish this, than to bring before them, as vividly and engagingly as we can, the never-ending love, the compassionating tenderness, the unchanging sympathy, alike in our joys and in our sorrows, manifested by the Eternal so touchingly and simply in the history of our female ancestors,—to lead them to know Him and love Him, not only through the repeated promises, but through the narratives of His word, and to glory in those high privileges which as children, retainers and promulgators of His holy law, are ours, over and above every other nation, past or present, in the history of the world!

FIRST PERIOD.

THE WIVES OF THE PATRIARCHS.

CHAPTER I.

EVE.

THE last and mightiest work of creation was completed. Man, in his angelic and immortal beauty, stood erect and perfect, fresh from the hand of his Creator; lord and possessor of the new formed world. Though formed of the dust, earth had not, as in the case of the inferior animals, brought him forth. Destined from the first to be made in the image of God, that is, to possess an emanation of the spiritual essence, and so become a living and immortal soul—the shrine of so glorious a possession was created by God himself. "And God created him," He did not "call him forth."

For man, the beautiful creation already wrought, was not sufficient; and "He planted a garden eastward in Eden, filling it with every tree that was pleasant for the sight, and good for food"—animate and inanimate creation brought together by the Eternal in one beautiful and perfect whole. Nor was this all: endowed with capabilities of love, happiness, and wisdom, as much above the other animals as the angelic nature is to man, still he needed more for the perfection of his felicity; and God in his infinite mercy provided for that want.

"It is not good for man to be alone," the Eternal said; "I will make him a help meet for him." And therefore woman was created, and brought unto man, who received her as the Eternal in His mercy had ordained, a being beloved above all others, whose gentler qualities and endearing sympathy should soften his rougher and prouder nature, and "help" him in all things "meet" for an immortal being.

The whole creation had had its origin in that Omnific Love which CREATED TO ENJOY,—called out of darkness and chaos a world teeming with life and beauty, that innumerable sources of happiness might spring forth from what had before been naught; but woman's creation was a still greater manifestation of love than all which had gone before it. She was created, not only to feel happiness herself, but to *make it for others;* and if that was the design of her existence in Eden, how deeply should we feel the solemn truth, that it is equally so now, and that woman has a higher and holier mission than the mere pursuit of pleasure and individual enjoyment; that to flutter through life without one serious thought or aim, without a dream beyond the present moment, without a feeling higher than temporal gratification, or an aspiration rising beyond this world, can never answer the purpose of her divine creation, or make her a help meet for man. Nor is it to wives only this privilege is accorded. Mother or sister, each has equally her appointed duty—to endeavor so to help and influence man, that her more spiritual and unselfish nature shall gradually be infused into him, and, raising him above mere worldly thought and sensual pleasures, compel him to feel that it is not indeed "good for man to be alone," but that woman may still fulfil the office of help and love for which alone she was created.

Although the Mosaic record of man's residence in Paradise is mournfully brief, we have sufficient scriptural authority for lingering a little while on Eve's innocent career. Placed in a garden with every capability of felicity within herself,—nature, meditation, commune with the Almighty in thanksgiving, or with Him direct, through the Voice which revealed the invisible presence, the sweet blessed intercourse of kindred spirits, springing from the love she bore to and received from her husband,—simple and imperfect as such sources of enjoyment may appear, they were more exquisite, more perfect, than we car dream of now.

The spirit which God had breathed within man when he became a living soul, was the likeness or image of God in which "made He man;" and this spirit, or essence, enabled both Adam and Eve to commune in close and beatified intercourse with the glorified Creator whence that essence sprang. No sin could fling its dark shade between the soul and his God; and so deaden spiritual joy. Naught of doubt could stagnate the love which must have been excited in their hearts towards their Father and their God. All *around* and *within* them bore such impress of His hand, as to excite naught but gratitude and devotion. If even now, when once we have realized the love of God and submission to His will—when once we can so put our trust in Him as to give Him "all our heart," and come to Him in sorrow and in joy, convinced that He knows and loves us better than ourselves—we experience a peace, a blessedness no earthly tempests can remove; how thrice blessed must have been the felicity of Eve!

Apart from the spirit which the Eternal gave to lead man to Himself, was the MIND which opened to the creatures formed in His image the inexhaustible resources of wisdom, imagination, knowledge—all that could create that higher kind of happiness, which is synonymous with mental joy. Sources of what is now termed wisdom, that of books and man, were indeed unknown to our first parents; nor did they need them. In the wonders of creation, the tree, the herb, the flower, the gushing rivers, the breezy winds; nay, from the mighty form of the largest beast, to the structure of the tiniest leaf; the flow of the river to the globule of the dew, which watered the face of the whole earth, there was enough to excite and satisfy their mental powers; enough to excite emotions alike of wonder and adoration. Their commune with the angelic messengers of their benevolent Creator, their tidings of Heaven and its hosts, must have excited the highest and purest pleasure of imagination, and so diversified and lightened the mental exercises of wisdom, which the palpable and visible objects of creation so continually call forth.

Nor was spiritual and mental felicity the only portion of Eve—the affections, the impulses of the *heart*, fresh from the creating Hand of Love, had full play—created, as the perfecting finish to man's happiness, beholding him, the lord of all on which she gazed—earth formed to yield him her fruits—water and air, to unite for his refreshment—every animal obeying his authority—instinctively feeling, too, the mighty power of his intellect, the strength of his mind and frame, the deepest reverence must have mingled with, and so perfected, her love. Nor would this acknowledgment tend to degrade woman in the scale of creation. Formed, like man, in the immortal likeness of the Lord, he was his equal in his responsibilities towards God and in the care of his creatures; endowed *equally* with man, but *differently* as to the nature of those endowments. His mission was to protect and guide and have dominion—hers to soothe, bless, persuade to right, and "help" in all things "meet" for immortal beings.

The existence of Eve, then, in her innocence, was, in a word, an existence of love—love towards God and nature and man, which none of the infirmities of our present state could cloud or interrupt. Do we err, then, in saying that, even in the brief record of Scripture, we have sufficient authority for delineating the felicity of our first parents in Eden? And will it not demonstrate appealingly to us, those pleasures which God Himself ordained, and which, even now, might so be cultivated as to bring us happiness, as infinitely superior to the amusements so called as innocence is to sin?

But beautiful as is this picture, we must turn from it to consider feelings and events of a sadly different nature. In the most conspicuous part of Paradise, the Eternal had called forth two trees, differing in their magnificence, perhaps in the halo with which they may have been encircled, as peculiar witnesses of their Creator, from every other in the garden. They were the Tree of Life and the Tree of Knowledge. Of the first so little is known that we are justified in supposing the intention of its existence was frustrated by the disobedience of man; a conjecture founded on the solemn fact, that as the Lord created not one thing in vain, that tree must also have had its use and intention, and from the words which follow at a later period, "Lest man put forth his hand, and take also of the tree of life, and eat and live for ever," we are quite authorized to suppose it possessed some qualities yet mightier than the Tree of Knowledge, with which its taste would have gifted man, had he not by rebellion frustrated the beneficent design of his Creator, and forfeited the privileges which might have been his own.

Of the Tree of Knowledge, its intention and its uses, we have sufficient information. The Eternal knew the nature of the creatures He had formed; that it was but an easy and slender trial of obedience and of love, if they had no temptation to rebel or disobey. Though subject to His sway, though deriving existence from His hand, and enjoying life and all its varied sources of felicity from the same infinite love, yet the Eternal, in

His wisdom and His justice, had endowed them with the power of free-will; of listening to and following, or struggling with and conquering, the seeds of corruption, which from their earthly shell were inherent, though as yet kept so completely under subjection from the divine and purifying nature of the soul, that, until he was tried, man himself was scarcely sensible of their existence. To have guarded him jealously from every temptation —to have surrounded him with naught but sources of pleasure and enjoyment, and so called forth only the grateful and adoring faculties of the spirit, was not according to that divine and perfect economy of love and justice which characterized the dealings of the Creator with his creatures. It was deeper, dearer love, to permit man to win his immortality, his eternal innocence, than to bestow them upon him unsought, and therefore little valued. They could be guilty of no crime in the world's parlance, so termed. They were the sole possessors of the newly created earth: in daily commune with their creator, and therefore in neither idolatry, blasphemy, Sabbath-breaking, dishonoring of parents, murder, adultery, theft, false-witness, or covetousness, could they sin. God knew that all the crimes which *might* devastate the earth would spring from one alone, DISOBEDIENCE; and therefore was it that His infinite wisdom ordained that the trial of man's love, and faith, and virtue, should simply be, obedience to His will.

"And the Lord God commanded the man, saying, of every tree of the garden thou mayst freely eat; but of the tree of the knowledge of the good and evil thou shalt not eat; for in the day that thou eatest thereof, thou shalt surely die." Whether this threatened chastisement was robed in mystery, or that Adam had beheld death in the inferior animals (for Holy Writ gives us no authority for believing that even they knew not death till after the fall), and so could have some idea of what he would become, even as a clod of the earth if he disobeyed, we may not here determine; suffice it, that the Eternal was too merciful, too just, to threaten His creature with a chastisement for disobedience which he could not comprehend.

Beautiful to look upon, and exquisite in its fragrance, we may imagine the Tree of Knowledge extending its rich foliage and tempting fruit in the most conspicuous part of the garden, no doubt frequently attracting the admiration of Adam and Eve, perhaps exciting wishes, which the spirit within them had as yet power to effectually banish, or entirely subdue. Alone, unprotected by the sterner, firmer qualities of her husband, Eve had walked forth, secure in her own innocence, in the consciousness of love lingering within, and all around her;—the young animals gambolling about her, calling forth her caresses and her smile—the little birds springing from tree to tree in joyous greeting, or nestling in her bosom without one touch of fear—the gorgeous flowers, in all their glowing robes and exquisite fragrance, clustering richly around her—the very buds seeming to look up into her sweet loving face, to reflect increase of beauty from the gaze, so may our fancy picture her, as she neared that tree under whose fair branches so much of misery lurked. Coiled at its root, or twisted in rainbow-colored folds around its trunk, lay the serpent, "who was more subtle than any beast of the field which the Lord God had made." And he said unto the woman, "Yea, hath God said, Ye shall not eat of every tree in the garden? And the woman said, We may eat of the fruit of the trees of the garden, but of the fruit of the tree which is in the midst of the garden, God hath said, Ye shall not eat of it, neither shall ye touch it, lest ye die. And the serpent said unto the woman, Ye shall not surely die, for God doth know, that in the day ye eat thereof, then your eyes shall be opened, and ye shall be as gods, knowing good and evil. And when the woman saw that the tree was good for food, and it was pleasant to the eyes, and a tree to be desired to make one wise, she took of the fruit thereof, and did eat;" and she gave also unto her husband with her, and he did eat.

Such are the brief, yet emphatic words in which the inspired prophet of the Lord detailed those incidents on which the whole after-history of the world is founded—the mournful detail of that first sin, from which every other sprang, DISOBEDIENCE. Of the various speculations and opinions concerning the instrumentality of the serpent we shall take no heed, save the humble endeavor to reconcile the ways of the Lord. He *permitted* the trial, but He *commanded* not the evil interposition of the subtlest of His creatures, the serpent, any more than He *commanded* the subtlety of Jacob in obtaining his father's blessing. Both events were permitted to take place; but the evil means of their accomplishment were NOT of the LORD, and consequently their agents were both subject to His displeasure, and condemned to punishment and wrath.

In one brief hour, the whole nature of Eve was changed—the seeds of frailty, of whose very existence she had been scarcely conscious before, sprang up into influencing poison. Curiosity, presumption, the overweening trust in her own strength, the desire to act alone, independent of all control—to become greater, wiser, higher than the scale of being, than the station in which God's love had placed her—discontent—scorn of the blessings which a moment before had seemed so precious, simply because imagination portrayed others more alluring—attracted by novelty, beauty, those idol shrines at which woman so often sacrifices her better, her immortal self—such (and are they not the characteristics of woman, even as she is now?)—such were the emotions excited by the wily tempter, through whose baneful influence she fell. Where, at that moment, was the voice of the spirit, warning her of the God she disobeyed? Where the whisper of the mind, telling her that the sources of wisdom, of knowledge, already open, were the purest and the best? Where the fond tones of the heart, urging her to seek the protection, the counsel, the support, of her earthly lord? Hushed, drowned, in the wild tumult of new and terrible excitement of feelings, whose very novelty fascinated and held her chained. The voice of the tempter was in her ear. Sight and smell were filled with the exquisite branch, the delicious fragrance; and if such were revealed, what must be its taste and touch, when to pluck and eat would make her as gods, knowing good and evil? Weak, frail, unguarded, for the still small voice of the soul was lost in that hour's tempest, was it marvel that she fell? Could she have done otherwise? The bulwark of FAITH was shivered, her heart was open and defenceless—she was alone, alone, for even the guardian within, if not fled, was silent. The God of infinite love and compassion beheld, but approached not; and wherefore? If He permitted, ordained, why did He punish? Oh, had the voice of his creature called on Him in that terrible hour; had but the faintest cry ascended for help, for strength, for mercy; had but the struggling murmur arisen, "Father, thy words are *truth*, let me but *believe*," strength, help, faith, would have poured their reviving rays into her sinking soul, and she had been saved—saved for immortality, saved to glorify her God! It was not that she had not the power so to pray. Free-will was her own—to obey, or disobey—to adhere, or to rebel. Of herself, indeed, she could not have resisted; but she had equal power to call upon the Lord, as to listen to the tempter. According to the path she chose, would have been the issue. Infinite, measureless, as is the love of the Eternal, yet how dare we believe He will grant us help and strength, unless they are implored? How dare we believe He will come forward to our aid, if we stand forth in our own strength, as if we needed naught; nay, through presumption, arrogance, self-righteousness, rebel against, and defy Him? He had said, "Eat not of the tree of knowledge, for on the day thou eatest thereof thou shalt surely die." He had not *commanded* only, though that should have been sufficient from a loving Father to his children; but the command was enforced with a warning, that love should be strengthened by reverential fear. He had given the power to resist temptation, by CALLING UPON HIM: but if that power were trampled upon and utterly disregarded; and the creature of His hand, whose whole existence, felicity, strength, wisdom, had their being but in Him, so depended upon *herself*, as to be satisfied with her own strength, believing it was in her power to become as a god, and so defying Him, is it contradiction to assert, that the All-wise, All-merciful, All-JUST, permitted, and yet punished? Surely, surely, there is not one portion of this mournful history, which, on mature consideration, will be found irreconcilable with the attributes of the Eternal, or with His dealings with His creatures.

"She took of the fruit thereof, and did eat." For a brief interval, we may suppose, the tumult within, the struggle between virtue and vice, innocence and guilt, was stilled in a strange, fearful intoxication of sinful joy. She had broken through the barrier which, at the words of the serpent, seemed suddenly of iron, it so degraded her by its harshness and injustice. She was INDEPENDENT, had acted by herself, had shaken off all control; and the full tide of guilty pleasure so swept over her soul as to permit for the moment no thought but of herself. But this lasted not long: the reaction came with the one thought—her husband. Terror of his anger was, in all probability, the first emotion—how might she evade it? Fear, notwithstanding her independence, deadened, banished, frustrated every feeling of remorse; repentance, sorrow—all would avail her nothing now; there was but one way to avert her husband's wrath—to make him disobedient as herself. The crime would appear less could another share it. She recollected the influence she possessed;

nay, that she had been created to be his help, to soften his sterner and less yielding nature, and would it fail her now? There was no pause, there could be none; guilt ever hurries on its victims. On her arguments, her persuasions, holy writ is silent. It was enough—"she gave also unto her husband with her, and he did eat."

The crime was consummated. Love itself, the purest, noblest, most influencing of those spiritual blessings vouchsafed to man by his Creator—love, deeper for the creature than the Creator, deeming the gift more precious than the Giver—love it was which to Adam was the tempter, and so converted the richest blessing to the direst curse. The specious offers, the dazzling allurements of the serpent had, perhaps, to his stronger, more steadfast nature, been of no avail. He had no need of ambition, for he was lord over the whole created world. A glance from his eye, a stern rebuke from his lips, had awed even the subtlest of the beasts into silence, and banished him for ever; but strength and firmness fled before the endearing influence of the being, whom, created to perfect his happiness, he loved better than himself. Excuse for his weakness, indeed, there is none; but if such may be the extent of woman's influence (and it is as powerful even now), how fearful is her responsibility, and how deep should be her humility, how fervent her petitions for grace to guide aright!

Not long might the triumph of guilt last. Day declined—the hour of evening came which they were wont so joyfully to welcome, for it brought with it the voice of God. Remorse had come with all its horrors, and now for the first time the extent of their sin stood before them. Terror banished all of love, as all of joy; and when the first sound of the Eternal's voice reached them, they fled in anguish to hide themselves amid the trees of the garden. Vain hope! but proving how all of spirit and of mind was crushed and buried in this first and awful sway of guilt. "And the Lord God called unto Adam, and said unto him, Where art thou? And he said, I heard thy voice in the garden, and I was afraid, because I was naked; and I hid myself. And the Lord God said, Who told thee that thou wast naked? Hast thou eaten of the tree whereof I commanded thee that thou shouldst not eat? And the man said, The woman thou gavest to be with me gave me of the fruit, and I did eat. And the Lord God said unto the woman,

What is this thou hast done? And the woman said, The serpent beguiled me, and I did eat."

Though to Him all was known, yet would not the beneficent, the ever-loving, aye, even at that moment still *loving* God condemn without question, judge without permitting defence. And how upbraiding, how loving the appeal, "What is this that thou hast done?" breathing a Father's sorrowing mercy in the very midst of justly deserved punishment. There was no consuming wrath, no terrifying anger, naught to betray that mighty and awful Being at whose first word might be annihilation.

The Eternal pronounced not sentence without requiring and *waiting* for reply: but what was that reply? Accusation of another, not self-abhorrence and lowly repentance. How fearful was the change wrought in the *heart*, as well as in the spirit of man, by his sin! Where now was his deep love for Eve, that he could say, vainly hoping to exculpate himself, "The woman thou didst give me, she gave me of the fruit, and I did eat?" She had led him by the power of his love into sin; but from that moment her power was at an end, and he cared not to give her up to justice, so he excused himself. How terrible a commencement of her punishment must have been her husband's words to the still loving heart of Eve! It was true she had done as he had said; but was he to be her accuser? And to her were those words of sorrowing compassion said, "What is this that thou hast done?" Hast thou indeed so used the power, the beauty, the influence with which I endowed thee for so different a purpose? She denied it not: she said not one word to justify her sin towards her husband; his words had entered her heart with the first sharp pang which human affection knew, and there was no attempt at defence or evasion;—"The serpent beguiled me, and I did eat." If Adam had stooped to lay the blame of his own weakness upon one whom he had loved, instead of bewailing his own sin, it was no wonder Eve, not yet awakened to what she should have done to avert the temptation, conscious but of increasing misery, thought only of what might seem excuse, "The serpent beguiled me." The Eternal knew she had spoken truth; and, still guided by that mercy and justice which in God alone are so perfectly united, there is no need of "man's ways" to reconcile them, proceeded to pronounce sentence according to the degrees of guilt.

This is not the place to enter into a dissertation on the punishment awarded to the serpent; suffice it that there seems no hidden or allegorical meaning in the inspired historian's simple words. The serpent, as a beast of the field, *beguiled*, and as a beast of the field was *punished*. Nor can an Israelite acknowledge any allusion to, or any necessity for, a crucified and atoning Saviour, in the very simple words, "I will put enmity between thee and the woman, between thy seed and her seed; it shall bruise thy head, and thou shalt bruise his heel." For a Hebrew, the words can only be taken in their purely literal sense. We are particular on this point; because thus early, in the perusal of the sacred Scriptures, the Jewish and Gentile readings differ; and from childish readings of Bible histories by Gentile writers, we may find ourselves giving credence to an assertion for which we have no Mosaic authority, and which, in after years, we would gladly root out from the mystical and contradictory opinions with which it confuses our ideas.

Eve's chastisement was severer than her husband's, and it was just that so it was, for she was the first transgressor. Death, indeed,—that the dust of which the *frame* was composed should return to dust,—was the awful sentence pronounced on both; for such had been threatened from the first if they disobeyed: but during their sojourn upon earth, the sharper and severer trial of pain, of multiplied sorrows, of sinking comparatively in the scale of strength and intellect, of becoming subject to her husband, not, as before, from the sweet obedience of love, but from the sterner mandate of duty; of being exposed, as a mother, to a hundred sources of anguish of which man knows nothing; for his deepest, dearest love for his offspring is not like a mother's, subject to the thousand petty anxieties and cares which, independent of severer maternal trials, fill her heart from the moment she hears the first faint cry of the new-born until death. And these trials *were* Eve's, and they *are* woman's. Man had, indeed, his work; the earth was cursed through his sin, and forbidden to yield her fruit without the severest labor; he was to go forth from the Paradise of innocence and love to till the ground whence he was taken—banished, and for ever.

The voice of their God, for the first time heard in reproachful though still forbearing inquiry, and then in fearful condemnation, removed the blackening veil of sin. The spirit burst from the chains of guilt and sin, and while it bowed in agony and remorse before the Father and the Judge, and acknowledged this awful sentence just, drew them once more to each other. Love was not given only for the happy: to the sorrowing, the repentant, it comes soothing while it softens, seeming, even while it deepens the heavy floods of grief, to banish all of hardness, of selfishness, and of despair. The justice of the Eternal marked the woman as the greater sinner—Adam's further wrath was needless; remorse too told him that, as the stronger, the firmer, he should have resisted her persuasions, that his disobedience was his own sin, not her's; and we may believe that, as weak, trembling, bowed to the very dust, not from the thoughts of her own chastisement so much as from the reflection of what she had hurled upon her husband, for such still is woman, Adam once more received her to his heart, the sharer of his future toils, the soother of his threatened cares, even as she had before been the helpmeet of his joy.

And already Eve needed all of strength and comfort her earthly lord might give. Still remembering mercy, the Eternal clothed them for their departure, endowing them with those faculties of invention, alike for their personal comfort as for the tillage of the ground, for which they had no need in Eden; but the very gift betrayed the bleak and desert world they were about to seek. Could they but remain in the home of their past innocence and joy, the anguish of the present might be sooner healed. Who that thinks a moment of what we now feel in turning from a beloved home, the scene of all our early hopes and joys and love, adorned with all of nature and of art, to seek another, impoverished, and fraught with toil and danger, apart from every object, animate or inanimate, which has twined round our hearts and bound us there,—who, that pictures scenes like these, will refuse our general mother the need of sympathy as she turned from Eden. A change perhaps her sin had wrought even there. The birds flew aloft, trembling to approach that gentle bosom which had before been their resting-place; the young animals fled in terror from her step; and there was that in the changed fierce aspects of the beasts of the field, which caused her heart to sicken with deadly fear. The very flowers hung their heads and drooped when gathered; they could not bear the touch of sin. Yet to that woman's heart Eden was Eden still—her *home*, the receiver of all those varied channels of love which could be spared from her husband; and to turn from it, never to approach it more, and from the consequences of her own act, how deep must have been her agony, how touching its remorse, and how necessary the support of love!

Though Moses, in his brief detail of past events, simply follows the expulsion from Eden by the birth of Cain, we have sufficient authority from the unchangeable attributes of the Eternal, to believe, that the same love which provided Adam and Eve with clothing, directed and blessed their wanderings; and though no longer revealing His gracious presence, as in Eden, yet still inspiring the power of prayer and belief in His constant omnipresence and protection. Their sin had indeed changed their earthly nature,—the *good* had been conquered by the *evil.* It was henceforth a difficult and weary task to subdue the evil inclinations, the proneness to disobedience and self-righteousness. It was a labor of toil and tears to bring the heavenly essence once more even to a faint and disfigured likeness of its God; the voice of the soul, once silenced as it had been, could only be heard after years of watching and prayer. The Eternal, in His prescience, knew this would be, not so much in Adam himself (for repentance and sorrow brought him back through his punishment to holiness and constant commune with his God), but in his offspring. Further and further, as the children of men advanced from their first father—as the tale of creation, of the Eternal's visible presence in Paradise, of all which His love had formed for His favored creature, man, became fainter and fainter in the distance of the past,—so would the likeness of the Lord in which man was made, become more and more effaced, and sin become more and more ascendant. For this reason then it was, that the Eternal, alike in His wisdom and justice and MERCY, ordained death as the end of all, the righteous and the wicked; for Solomon himself telleth us "there is no man that sinneth not:" and we read in the narrative of Moses himself (Gen. vi. 6) that every imagination of man's heart was only evil continually, and it repented the Lord that he had made man on the earth, and it grieved him at his heart; and again (Gen. viii.), "I will not curse the ground any more for man's sake; for the imagination of man's heart is evil from his youth."

But the Mosaic creed of love and perfect justice goes no further. We utterly repudiate, deny, and hold in abhorrence, the awful creed which condemns every man's soul for the sin of Adam. To use the language of our own venerable sages:—

"Although the descendants of Adam inherited the body from him, and with it the maledictions attached thereto, it is not because they received corporeal existence from him that the souls of all mankind are condemned, for *they had not existence from Adam*, but *are a direct emanation from God*. Therefore Noah, Shem, Abraham, Isaac, and Jacob, and all the other just, *did not* pay the *sin of Adam*, nor were their souls condemned." * And still more convincing proof from the Word of God; Pentateuch, History, Psalms, Proverbs, and Prophets, almost every page bears witness that *each man is responsible for his own individual acts.*—" See, I have set before you this day LIFE and GOOD, DEATH and EVIL; therefore choose *life*, that thou and thy seed may LIVE" (Deut. xxx. 15 and 19). "Then they that feared the Lord spake often one to another; and the Lord hearkened, and heard it: and a book of remembrance was written before Him for them that feared the Lord and thought upon his name. And they shall be mine, saith the Lord of hosts, in that day when I make up my jewels; and I will spare them, as a man spareth his own son that serveth him. Then shall ye return, and discern between the RIGHTEOUS and the WICKED; between him that *serveth God, and him that serveth him not*" (Mal. iii. 16, 17, 18). "*Repent*, and turn yourselves from all your transgressions; *so iniquity shall not be your ruin.* Cast away from you all your transgressions, whereby ye have transgressed; and make you a new heart and a new spirit: for why will ye die, O house of Israel? For I have no pleasure in the death of him that dieth, saith the Lord God: therefore turn yourselves, and live ye" (Eze. xviii. 30, 31, 32). "Turn ye unto me, saith the Lord of hosts, and I will turn unto you" (Zach. i. 3).

It would be useless transcribing all the passages in the Bible similar to the above—and teeming with the doctrine of individual responsibility, and individual power to regain the favor of the Eternal—which is completely opposed to the Gentile creed. But while we reject, wholly and utterly, all belief in the Nazarene doctrine, that we are each and all, even the new-born babe, condemned to everlasting misery unless we acknowledge Jesus—reject it, because it is contrary to the doctrines of Moses;

* The Conciliator, vol. ii. page 214. Translated from the Spanish of Manasseh Ben Israel, by E. H. Lindo, Esq.

contrary to the whole spirit of the Bible; contrary to every attribute of a just and merciful God; we equally reject the mistaken and sceptical belief that the disobedience of our first parents in no way affects us now. If its effects were only confined to them, where is the mercy, the justice of the Lord, in condemning *all their seed* to return to the dust? Who that looks into himself and knows the "plague of his own heart," the difficulty to realize spirituality and holiness—who that reads his Bible with faith and prayer, and marks the prevalence of evil even there, the failings and the weaknesses of the holiest men, even those hallowed by the appellation of the "friends of God," will still refuse belief that the disobedience of our first parents so far altered our nature as to give the *body* more powerful dominion than the *soul;* and thus, by deadening the spiritual influence within us, exposing us to temptation of every kind, and consequently but too often to sin; and rendering it a difficult and often desponding task to give the *spiritual* dominion over the *corporeal*, and to devote our whole hearts—not alone in our closets, but in the duties and occupations of the world still to serve and love our God. What would have been the glorious nature of Adam and Eve if they had not sinned, we know not; for it is a subject far too holy for speculation or conjecture: but that their transgression produced consequences which demanded that not only themselves but their seed should return to dust, is a scriptural truth which no one who believes in Moses and the Prophets can, we think, have sufficient boldness to deny. But the SOUL it touched not.—An emanation from God Himself, it will return to Him, untouched by any sin but those of the body in whom it was breathed; and there, at the bar of God, our own acts, purified by mercy, judged by the ways and thoughts of the Lord—which are not the ways and thoughts of man—guided by the law his mercy gave, hallowed by faith and justified by love—our own acts must be our witness or our condemnation. Nor is this an individual doctrine lightly and carelessly entered upon or produced from one particular class of reading. It has been the thought and study of long years, based on an earnest and prayerful study of the Holy Scriptures, and on the spirit pervading the writings of every Hebrew sage which are accessible to woman. We have brought it strongly forward; because, unless we know exactly what we do believe and what we do not believe from the very beginning of the Holy Scriptures, our readings must always be attended with obscurity and pain, and the very attributes of the Eternal difficult to be realized amid the awful scenes of wickedness which the historical books present. We will now proceed with the more private history of Eve.

Years must have rolled over the heads of our first parents since their expulsion, ere the fearful event took place, which, although it mentions not their names, must recall our attention to them. Although, in comparison, they had become degraded, and the recollection of their sin must ever have remained with its stinging remorse,—still, repentance and real sorrow, meek submission to their chastisement and acknowledgment of its justice, raised them from their first abject misery, and permitted them once more, through prayer and thanksgiving and sacrifice, to commune with the Lord. Eve's exclamation on the birth of Cain—"I have gotten a man from the Lord," proves how closely and devoutly she still traced all blessings from His gracious hand:—hallowing her maternal joy by gratitude to Him. His love had bestowed on her a blessing unknown even in Eden—a child—a *possession* peculiarly her own and her husband's; and in the exultation of her grateful joy she calls his name קין Cain, from קָנֹה, to possess or to acquire. In his early infancy, ere he became awake to right and wrong, his parents could but feel enjoyment to train him up so as to know no sin, to love and serve the Lord, and to give them love and reverence in return for the deep, endless fondness they lavished upon him. But by the name bestowed upon their second son, Abel, we may almost suppose that they had already felt the *vanity* of these hopes and wishes; that even in his boyhood Cain manifested those evil passions and that headstrong will, which led in after years to such fearful consequences.

The effects of Eve's disobedience were now to be displayed in her own offspring—the child of exultation and joy—whom she had welcomed with such delight, that she almost felt as if no sorrow or suffering could assail her more, was the instrument in the Eternal hand to bring her back meekly and submissively to Him, in prayer for that beloved one, in recognition that her sin was working still. The passions and rebellion of her first-born brought all the agony of remorse fresh upon her heart; and deep as was the joy with which she had hailed his birth, was the anxiety, the suffering, his dawning character called forth.

Actuated by such emotions, it was with sorrow, then, more than joy, that the birth of her second boy was hailed. She had already felt the vanity, the transientness of her hopes; and mournfully she called his name הֶבֶל Hebel—transientness or vanity, from הָבַל, which signifies to follow a vain thing, to cherish vain thoughts. But as is the case (how often even now!) the child of tears and anticipated sorrow, proved as dear and precious a blessing as the son of exultation was of grief. She saw in him the ascendency of the spiritual, the deathless part of their mingled nature, that evil could still be subdued, and man be still acceptable and worthy in the sight of his Creator. The compassionate love of the Eternal, while He chastised through Cain, gave hope and trust and comfort through Abel. He showed through these varying natures, that free will to choose the good and eschew the evil was still given; and that though the latter to the eyes of the world might seem, nay was, the ascendant, He would yet preserve his witnesses among mankind, to keep alive the knowledge of the Lord, and prove the pre-eminence, the beauty, the glory, and the consolation of piety and virtue.

So years rolled on: the boys grew up to manhood. And though it is not specifically mentioned, it is evident that Eve must also have borne a daughter, who, as was absolutely necessary in the early stages of the world, became the wife of Cain. Some writers believe that Cain and Abel were both born with twin sisters. It may or may not be, as it must be only conjecture—though Cain's wife only is mentioned.

The words of scripture "and he (Adam) begat sons and daughters," are sufficient for our information. In all probability his family was a large one,—that his seed might fulfil the intention of the Eternal in peopling the world; but how many daughters he had before the death of Abel does not appear, and is of little consequence.

During the growth of their elder children, the lives of our first parents differ little in feeling from those of the present day. Their employments, indeed, were as unlike as patriarchal simplicity is from worldly interest and luxury—the peace of nature from the contention of the world. In reading the narratives of the Bible, we often blend *situation* with feeling, and believe that as the one is too antiquated for interest and example, so is the other for sympathy and love. But the Bible tells of no character above human nature; and why not then, in perusing the circumstances of their simple lives, try their feelings by the standard of our own? Who that is a mother, does not feel anxiety, pleasure, grief, joy, despondency, and hope, almost all at the same time, according to the differing dispositions of her children? Who that is a parent does not acknowledge that maternal love may combine the intensest joy with the intensest grief? And will they not then sympathize in the feelings of Eve?—at one time bowed to the very dust in the anguish occasioned by the sinful inclinations and rude temper of her first born, in self-accusation that she, perhaps, was the original cause, even as an affectionate mother very often accuses herself for the faults of her offspring—at another, weeping tears of sweet joy, and love, and consolation, on the gentle bosom of her Abel, whose whole life and thoughts were directed to piety and virtue to God and to his parents—whose very existence, as her own had been in Paradise, seemed bright with reverence and love?

But even this life of mingled grief and comfort might not last. Not yet had Eve sufficiently atoned for her disobedience, and proved her love and faith, to pass through the awful portals of death to the home prepared for her in heaven. Death, as concerned herself, her husband, her children, was still the dark shadow through which as yet no *certain* light had beamed. The Eternal, in His mercy, had prepared to reveal it, but through clouds of denser, more appalling blackness than had yet gathered round His creatures.

Wrought up to phrensy by the preference manifested towards the pious offering of his younger brother—refusing to acknowledge that it was the temper of his own mind at fault, and that he had himself trampled on, and defied the favor he yet coveted, when shown to another—still sullenly and obstinately encouraging the evil, even when the Lord, in infinite mercy, condescended Himself to speak with his rebellious servant, and asking why he was wroth, informed him that though sin was ever crouching beside him, he (Cain) *had the power to rule over and subdue it*, still disregarding even this, listening but to the fearful instigations of his own heart,—"it came to pass, when they were in the field together, that Cain rose up against his brother Abel, and slew him."

The dark terror of death was mysterious no longer. In its most fearful, most appalling shape, it had descended upon earth—the bright, the beautiful, the loving, and the holy, there he lay before the eyes of his agonized parents, his life-blood dyeing the green-sward—that face so fair, so sweet an index of the pure glorious soul—those limbs, so soft and round and graceful, whose every movement had brought joy to his mother's heart—they gazed upon them still, beautiful as if he slept, save that there was a stillness and a coldness as the earth on which he lay. This, then, was death, and it had been dealt by a *brother's* hand. Can any woman, much less a mother, reflect on Eve's immeasurable agony, and yet pass lightly and heedlessly over this first narration of Holy Writ, refusing sympathy, even interest, in the deep dark floods of misery, with which, though her name is not mentioned, those few words of a brother's hate and wrath and murder teem? Not alone a mother's anguish, deprived of both her children in one fearful day—not, not alone the wild yearnings of affection towards the guilty and the exile, struggling with the passionate misery for her own bereavement, but more crushing, more agonizing still—it was her work—she had disobeyed to obtain the knowledge of good and evil,—and how appallingly had that forbidden knowledge poured back its stinging poison into her own heart! Her beautiful had fallen—she might never, never gaze upon him, list his sweet voice more—the dust had gone to its dust—sent to his grave in his youth, his sinlessness—the helpless and the innocent crushed by the strong hand of the guilty—and the Eternal had looked down from his awful throne and interfered not. Why had the *only innocent*, the *only righteous*, being the first to pay the penalty of death, when his guilty parents and yet more guilty brother were permitted still to live? Nay, the doom of Cain, which the hardened one himself declared "was greater than he could bear," was not to die, but live as a wanderer whom none might slay. Why might such things be? Were they reconcilable with those attributes of justice and of love and long suffering, which the Eternal had already proclaimed, through

His conduct, to his creatures? They were: for in the death of the innocent, IMMORTALITY was proclaimed!

The disobedient looked on the death their sin had brought—they felt, in their own bosoms, the deepest agony of bereavement—they saw not the terror, only as the *end* of *existence;* but by the scythe cutting down the young in his first beautiful spring, and in the full prime of holiness and good, they learned what their own death, at the moment of disobedience, could not have taught—that the righteous must also be cut off, as well as the guilty—that death was not only chastisement for itself *alone*, but in the deep agony it inflicted upon the *living*, in the awful trial of separation and bereavement, and the utter loneliness of heart when a beloved one goes; and, this learned, the world beyond death, the dwelling of the righteous, the reunion of the divine essence with its parent Fount—immortality—was revealed!

That the caviller, the sceptic, the thoughtless will deny this, because we can bring forward no *written proof* of its truth, we are perfectly aware: but we write for the believer, for the Israelite, who not only *reads* the words of his Bible, but *explains* them by one only unerring test, the ATTRIBUTES of God. The question is simply this—Do we believe in a God? That He is, as He proclaimed Himself, "merciful and gracious, long-suffering, and abundant in goodness and truth, keeping mercy for *thousands*, forgiving iniquity and sin, yet clearing not the guilty," without repentance and amendment? Do we believe in Him, as in every page of His Holy Word He is revealed, or do we not? If we do not—if we deny the existence of a just and merciful, though in many instances inscrutable, God, then indeed we may deny our immortality; but if we acknowledge there is a God, aye, and one whose justice and whose love are infinite and perfect as Himself, we must not only believe in our own immortality, but trace its doctrine running through the Holy Scriptures, alike from the death of Abel to the last verses of Malachi, pervading, vivifying, spiritualizing its every portion, even as our mortal frame is pervaded, vivified, and spiritualized, by the *invisible*, yet ever breathing SOUL. We do not doubt and question that we have a soul, because we have nothing palpable and evident by which to *prove* it; and even as the soul is the *essence*, the spirit of our being, so is immortality the essence and the spirit of the Bible.

Where was the mercy, nay, the *justice* of the Eternal, had he punished with *eternal* death the only righteous of His creatures? We can scarcely even dwell upon the idea for a moment without impiety. Abel was taken, that while death in his most fearful form was revealed to manifest all the terrible evil and anguish Eve's sin had brought, the hope and promise of immortality might be given, and the agonized parents comforted. He was removed "from the evil to come," to that world, where "light had been sown for the righteous" from the beginning, and would be for ever.

But though this revelation must have brought with it comfort unspeakable, yet the heavy trial of Eve might not even, through this beneficent assurance, be entirely assuaged. She could not now, as she had done in Eden, realize so blessedly the pre-eminence of the spirit over the feelings of the clay. Though comforted, the weakness of humanity must still have been too often in the ascendant, and taught her all the bitterness of grief. Even though the thought of Abel might, through the unselfishness of woman's love, be tranquillized by the idea, that however she might suffer, he was happy, as she had been in Eden, no such comfort could attend the thought of Cain. It was vain to measure maternal love by the worth or unworthiness of its objects. It was not only that he was exiled for ever from her sight, that her yearning heart might never seek to soothe him more; but she knew that he was, he must be a wretched wanderer, and the mother felt his wretchedness, though she saw it not, in addition to her own. Mercy, indeed, had tempered his chastisement, for he had not been cut off in his sin—he had been doomed to length of days on earth, that he might repent and atone; but this, to a weak and suffering parent, though she might struggle to lift up her heart in gratitude, could not afford consolation.

There is little more to narrate in the life of Eve; but that little, as every other incident in her life, proves forcibly the Eternal's still compassionating love. To remove all of utter bereavement from His first created, first beloved, when the first agony of Eve's heavy trial was over, God gave her another son. And she called his name שֵׁת Seth, because she said, God has appointed me another seed instead of Abel, whom Cain slew." And as from Seth descended a line of venerable patriarchs, one of whom was taken up to heaven, without dying, for his righteousness; and from them came Noah, who alone was saved from universal destruction; then through him Abraham, the favored servant and friend of the Eternal—Abraham, for whose sake Israel was the chosen, and is still the beloved of the Lord, we may quite believe that Eve was not only comforted by the gift of a son, but that even as Abel he was righteous, and that he was the comforter of his parents—that in beholding his opening manhood, the dawning virtue and graces of his spirit, the fiery trial of their early life was soothed, and they could trace the hand of the Lord bringing forth good out of the very midst of evil, and rest satisfied, that however the strong and the guilty might seem to prosper, He would never leave Himself without witnesses upon earth.

Although there is no mention of the death of Eve, the words of Holy Writ, informing us that "Adam lived eight hundred years after he had begotten Seth, and had sons and daughters," would prove that she, too, lived that period, there being no mention whatever, as is often the case with the other patriarchs, of Adam taking another wife. The former temptations, trials, and sorrows of our first parents, must have then been looked back upon by them in their old age, as we should look on the events which may have befallen us before the age of twenty, when we have reached the venerable years of fourscore. That long life was evidently granted in mercy. Had they been cut off on the instant of their transgression, it must have been for eternity, or death would have been no punishment. Had they been taken sooner, we will suppose before the death of Abel, though they might have been spared that bitter sorrow, still darkness, and fear for themselves, and doubt as to the ways and attributes of the Eternal, must have crowded round them, and filled them with despair as to the probable effects of their sin on their offspring, and their offspring's seed. Long life, through the infinite mercy of the Eternal, removed these evils. While they felt, in all the bitterness of remorse, all the evil they had wrought, they were yet comforted by the revelation of immortality, and the consequent incentive for the struggling after righteousness, which, without such blessed incentive, man could never have achieved. They beheld, that though the likeness of God within them had been dulled in all, and in some would be almost entirely effaced, it might in heaven be regained, if while on earth it was sought with faith and works. They learned, that though discord, strife, and oppression, and labor, and care, would reign tumultuously on earth, to the extinction, in *appearance*, of all that was spiritual and good, there was yet in heaven an omnipresent and ever-acting love, which would so over-rule the world, that even from "transitory evil" would spring forth "universal good," and every seemingly dark and contradictory event below, tend to the glory, the extension, and the perfection of the divine economy above.

To obtain this knowledge our first parents were spared, and not cut off in their sin; and can we, their offspring, even at this length of time, peruse their eventful history, without feeling our hearts glow with grateful adoration of the love which guided and hallowed them throughout? The stream of time which divides us is indeed so wide, that we are apt to feel that events so far distant can concern us little. Yet while we trace in our mortal frame, and painful infirmities, the *effects* of their *disobedience*, shall we not acknowledge, with grateful and adoring faith, that the same love which guided, blessed, and pardoned them, is still extended unto us?

To dwell in paradise, to be blessed with direct communings with the Eternal and His heavenly messengers, are indeed not ours; but many a home—aye, many a lot is a sinless paradise to a young and gentle girl; and loving parents will so throng her path with care and blessings, that of evil she knows little, and temptation is afar off. And often, too often, like Eve, these blessings are undervalued and sacrificed, not through her sin and disobedience, but from woman's unfortunate desire to grasp *something more than is her allotted portion*;—her discontent with the lowlier station which her weaker frame and less powerful mind mark imperatively as her own—her mistaken notion, that humility is degradation; and unless she *compels* man to accede to her her rights, they will be trampled on, and never acknowledged—her curiosity leading her too often to covet knowledge which she needs not for the continuance of her happiness. Oh! let not woman deny that such too often are her characteristics, and exclaim with scorn of Eve's weakness, that had she been in Eve's place, surrounded with felicity as she was, the forbidden tree might have remained for ever ere she would have touched it. She who thus thinks, commits unconsciously Eve's first sin, trusting too much in her own strength;

and, in consequence, is just as likely to fall beneath the very first temptation which assails her.

Let her not quiet such fears by the thought that Eve's particular temptation cannot be hers. No; but snares innumerable, and equally fearful, surround us. Each day brings its own temptations, each day calls upon us to pray against them; for we know not how or in what shape they may arise, and how soon, if we trust in our own strength, they may triumph and lead us to perdition. Had Eve been truly *humble* she had not sinned. And if in Eden HUMILITY was needed, if even there, without such panoply of proof, woman fell, how much more should we encourage it now! Humility is to woman her truest safeguard, her loveliest ornament, her noblest influence, her greatest strength. Teaching her her true station in regard to man, it leads her ever to the footstool of her God, thence to derive firmness, devotedness, fortitude, consolation, hope, all that she needs. While such privilege is hers, let her not repine that God lowered Eve and made her less than man; let her not look back with anger that the sin of one woman should thus punish her descendants. From the very first she was endowed differently to man; had she not been the weaker, the serpent had not marked her as his easier prey. And, as our own nature is even now as Eve's, let us rather thank God that his love has granted us that lowly station where our natural qualities may best be proved, and our weaknesses and failings have less power to work us harm. Let us cultivate, with all our heart and soul and might, the lovely flower of humility, which, by teaching us to think lowlily of ourselves, will render us contented and thankful for the blessings around us, the gifts bestowed on us, instead of urging us to covet more;—the sweet flower on whose breath our souls are enabled more continually to ascend to God, and whose petals, seemingly so frail and tender, have yet more power to guard us from temptation and presumption than an unsheathed sword. Let us not pause till it is found and worn; and if it make us invisible as itself, save to those who seek and value us, it will shed around us an atmosphere of love and peace and joy, with which no other flower can vie; and in death, as in life, we shall bless God for its possession, as for the dearest gift He has vouchsafed.

Would I then, some may exclaim, deny all privileges to women—refuse to acknowledge their equality with man—degrade them as the Jewish religion is falsely accused of doing? No! for in the sight of God, in their *spiritual* privileges, in their peculiar gifts and endowments, the power of performing their duties in their own sphere, in their *responsibility*, they are on a perfect equality with man. But I would conjure them to seek humility, simply from its magic power of keeping woman in her own beautiful sphere, without one wish, one ambitious whisper, to exchange it for another. *While there*, while satisfied and rejoicing in the infinite love and wisdom which placed us there, we are not only in the privileges enumerated above, man's equal,—but however in strength of frame, immense capability of physical and mental exertion, in might and grasp of intellect, his inferior; yet in the depth and faithfulness of love, in the capability of *feeling* and *enduring*, in devotedness and fortitude —alike in bodily and mental trial—we are unanswerably his superior. Then has not woman enough to call for gratitude? Endowed with influence over the heart of man,—oh! let her remember for what fearful end Eve used that influence, and keep a constant guard of watchfulness and prayer over her heart to preserve her from its similar abuse. Let her remember the employments of Eve in Eden, and so cultivate her intellectual faculties in the study of God and nature, both animate and inanimate, that her mind may be strengthened, and in the contemplation of the beauties of creation, she may learn the true value of the beauty which may be hers. How small is its *relative* proportion, and yet how blessedly it may be used, even as the beauty of creation, for the glory of God, in its mild, soothing, and benignant influence upon His creatures!

Above all, let the history of Eve impress this truth upon the hearts of her young descendants—that however weak and faulty and abased, however sorrowing and bereaved, however reaping in tears the effects of indiscretion or graver error,—yet still the compassion, the long suffering, the exhaustless love of their Father in Heaven is theirs; that no circumstance in life can deprive them of that love, can throw a barrier between woman's yearning heart and the healing compassion of her God. No; not even departure from Him, neglect, forgetfulness, will make Him forget or cease to compassionate, if she will but return in true repentance, and clinging faithfulness to his deep love once more. We cannot measure that exhaustless fount—for as high as the heaven from the earth, so great is its extent. We cannot weary that never-ceasing mercy—for as far as the East is from the West, so far, when we return to Him, doth He remove our transgressions from us. And will woman—whose whole existence still is love—neglect or despise these thrice-blessed privileges; will the exile, the despised, the persecuted—for such has been, and is, the woman of Israel—will she not receive with grateful adoration the love vouchsafed, and come and make manifest the Sustainer, the Comforter, the Mainspring of her being? To woman of every creed, of every race, of every rank—life, though it may seem blessed, is a fearful desert without God. What then, without Him, is it to the woman of Israel, the exile and the mourner, who hath no land, no hope, no comforter but Him?

CHAPTER II.

SARAH.

So varied and so important are the incidents comprised in the life of Eve, that, on a mere superficial view, Sarah's biography appears somewhat deficient in interest. Yet, as the beloved partner of Abraham, she ought to be a subject of reverence and love to her female descendants; and we will endeavor to bring her history forward, that such she may become. Much of the Eternal's love and pity towards His female children is manifested in her simple life, and also in the life of her bondwoman, Hagar, which is too closely interwoven with hers to be omitted.

The real relationship between Abraham and Sarah, before marriage, has never yet been clearly or satisfactorily solved; some commentators asserting she was his niece, the daughter of Haran his elder brother; and others, that she was, as Abraham himself declares, his half-sister—"She is the daughter of my father, but not the daughter of my mother and she became my wife." We believe the latter assertion much more likely to be the correct one, because, in the first place, there is no foundation whatever for the idea that she was Haran's daughter, except the supposition that Iscah means Sarah (Gen. xi. 29); and, in the second, it is not probable that when questioned by Abimelech, Abraham would have condescended to utter a falsehood. The Bible mentions Lot only as the child of Haran; and Abraham himself says, Sarah was his half-sister. The latter relationship, as preventing marriage, is no proof in favor of her being his niece, as no laws of marriage had yet been issued; and in the early stages of the world, such connexions were not considered sin.

Leaving this difficult decision to more curious speculators, we will proceed to subjects of greater interest. The first notice we have of Sarai is her accompanying her husband and Lot from the home of her kindred to a strange country, among all strange people, in simple obedience to the word of God. Holy writ is silent on the youth of Abram; but it is the opinion of our ancient fathers, that his earnest desire after divine knowledge—his pure and holy life—his affectionate and virtuous conduct, attracted towards him the blessing of the Lord, and caused him to be selected as the promulgator of the Divine Revelation. That Abram was exposed to many dangers on account of his loving obedience to the one sole invisible God, instead of acknowledging the idols of his race, is indeed very possible, and probably originated the first removal of his family to Charran, where also his father accompanied him. At Charran they seem to have dwelt in peace and prosperity, secured from former persecutors, so that it must have been no little trial to go forth again, more particularly without any definite cause for the removal.

To Sarai the trial must have been more severe than to her husband. She was to go forth with him indeed; but it is woman's peculiar nature to cling to home, home ties, and home affections—to shrink from encountering a strange world, teeming with unknown trials and dangers. Rather than the parting from a husband, indeed, all other partings may seem light; but yet they are trials to a gentle woman: and the heart that can leave the home and friends of a happy youth—the associations of years—without regret, proves not that its affections are so centred on one object as to eschew all others; but that it is too often wrapped in a chilling indifference, which prevents strong emotions on any subject whatever. We have enough of Sarai in the Bible to satisfy us that such is not her character.

One cause for the love of home ties and associations, in the heart of a right-feeling woman, originates in the belief that there she can do so much more good than elsewhere—that, unfitted by the weakness and infirmities of her frame from active toil, and the pursuit of goodly service, as falls to the lot of man, she can yet benefit her friends, children, and domestics, in the hallowed circle of home; and better manifest the blessings of the Lord and the love she bears Him, there than amongst strangers. And this was especially the case with Sarai. By one of our ancient fathers it is said, that as Abram and Lot were permitted to turn many of their own sex from idolatry to the knowledge of the one true God, so also was Sarai granted the hallowed privilege of leading many of her female friends and domestics to the same blessed Fount. It was therefore, no doubt, a source of questioning and wonder in her mind, why the Eternal's mandate to go forth should be given. She had not even *experience* in the Eternal's glorious attributes, as displayed in His dealings with His creatures, and through His word, to comfort and be her guide. All was mental darkness in the world around her, except her husband and those few whom he had been enabled to teach a partial knowledge of his God. They stood alone in their peculiar faith; and how often, in such a case, do doubts and fears enter the breast of woman! Yet it was enough that her husband prepared without question or hesitation to obey his God—to leave his aged father, his kindred, and his friends; and, with simple and loving faith, she went with him where the Lord should lead. Well is it for us when we can do so likewise; when, in some of those bitterest trials that woman's heart can know, the change of home or land, be it with our parents, or, husband, or more fearful still, *alone*, we can yet so stay upon our God that we can realize His presence, His loving mercy directing our weary way, and resting with us still. His direct communing by voice or sign, or through angelic messengers, is indeed no longer ours; but those that seek to love and serve Him may yet hear His still small voice breathing in the solemn whisper of their own hearts, and through the *individual* promises of His word.

Accompanied by Lot and their household—expressed in the term, "the souls they had gotten in Charran," who were probably those whom they had instructed in the true faith—and carrying with them the substance they possessed, Abram and Sarai "went forth into the land of Canaan," which was inhabited by a fierce people, and gave little hope of ever being possessed by the patriarch and his family, for by their constant journeyings it would seem as if they could not even obtain sufficient land to fix their home. Yet, there again the Lord appeared to the patriarch and renewed His promise—thus proving His tender compassion for the human weakness of His creatures, and encouraging their faith, when, without such encouragement, He knew it must have failed. To add to their numerous *human* discomforts and trials, a famine broke out in the land, so severe and grievous that Abram sought the land of Egypt; and there, rendered fearful by the exceeding beauty of his wife, and the supposed barbarity of the land, he bade Sarai call herself his sister, not his wife.

In this first deception, however, Abram was much more to be excused than in the second. He had not yet had all the convincing proofs of the Eternal's tender watchfulness and care, as he had afterwards. He had gone to Egypt *without* the express command of the Lord, and this very fact, to one accustomed to divine guidance, and not yet perhaps feeling himself sufficiently strong spiritually to go alone, rendered him more fearful than he would otherwise have been. He might also have thought, that as he was destined for a great end, it was his duty to use any means to preserve the life so appointed, without sufficiently considering that life and death were equally in the hands of the Eternal, and that He would preserve His servant alive, without the intervention of human means. Spiritual advancement requires effort, perseverance, and experience, as well as every other; and Abram himself, though the elect of the Eternal, could not obtain perfection and firmness in faith without some human tremblings, which it is enough for us to know, were overruled, compassionated, and forgiven. We perceive by the sacred narrative, that his intention was frustrated, and his words caused the very evil he dreaded;—which is sufficient warning for us to avoid all departure from the straight line of truth—while the continued care and favor of the Lord should check our presumptuous condemnation, and remind us. that if His justice and mercy thought proper to overrule and forgive, and continue, nay increase, His long tenderness towards Abram and his family, it is our part, instead of marvelling, to thank God that such weakness is recorded, that we may not feel it is human perfection *alone* which calls down His blessing, and so shrink back in terror and despair.

This part of Sarai's history gives us information generally very interesting to young female readers—that she was very beautiful. We are wont to imagine that the charms of sixty-five could not be very remarkable; but reckoning according to the age to which mortals then lived, she was not older than a woman of thirty or five-and-thirty would be now, consequently in her prime; endowed, as her history gives us authority to suppose, with a quiet, retiring dignity, which greatly enhanced her beauty, and rendered it yet more interesting than that of girlhood.

Protected from this danger, his substance greatly increased by Pharaoh's gifts, Abram, his wife, and household, retraced their steps to where "his tent had been at first, between Bethel and Hai." The altar which he had originally erected was still there, and again he and his family "called on the name of the Lord." The command of Pharaoh—"Go thy way," was most probably regarded and acted on by the patriarch as a warning, that his safest and most hallowed home was in the land to which the Lord had originally guided him.

In the events which follow—the separation of Abram and Lot—the battle of the kings—the imprisonment and rescue of Lot—the blessing of Melchisedek—Holy Writ makes no mention of Sarai. She was performing those duties of an affectionate wife and gentle mistress of her husband's immense establishment, which are nothing to write about, but which make up the sum of woman's life, create her dearest and purest sources of happiness, and bring her acceptably before God. Her home was still an unsettled one. The Lord had again appeared to renew His promises to Abram—comforting him in the sorrow which Lot's choice of a dwelling in the sinful Sodom had occasioned him, by the assurance that all the land which he saw, northward and southward, eastward and westward, would He give unto him and to his seed, and his seed's seed for ever. That he was to "Arise, and walk through the land, in the breadth of it and in the length of it, for I will give it unto thee." In consequence of which, the tent of the patriarch was removed southward, to Mamre in Hebron, and an altar built, at once to claim the land in the name of the Lord, and give to Abram and his household a place where to worship. The extent of the patriarch's household may be imagined by the fact, that at his word, no less than three hundred and eighteen servants, born in his house and trained to arms, accompanied him to the rescue of his nephew. Those who were left to attend to his flocks and herds, which he possessed in great numbers, must have been in equal proportion; and over these, during his absence, Sarai, assisted by the steward, had unlimited dominion.

The beautiful confidence and true affection subsisting between Abram and Sarai, marks unanswerably their *equality;* that his wife was to Abram friend as well as partner; and yet, that Sarai knew perfectly her own station, and never attempted to push herself forward in unseemly counsel, or use the influence which she so largely possessed for any weak or sinful purpose. Some, however, would have found it difficult to preserve their humility and meekness, situated as was Sarai. A coarser and narrower mind would have prided herself on the promises made her husband, imagining there must be some superlative merit, either in herself or Abram, to be so singled out by the Eternal. There is no pride so dangerous and subtle as spiritual pride, no sin more likely to gain dominion in the early stages of religion —none so disguised, and so difficult to be discovered and rooted out. But in Sarai there was none of this; not a particle of pride, even at a time when, of all others, she might have been *almost* justified in feeling it. She was, indeed, blessed in a husband whose exalted, yet domestic and affectionate character must ever have strengthened, guided, and cherished hers; but it is not always the most blessed and distinguished woman who attends the most faithfully to her domestic duties, and preserves unharmed and untainted that meekness and integrity which is her greatest charm.

Abram's warlike expedition was the only one in which his wife did not accompany him. With what joy she must have welcomed her warrior lord! How gratefully must her loving heart have delighted to ponder on his magnanimity, in going instantly to the rescue of his weak and little grateful nephew;—on his courage—his success; and yet more on his noble refusal of all gifts from the king of Sodom, lest the glory should be taken from the Lord, and any mortal should say, "I have made Abram rich." We dwell with delight on the stirring records of chivalry; and it is right we should do so, for the study of all honorable, unselfish, and unworldly deeds must do us good; but where shall we find, in the whole history of chivalry, an instance of such perfect nobility and magnanimity, unstained by one action from which mind or heart could revolt, as in the only warlike expedition of Abram? It was indeed enough for a woman to glory in: and, though nothing is said, for the record of Moses is too important to descend to the thoughts and feelings of woman, we may well imagine the grateful and rejoicing feelings of Sarai, as she welcomed her husband home—forgetting all the pangs of parting and loneliness of separation, in the triumph and delight of such a meeting.

It was after these things, that we have the first allusion to the patriarch's being childless. And by the words in which the Lord addressed him—"Fear not, Abram, I am thy shield, and exceeding great reward," we are led to suppose that some anxious thoughts, and perhaps doubts, natural to humanity, were occupying his mind. *We*, weak and frail as himself, might exclaim, What, still doubting, still fearing, when he has had so many proofs of the Eternal's providence and care! But God, whose "thoughts are not as our thoughts," instead of *reproving*, addresses him in terms of the tenderest love and encouragement, for He knew the nature of His creatures, and that faith could *not* be perfectly attained without years of watchfulness and prayer; that if it were, man would cease to be man, and this life be no longer what it was intended—a life of trial. Abram's instant reply reveals the painful thoughts which had engrossed him:—"Lord God, what wilt thou give me? seeing I go childless, and the steward of my house is this Eliezer of Damascus. Behold, to me thou hast given no seed, and lo, one born in my house is mine heir." God had promised that the land should be his and his *seed's*, but Abram in sorrow beheld years pass, and still he had no child. Sarai had long passed the age when, humanly speaking, she could be a mother. It was much more natural—truly pious and faithful as he was—that Abram should be harassed with contradictory fears and doubts, than that he should have had none. God had promised, but how was that promise to be fulfilled?—unless, indeed, not his own child, but "one born in his house" was to be his destined heir. This appeared perhaps the most probable, though it was painfully disappointing; and to soothe this fear and remove it, the Lord addressed him as we have said. The gracious and most blessed promise directly followed—that not one born in his house, but his own son should be his heir; and, bidding him look up at the stars—as countless and numberless they gemmed the clear, bright heavens—promised, that "so should his seed be." And then it was, that—all of doubt and mist and fear dissolving in the heart of the patriarch, before the words of the Lord, as snow before the sun—HE BELIEVED: and that pure FAITH was accounted to him as RIGHTEOUSNESS. How blessed are those words! In every station of life, however tried, and sad, and mourning, and deprived of all power to *serve* the Lord as our hearts dictate, we may yet BELIEVE, and Faith is still accounted RIGHTEOUSNESS.

On the glorious prophetic vision which followed when the sun went down, we may not linger, as it will take us too far from the subject of our narrative.

Great must have been Sarai's joy when this gracious promise was made known to her. If to Abram the being childless was a source of deep regret, it must have been still more so to her. Loving and domestic, as her whole history proves she was, how often may she have yearned to list the welcome cry of infancy; to feel one being look up to her for protection and love, and call her by that sweet name—Mother. But this joyful anticipation could only have been of short duration. Sarai, as is woman's nature, in all probability imagined the *fulfilment* would immediately follow the *promise*. The most difficult of all our spiritual attainments is to *wait* for the Lord: to believe still, through long months, perhaps years, of anticipation and disappointment, that as He has said it, so it *will be*, so it *must be*, though our finite wisdom cannot pronounce the *when*. Did the Eternal fulfil His gracious promises on the instant, where would be the trial of our faith, and of our confidence and constancy in prayer?

Finding still there was no appearance of her becoming a mother, we are led to suppose, by the events which follow, that all Sarai's joyous anticipations turned into gloomy fears, not merely from the belief that she herself would not be blessed with a child, but that Abram might, as was and is the custom of Eastern nations, take another wife; an idea excited, perhaps, by the recollection that *her* name had not been mentioned as the destined mother of the promised seed, but precisely the most painful which could find entrance in a heart affectionate and faithful as her own. To prevent this misfortune, and yet to further (as she supposed) the will of the Eternal, Sarai had recourse to human means.

All women in her position, and influenced as she was by the manners and customs of the East, would have both felt and acted as she did, but few, we think, would have waited so long. It was ten years after Abram had left Egypt to fix his residence in Canaan, before Hagar became his wife. The separation of himself and Lot appears to have taken place in the first year after their settlement in Canaan, the expedition against the kings in the second or third year following. And we are expressly told, that it was *soon after these occurrences* that the Lord appeared unto the patriarch, and promised him an heir in his own child; the Hebrew word, אַחַר (after), signifying, according to Rashi, that the event about to be related took place *soon after* the period of the former narration; but when a *long period* has intervened, the expression אַחֲרֵי is used.*

According to this reckoning, then, full five, or at the very least three, years must have elapsed between the promise made to Abram and his taking Hagar, at Sarai's own request, to be his wife; and few women would have beheld year after year pass, each year increasing the improbability of her becoming a mother, and yet so believed as to adopt no human means for the furtherance of her wishes. In perusing and reflecting on the blessings promised, and revelations made to the favored servants of the Lord, we are apt to suppose that their lives were preserved from all trouble, all trial of delay, from the fearful sickness of anticipation disappointed, and hope deferred; whereas, a more intimate study of the holy Scriptures would convince us, that though indeed most *spiritually* blessed, their *mortal* lives were not more exempt from labor, and all the sorrows proceeding from human emotions, than our own. We only see those periods on which the broad light of sunshine falls. The darker

* See "The Sacred Scriptures, Hebrew and English," translated by the Rev. D. A. De Sola, &c. Note to verse 1 of chap. xvi.

shades of human doubt, the often supposed blighting of hope, the struggles and terrors of the spirit alternating with the rest and confidence which it sometimes enjoys; these we see not, and, therefore, pronounce them unknown to our forefathers; whereas, did we examine more closely, we should not find severer trials in our own lives than in theirs: nor cease to believe, for a single moment, that the God who guided them through the dark shadows of human trials, and strengthened them with the light of His presence, does not equally guide and reveal Himself to us.

The first human evidence that Sarai's scheme would be productive of vexation and sorrow, as well as of joy, was her disappointment with regard to Hagar's continued humility and submission. Forgetful that it was to her mistress, humanly speaking, she owed the privileges now hers, the Egyptian so far forgot herself, as to feel and make manifest that Sarai "was despised in her eyes." Alas, how mournfully does that brief sentence breathe of woman's fallen nature! How apt are we to exalt ourselves for imaginary superiority—to look down on those who have served us, when God has bestowed on us privileges of which they are deprived. We forget, often through thoughtlessness, that those very things of which we are so proud, come not from ourselves, but from Him who might equally have vouchsafed them to others. We may not indeed have the same incitement to pride and presumption as Hagar, but have we *never* despised others for the want of those accomplishments, those advantages, that beauty, and other gifts from God, which we ourselves may possess? Aye, sometimes, though we trust such emotions are rare as they are sad, the parents who have toiled and labored to give us advantages of dress and education far above what they possessed themselves—the elder sister, who is contented and rejoiced to remain in the background, that younger and fairer ones, whom she loves with almost a mother's love, may come forward—the homely and older-fashioned aunt, to whom, perhaps, a sister's orphan family owe their all—these are the beings whom the young and thoughtless but too often secretly despise, as if their superior advantages had come from themselves, not from God, through loving relatives and friends.

And this was the case with Hagar. A superficial reading of the Bible often causes Sarai to be most unjustly blamed for undue harshness. We think only of Hagar's wanderings in the wilderness, and pity her as cruelly treated, and suppose, that as the Most High relieved her through His angel, she had never been in any way to blame. Now, though to sympathize with the sorrowing and afflicted be one of our purest and best feelings, it must not so blind us as to prevent our doing justice to the inflictor of that affliction. We candidly avow, that until lately we too thought Sarai harsh and unjust, and rather turned from than admired her character: but we have seen the injustice of this decision, and, therefore, without the smallest remaining prejudice, retract it altogether: retract it, simply because the words of the angel are quite sufficient proof that Hagar had been *wrong*, and Sarai's chastisement *just*, or he would not have commanded her, as Sarai's *bondwoman*, to return and submit herself to her mistress's power, without any reservation whatever.

It must indeed have been a bitterly painful disappointment to Sarai, that instead of receiving increased gratitude and affection from one whom she had so raised and cherished, she was despised with an insolence that, unless checked, might bring discord and misery in a household which had before been so blessed with peace and love. Sarai's was not a character to submit tamely to ingratitude. There was neither coldness nor indifference about her. In no part of the Bible, either in character or precept, do we perceive the necessity or the merit of that species of cold indifference, which is by some well-meaning religious persons supposed to be the self-control and pious forgiveness of injuries most acceptable to God. The Patriarchal and Jewish history alike prove, that natural feelings were not to be trampled upon. The Hebrew code was formed by a God of love for the nature of *man*, not angels—formed so as to be *obeyed*, not to be laid aside as impracticable. The passions and feelings of the East were very different to those of the calmer and colder North; and nowhere in Holy Writ are we told that those feelings and emotions must be annihilated. *Subdued* and *guided* indeed, as must be the consequence of a true and strict adherence to the law of God, and impartial study of His word; but in the sight of a God of love, indifference can never be, and never was, religion.

Yet even this, an affair of feeling entirely between herself and Hagar, could not urge Sarai to any line of conduct unauthorized by her husband. Naturally indignant, she complained to him, perhaps, too, with some secret fear that Hagar, favored so much above herself by the hope of her giving him a son, might be unduly justified and protected. But it was not so. Abram's answer at once convinced her that Hagar had not taken her place; nay, that though Abram could not do otherwise than feel tenderness and kindness towards her, he at once recognised Sarai's supremacy, both as his wife and Hagar's mistress, and bade her "do with her what seemeth good to thee." We have so many proofs of Abram's just, affectionate, and forgiving character, that we may fully believe he would never have said this, if he had not been convinced that it was no unjust accusation on the part of Sarai. He knew, too, that she was not likely to inflict more punishment than was deserved, particularly on a favorite slave; and, therefore, it was with his full consent "Sarai afflicted her, and she fled from her presence."

Whatever the nature of this affliction, it could not have been very severe—neither pain nor restraint—for Hagar had the power to fly. Reproof to an irritable and disdainful mind is often felt as intolerable, and given too, as it no doubt was, with severity, and at a time when Hagar felt exalted and superior to all around her, even to her mistress, her proud spirit urged flight instead of submission, and not till addressed by the voice of the angel did those rebellious feelings subside.

There was no mistaking the angelic voice, and his first words destroyed the proud dreams which she had indulged. "Hagar, Sarai's bondwoman!" he said, and the term told her in the sight of God she was still the same, "whence camest thou, and whither art thou going?" It was not because he knew not that he thus spoke. The messengers of the Lord need no enlightenment on the affairs of men, but their questions are adapted to the nature of men, to awaken them to consciousness, to still the tumult of human passion, and by clear and simple questioning *compel* a clear and true reply. Had his command to return been given without preparation, Hagar's obedience would have been the effect of fear, not conviction. But those simple questions, "whence camest thou? whither art thou going?" startled her from the tumultuous emotions of rebellion and presumption. Whence had she come? From a happy, loving home, where she had been the favorite of an indulgent and gentle mistress; a home which would speedily be to her yet dearer, as the birthplace of her child; that child who was to be the supposed heir to her master and all his sainted privileges; from friends, from companions, all whom she had loved: and she had left them! And whither was she going? How might she answer when she knew not? Was she about to resign all of affection, privilege, joy, to wander in the wilderness, helpless and alone? How idle and impotent now seemed her previous feelings. Those simple questions had flashed back light on her darkened heart, and humbled her at once; and simply and truthfully she answered, "I flee from the presence of my mistress Sarai;" thus meekly acknowledging that Sarai was still her mistress, and that her derision had indeed been wrong. Reproof, therefore, followed not; but the angel bade her, "Return to thy mistress, and submit thyself to her power." And, perceiving that her repentance was sincere, and would lead to obedience, he continued graciously to promise that her seed should be multiplied, so that it should not be numbered for multitude; that her son should bear a name which would ever remind her that God had heard her affliction, with other promises concerning that son, *yet none* which might lead her to the deceitful belief that he would be Abram's promised seed.

Inexpressibly consoled, in the midst of her bitter self-reproach, and convinced, by his supernatural voice and disappearance, that it was indeed an angel direct from the Lord with whom she had spoken, it is evident from the context, although not there mentioned, that Hagar must have unhesitatingly obeyed, and returned to her mistress—convinced of her error—submissive and repentant, and been by Sarai received with returning confidence and full forgiveness.

In due course of time the promise was fulfilled, and Hagar, to the great joy of Abram, had a son, whom *Abram* called Ishmael, thus proving that Hagar must have imparted the visit of the angel, and his command as to the name of her son.

Before we proceed, we would entreat our younger readers to pause one moment on the simple facts we have related; and so take it to their hearts, that the first words of the angel may become theirs as well as Hagar's. We have not indeed the direct communings with the messengers of the Lord, as is recorded in the Bible; but we are not left unguided and unquestioned. We have still an angelic voice within us, that, would we but encourage it to speak—would we but listen to it—can, even as the angel's, still the wild torrent of passion, awaken us to our neglected duty, and lead us, repentant and sorrowing, to those whom we may have offended. God has not left us without His witness. The VOICE OF CONSCIENCE may be to us what angel visits were to our ancestors of old. There is no period of our lives in which it is wholly lost; but in youth it is strongest and most thrilling. In youth it is, that we awake from the (often) stagnant sleep of earlier years;—we awake to a consciousness of bright, glowing, beautiful existence;—we become conscious of a deep yearning after the *good*, and at the same time sorrowfully feel, that it is not quite as easy to attain as we believed it. As our emotions and feelings spring into life, so does conscience. We become aware of a peculiar thrilling sense of joy, when we have accomplished good, either in conquering ourselves—in giving up a selfish inclination—or in showing kindness, affection, and respect to others. There is a glowing sense of joy, when conscience tells us we have done well, unlike the joy proceeding from any other cause; and as it approves, with an angel voice that *will* be heard, so does it disapprove. We may stifle it—we may refuse to listen to its still small tones—yet we cannot shake off the depression and the sadness which it leaves. We may *refuse* to know wherefore we thus feel; but it is *conscience* still. How much better, then, to permit its having voice and power, and, as it dictates, do—to encourage it at times to speak, and ever keep its silent watch, for we need it, oh! how powerfully we need it. How fearful is our responsibility if we permit it to lie unused; for more strongly than aught else does it breathe our approval, or our condemnation, in the sight of the Lord. Is there one amongst us that has not felt, at one time or other, emotions similar to those of Hagar—anger at reproof, scorn of those who reprove, rebellion against their dictates; and we would fly from their presence with wrath at our hearts, and rebellion on our lips; and at such times does the voice of conscience never steal over us with questions similar to these? "Whence comest thou? Whither wouldst thou flee? What wouldst thou do?" startling us from wrath, often and often into a burst of passionate and self-reproachful, though, as yet, only half-repentant tears. And when that passion in a degree is stilled—when affection and reason softly and pleadingly resume their sway, does not the angel voice bid us also "return" unto those whom we have offended? submit to their control? It is wisest, best, though our wayward spirits shrink from it, proud of their own will, desirous of undue freedom. And at such times, oh! well it is for us, now and hereafter, if, even as Hagar, we return and submit, and thus acknowledge the power of that inward voice! Its angelic whisper will come to us again; we need not fear them, nor shrink from a lonely path—we have within us the "angel of the Lord." But those who hear yet refuse to heed, drowning that heavenly whisper by plunging anew into gaiety and pleasure, or stifling it by unwonted industry, are exposing themselves to distant but untold of sorrows. It will, indeed, be long ere conscience becomes so silenced as not to intrude, but she will at length; and then, when, in agony of spirit, we wake from our vain dream, and would give worlds, if we had them, to feel as we have felt—to hear once more the voice of conscience thrilling and directing as in happier years—to be awake to the consciousness of our faults, that we might correct and subdue them—and feel once more the glowing approval of our strivings after good, oh! how agonizing must be the conviction—it is we who have spurned, neglected, and so silenced the angel of the Lord, that it must be a long, long, and weary interval of pain, and toil, and watching, ere we may list those sweet low spiritual tones again. Better, far better, the momentary pain and humility of acknowledgment and submission. Better, far better, the too tender conscience, giving pain, in some cases apparently unnecessarily, than its silence and stagnation; for it MUST one day awake, and dreadful will be that waking. To obtain this blessed influence—to feel that to us is sent, as to our ancestors, "the angel of the Lord"—we have but to study the word of God and ourselves. It may cost us at first many sad and weary hours—many bitter tears—and many a secret pang; for it is hard so to know ourselves as to see faults and failings which others see not.—It is hard to restrain the too frequent indulgence of favorite pleasures, because *we* know they will do us harm.—It is hard sometimes to perform a disagreeable, nay a painful duty, *only* because we feel we ought, though our friends see not the necessity;—hard, when friends approve, for our hearts to disapprove; and all this we must encounter, would we study ourselves and God's word, till our hearts become shrines for his guiding angel. But oh! and depressing as all this may seem, it is but a grain in the balance compared to the deep thrilling joy which is its accompaniment. Those who have once felt the glow of approving conscience—the strength, encouragement, consolation, hope, which it gives when all around is desolate and dark, who feel that, hand-in-hand with faith and prayer, it is leading us safely and blessedly through the stony paths of earth, even through the dark valley of death, up to the glowing and immortal light of heaven, will welcome even its severest pang to call it theirs, and hail it as, indeed, the angel of the Lord.

It may be that Sarai's correction of Hagar was unduly harsh, although we have no warrant in Scripture for so believing; but it is evident, as there is no further mention of contention and disagreement between them, that she received her submission with gentleness, and restored her to favor. It is well when forgiveness is thus recorded: many and many a young meek spirit would obey the voice of the angel and return, in humility and love, could they but be sure that submission would be gently and lovingly received; and shrink from it only because the chilling reception, the *uttered* but not *felt* reconciliation, falls upon their still quivering hearts with a pang and degradation which they feel that as yet they cannot bear. The spirit of that healing and consoling love which has its birth in religion, must guide both the offended and the offender, or reconciliation never can be complete; nor the latter be securely and convincingly led back to that better path to which the angel points. The pang of unrequited confidence, chilled affection, and all the bitterness of unnecessary degradation, will be stronger at first than the approving glow of conscience; while a contrary reception, even though it may heighten the pang of self-reproach, will soothe and encourage, for the inward voice whispers—we have done well; and, from that moment, the heavenly messenger assumes her mild dominion in the heart, never to be lured thence again.

For thirteen years Abram and Sarai must have looked upon Ishmael as the promised seed; for though, not actually so said, there was neither spiritual sign nor human hope of the patriarch having any other child. At the end of that period, however, the Most High again appeared unto Abram, proclaiming Himself as the ALMIGHTY,—a fit introduction to the event He was about to foretell; and bidding His favored servant, "Walk before me, and be thou perfect," perfect in trust, in faith, without any regard to human probabilities, for, as Almighty God, all things were possible with Him. The name of the patriarch was then changed, as a sign of the many nations over whom he was appointed father—the land again promised him—and the covenant appointed which was to mark his descendants as the chosen of the Lord, the everlasting inheritors of Canaan; and bear witness, to untold-of ages, of the truth of the Lord's word, and the election of His people. This proclaimed and commanded, the Eternal commenced His information of the miracle He was about to perform, by desiring Abraham to call his wife no longer Sarai שָׂרַי but Sarah שָׂרָה—a change which our ancient fathers suppose to mean the same as from Abram to Abraham. "Sarai, signifying a lady or princess in a restricted sense, imported that she was a lady, or princess, to Abram only; whereas the latter name signifies princess or lady absolutely, indicating that she would thus be acknowledged by many, even as Abraham was to become the father of many nations."* A meaning perfectly reconcilable with the verse which follows: "And I will bless her, and give thee a son also of her: yea, I will bless her, so that she shall be a *mother of nations; kings of people* shall be of her." She was, therefore, no longer a princess over Abraham's household, but a princess in royal rank, from whom *kings* should descend. Joy must have been the first emotion of Abraham's heart at this miraculous announcement, mingled with a feeling of wonder and astonishment how such a thing could be; but then, in his peculiarly affectionate heart, came the thought of his first-born Ishmael, and with earnestness he prayed, "Oh! that Ishmael might live before thee!" And though the Eternal could not grant this prayer, for the seed of Abraham, from whom His chosen people would spring, must be of pure and unmixed birth, He yet, with compassionating tenderness, soothed the father's anxious love, by the gracious promise that, though Sarah's child must be the seed with whom His covenant should be established, yet Ishmael also should be blessed and multiplied exceedingly, and become, even as Isaac, the father of a great nation. "And for Ishmael I have also heard thee." How blessed an encouragement for us to pour forth our prayers unto the Lord, proving, how consolingly, that no prayer is offered in vain; for if He cannot grant as our infinite wishes would dictate, He will yet hear us—yet fulfil our prayer far better for our welfare, and the welfare of our beloved ones, than our own wishes could have accomplished, had they been granted to the full.

The acceptance of the covenant throughout Abraham's house-

* See note to Gen. xvii 15, in the Rev. D. A. De Sola's translation of the Bible.

hold, and the change in her own name, must, of course, have been imparted by Abraham to his wife, with the addition of the startling promise, that she too, even at her advanced age, should bear a son. Yet by her behavior, when the promise was repeated in the following chapter, it would appear that, though informed of it, she had dismissed it from her mind as a thing impossible. Accustomed to regard Ishmael as the only seed of Abraham—to suppose her scheme had been blessed, more particularly as she had never been named before as the mother of the chosen seed—the hope of being so had long since entirely faded; and, not having attained the simple questionless faith of her husband, she, in all probability, dismissed the thought, as recalling too painfully those ardent hopes and wishes, which she had with such difficulty previously subdued. Engaged, as was her wont, in her domestic duties, she was one day interrupted by the hasty entrance of her husband, requiring her "quickly to prepare three measures of fine meal, knead it, and make it into cakes." Patriarchal hospitality was never satisfied by committing to hirelings only the fit preparations for a hearty welcome. We see either Sarah herself making the desired cakes, or closely superintending her domestics in doing so; and the patriarch hastening, in the warmth of his hospitality, himself to fetch a calf from the herd, to give it to a young man to dress it, though he had abundance of servants around him to save him the exertion. Yet both Abraham and Sarah were of the nobility of the Eternal's creating. He had raised them above their fellows, and bestowed on them the patent of an aristocracy, with which not one of the nations could vie, for it came from God Himself. He had changed their names to signify their royal claims—to make them regarded in future ages as noble ancestors of a long line of prophets, kings, princes, and nobles; and there was a refinement, a nobleness, a magnanimity of character in both the patriarch and his wife, which, breathing through their very simplicity, betrayed their native aristocracy, and marked them of that princely race which has its origin in the favor and election of the King of kings. The primitive simplicity of our first fathers generally impresses the mind with the mistaken idea of their being simply farmers or agriculturists, both of which they certainly were, but not these alone, as supposed in the present acceptation of the term. They were princes and nobles, not only in their mental superiority but in their immense possessions—in their large and well ordered household, in the power they possessed both in their own establishments and in the adjoining lands, and in the respect and submission ever paid them by the nations with whom they might have held intercourse. Abraham was never addressed save as "My Lord," either by his own domestics or other nations; thus acknowledged as superior, and of noble if not royal rank, by those who could scarcely be supposed to understand why he was so, save by the outward signs of landed possession and large establishment. Those who think so much of noble descent and princely connexion, would do well to remember this—that impoverished, scattered, chastised, for a "little moment," as we are—yet, that if we are children and descendants of Abraham —ISRAELITES not only in seeming but in heart—we are descended from the aristocracy of the Lord—from a higher and nobler race than even Gentile kings may boast; a privilege and glory of which no circumstance, no affliction, no persecution can deprive us—ours, through all and every event of life, unless we cast it from us by the dark deed of forsaking, for ambition, or gold, or power, the banner of our blessed faith—the religion of our God.

Yet noble, even princely, as were Abraham and Sarah, it was no sign of rank, with them, to be cold and restrained by false artificial laws. In the Bible, nobility was nature and *heart*, simplicity and benevolence, cordiality and warmth; no coldness, no indifference, no folding up the affections and the impulses of feeling in the icy garment of pride and fashion, which so often turns to selfishness, and so utterly prevents all of benevolence and social good. Abraham knew not, at his first invitation, the rank or mission of his visitors. His address was one of the *heart's respect*, not the mere politeness of the lip; and the warmth of his welcome would not permit of his sitting idly down while hirelings prepared their meal—nay, we find that, even while they sat down to partake of it, their host stood,—a mark of profound respect, which a further consideration of their majestic aspect prompted, by the supposition that they were more than ordinary mortals.

Sarah joined not her husband or his guests. The modest and dignified customs of the East prevented all intrusion, or even the wish to intrude. Unless particularly asked for, the place of the Eastern and Jewish wife was in the retirement of home; not from any inferiority of rank, or servitude of station, but simply because their inclination so prompted. The strangers might have business with Abraham, which, if needed, he would impart to her; there was no occasion for her to come forward. But, while seated in the inner tent, engaged in her usual avocations, she heard her own name, "Where is Sarah, thy wife?" and her husband's reply, "She is in the tent," followed by words that must indeed have sounded strange and improbable, "Sarah, thy wife, shall bear a son;" yet, improbable as they might have seemed, there is no excuse for the laugh of incredulity with which they were received. Already prepared by the previous promise of the Lord, the words should at once have revealed the heavenly nature of those who spake, and been heard with faith and thankfulness; but Sarah thought only of the human impossibility. Strange as it is, that such unbelief should be found in the beloved partner of Abraham, yet her laugh proves that even she was not exempt from the natural feelings of mortality—the looking to human means and human possibilities alone; forgetting that with God all things are possible. Yet, to us, the whole of this incident is consoling. It proves that even Sarah was not utterly free from human infirmities; and yet that the Eternal, through His angel, deigned graciously to *reprove*, not to *chastise*. It proves that God has compassion on the nature of His erring children; for he knows their weakness. *Man* would have been wroth with the laugh of scorn, and withdrawn his intended favor; but "the Lord said unto Abraham, Wherefore did Sarah laugh, saying, Shall I, who am old, indeed bear a child? Is anything too mighty for the Lord? At the time appointed I will return unto thee, and Sarah shall indeed have a son." The gracious mildness of the rebuke—the blessed repetition of the promise—must, to one so affectionate as Sarah, have caused the bitterest reproach; but, weakly listening to fear instead of repentance, she denied her fault, seeking thus mistakenly to extenuate it. But He said, "Nay, but thou didst laugh," proving that her innermost thoughts were known; and, silenced at once, left to the solitude of her own tent, for Abraham accompanied his guests on the road to Sodom, we know quite enough of Sarah's character to rest satisfied that repentance and self-abasement for unbelief, mingled with, and hallowed the burst of rejoicing thankfulness with which she must have looked forward to an event so full of bliss to her individually, and so blessed a revelation of the Lord's deep love for Abraham and herself. Nearly twenty years had passed since the first promise of an heir in his own child had been given. Years, long, full of incident and feeling, seeming in their passing an interval long enough for the utter forgetfulness of the promise, save as it was supposed fulfilled in the birth of Ishmael; but now, in the retrospect, the promise flashed back with a vividness, a brightness, as if scarce a single year had passed ere it had been given: and Sarah must have felt self-reproached in the midst of her joy, that she had not waited, had not trusted, had not believed unto the end And many a one, ere life has closed, will feel as she did; not indeed, from the same cause—but often and often a prayer has been offered up, a promise given from the word of God, and both have been forgotten, neglected, mistrusted, through long weary years—as vainly prayed and vainly answered—and yet, ere life has closed, recalled as by a flash of sudden light, by the divine answer to the one, and gracious fulfilment of the other.

Before the birth of Isaac, however, Abraham and his family once more removed their dwelling, partly, it may be supposed, to fulfil the words of the Lord previously spoken: " Arise, walk through the land, in the length of it and the breadth of it, for I will give it unto thee;" and partly from the desolate appearance and poisonous vapors of the once beautiful vale of Sodom, and in consequence of the cessation of travellers, to whom Abraham had so delighted to show hospitality. We shall pass lightly over the next event in the life of Sarah, having already made our remarks on a similar occurrence. The fault of the patriarch in again passing his wife for his sister, was indeed much greater than it had been at the first. He had now no longer the excuse of not sufficiently knowing the ways of the Lord to trust in Him, even in the midst of those dangers incidental to mankind, yet seeming too trivial for the interference of the Most High. He had had nearly thirty years' experience that he was in truth the chosen servant, and the well-beloved of the Lord—that there was not an event in his life which had not been ordered and guided by a special providence; and he ought to have known that this danger, as every other, would be overruled. Yet, while we *regret* that this incomprehensible weakness should overshadow the beautiful character of our great ancestor, we may not condemn: for, at this distance of time, and complete change in manners and customs, it is impossible for us to know the temptation he may have had to act as he did, or the extent of danger to which he was exposed. The most truly pious, the most experienced in religion, have often to mourn their "iniquities in holy things." The painful struggle is always to realize faith, to trust without one doubt, and more particularly in the smaller trials of life, which they deem too trivial for the notice, compassion, or interference of the Eternal. Nor can even *proofs* of a superintending providence always conquer the weakness of human nature. In this world, the likeness of God will at times be completely hidden in the earthly shell, however it may stand forth at others, as if naught of clay could dull it more. And this was the case with Abraham, who, though the beloved of the Lord, was yet *human*, and liable to all the weaknesses and frailties of human nature. We are not therefore to condemn, and so withdraw our admiration of his great and most consolingly beautiful character, because in two instances he falls short of our ideas of perfection —but rather thank God that in His Word human nature is recorded as *it is*, simply that we may not despair. It is enough for us, in this part of our narrative, to notice that our gracious God demands no more of His creatures than He knows they can perform; that Abraham's faulty weakness in this one instance, could not blot from the recollection of the Lord his pure and simple faith in every other; and that he permitted all that occurred in the kingdom of Gerar to make manifest, alike to Abraham and the nations, His continued watchfulness and miraculous interposition in favor of those whom He loves —His power to protect them from all harm, and also, that nothing was too wonderful for Him. Sarah had imagined she was too old to enjoy the felicity of becoming a mother—too old in any way to excite admiration, save to the beloved husband of her youth; and, ignorant that her beauty had been supernaturally renewed, neglected to assume the veil, which was worn by all Eastern women dwelling in towns. This explains Abimelech's present of a "covering for the eyes," and the words, "thus she was reproved," or warned, that her beauty subjected her to as much danger as had been the case in her youth.

Miraculously protected by the Eternal, and publicly vindicated from all dishonor by the King of Gerar, Sarah and her husband continued to dwell in Abimelech's dominions, some few miles to the south of Gerar; a place afterwards called Beer-Shebang, or Well of the Oath, from the covenant of peace there made between the patriarch and the king. Here it was that at the appointed time "God visited Sarah as He had said;" and the promised seed—the child of rejoicing—Isaac was born. What must have been the emotions of Sarah on beholding him? Not alone the bliss of a mother; but that in him the infant claimer of a love and joy which she had never so felt before, she beheld a visible and palpable manifestation of the wonderful power and unchanging love of the Most High God. Devoted, as Sarah had been, to the service and love of the Lord, how inexpressibly must those emotions have been heightened as she gazed upon her babe, and held him to her bosom as her *own*, her granted child! To those who really love the Lord, joy is as dear, as bright, as close a link between the heart and its God, as grief is to more fallen natures. We find the hymn of rejoicing, the song of thanksgiving, always the vehicle in which the favored servants of the Lord poured forth their grateful adoration, thus proving that the thought of the beneficent Giver ever hallowed and sanctified the gift; and therefore we believe with our ancient fathers, that though *not translated metrically*, Sarah expressed her joy in a short hymn of thanksgiving. The peculiar idiom of the Hebrew text confirms this supposition,* and we adopt it as most natural to the occasion. Her age had had no power, even before she became a mother, to dull her feelings, and her song of thanksgiving well expresses every emotion natural, not alone to the occasion, but to her peculiar situation. As a young mother, full of life, of sentiment, of affection, she felt towards her babe—giving him his natural food from her own bosom—tending his infant years—guiding him from boyhood to youth—from youth to manhood, and lavishing on him the full tide of love which had been pent up so long. The very character of Isaac, as is afterwards displayed—meek, yielding, affectionate almost as a woman's—disinclined to enterprise—satisfied with his heritage—all prove the influence which his mother had possessed,

* See the Rev. D. A. De Sola's translation, and note thereon.

and that his disposition was more the work of her hand than of his father's.

"The child grew and was weaned," Holy Writ proceeds to inform us; "and Abraham made a great feast the day Isaac was weaned,"—a feast of rejoicing that the Eternal had mercifully preserved him through the first epoch of his young existence. He was now three years old, if not more—for the women of the East, even now, do not wean their children till that age. The feast, however, which commenced in joy, was, for the patriarch, dashed with sorrow ere it closed. Educated with the full idea that he was his father's heir—though the words of the angel before his birth gave no warrant for the supposition—to Ishmael and his mother, the birth of Isaac must have been a grievous disappointment. And we find the son committing the same fault as his mother previously had done—deriding, speaking disrespectfully of Sarah and her child. The youth of Ishmael, and Sarah's request that the bond-woman might also be expelled, would lead to the supposition that it was Hagar who had instigated the affront. The age of Sarah, and the decidedly superhuman birth of Isaac, must, to all but the patriarch's own household, have naturally given rise to many strange and perhaps calumniating reports. In the common events of life all that is incomprehensible is either ridiculed, disbelieved, or made matter of scandal; and, therefore, in a case so uncommon as this, it is more than probable reports very discreditable both to Sarah and Abraham were promulgated all around them. Hagar, indeed, and Ishmael must have known differently:—that it was the hand of God which worked, and therefore all things were possible; but it was to Ishmael's interest to dispute or deny the legitimacy of Isaac; and therefore it was not in human nature to neglect the opportunity. No other offence would have so worked on Sarah. We are apt to think more poetically than justly of this part of the Bible. Hagar and her young son, expelled from their luxurious and happy home, almost perishing in the desert from thirst, are infinitely more interesting objects of consideration and sympathy, than the harsh and jealous Sarah, who, for seemingly such trifling offence, demanded and obtained such severe retribution.

We generally rest satisfied with one or two verses; whereas, did we look further and think deeper, our judgment would be different. In a mere superficial reading we acknowledge Sarah does appear in rather an unfavorable light; as if her love for Isaac had suddenly narrowed and stagnated every other feeling; and, jealous of Ishmael's influence over his father, she had determined on seizing the first opportunity for his expulsion. That this, however, is a wrong judgment is proved by the fact, that the Eternal Himself desires Abraham to hearken to the voice of Sarah in all that she shall say; for in Isaac was to be the promised seed, though of Ishmael also would He make a nation, because he was Abraham's son. That Sarah's advice was not to be displeasing to him, because of the lad and his mother.

Now, had Sarah's advice proceeded from an undue harshness, a mean and jealous motive, the Most High would, in His divine justice, have taken other means for the fulfilment of His decrees. He would not have desired His good and faithful servant to be so guided by an evil and suspicious tongue. There are times when we feel urged and impelled to speak that which we are yet conscious will be productive of pain and suffering to ourselves. All such impulses are of God; and it must have been some such feeling which actuated Sarah, and compelled her to continue her solicitation for the expulsion of Hagar and Ishmael, even after the moment of anger was passed. We know that Hagar had ever been her favorite slave; it was impossible for one affectionate as was Sarah, to have regarded Ishmael as her son for thirteen or fourteen years and yet not have loved him, though of course with less intensity than his father. The birth of Isaac naturally revealed yet stronger emotions; still Ishmael could not have been so excluded from her affections as to render her separation from him void of pain. And still she spoke, still urged the necessity, conscious all the time she was inflicting pain not only on her husband but on herself. This appears like contradiction; but each one who has attentively studied the workings of his own heart, will not only feel but pronounce it *truth*. Anger caused the demand: "Expel this bondwoman and her son; for the son of this bondwoman shall not inherit with my son, even with Isaac;" and calmer reflection continued to see the necessity. Abraham's possessions were sufficient for the heritage of both his sons; but as the course of nature was changed, and the younger, not the elder, was to be the heir of promise, confusion and discord would have ensued, and the brothers continually have been at war. Sarah's penetration appears to have discovered this; and as it was necessary for Ishmael to form a separate establishment, it was an act of kindness, not of harshness, to let him depart with Hagar, instead of going forth alone. From her own feelings she now knew the whole extent of a mother's love; and therefore, though Ishmael had been the sole offender, and the only one whose claims were likely to clash with Isaac's, she would not separate the mother from the son, and so urged Abraham to separate from both.

There is something touchingly beautiful in the patriarch's love for his elder son, and yet his instant conquest of self at the word of the Lord. His deep affection had blinded him to the probable discomforts which might ensue from his sons remaining together. His gentle and affectionate nature shrank from the pang of separation, causing even displeasure against Sarah for the first time in their long and faithful intercourse. Yet when God spake there was neither complaint nor murmur, nor one word of supplication that the heavy trial might be averted from him. It was enough that the Most High had spoken; and though all was dark before his son, to the fond anxious gaze of parental affection, he knew even from that darkness God *could* bring forth light, and *would* do so, for He had promised.

We are sometimes surprised at the small provision with which Abraham endowed his son at his departure. The riches of the patriarchs consisted of land, flocks, herds, and servants; nothing which could easily be bestowed. Besides which, Ishmael was to become the ancestor of a nation, through *the direct agency of the Lord*, not from any provision made him by his earthly father. Had Abraham endowed him, the interposition of the Eternal would not have been so clearly and unanswerably demonstrated. There would have been many to have traced his riches and the princely rank of his descendants from the gifts and power of Abraham, and denied altogether any interposition of the Lord; whereas, sent forth as he was, with nothing but sufficient provision to sustain him till he reached his appointed resting, it was impossible even for the greatest sceptic to trace his future prosperity and wealth to any earthly power alone. The bread and water must not be supposed as meaning only what we now regard them. In the language of the Bible bread is used indiscriminately for every kind of food, and the bottle of water signifies a skinful, such being used by Eastern travellers even now, and containing much more than we imagine is comprised by the term "bottle." Yet even these were to fail, that the miraculous power and compassionate love of the Eternal might still more startlingly be proved. It was as easy for the Most High to have guided Ishmael and his mother at once to their destined dwelling, as to try them as He did in the ordeal of alike physical and mental suffering. But He chose the latter, at once to prove His love to them, and to give to future ages, through his unerring word, comfort in their darkest hours; for as He relieved Hagar, so will He them. The God of the bondwoman is ours still; no time, no change can part us from Him.

The narrative of Hagar's wanderings in the wilderness, her maternal suffering and miraculous relief, is one of the most beautiful and most touching amongst the many beauties of the Bible. Hagar was not of Abraham's race, but one of a heathen and benighted nation, a bondwoman and a wanderer, a weak and lonely female, exiled from a home of love, overwhelmed with anxious fears for her child, perhaps, too, with self-reproaches for the unguarded words which she encouraged her boy to speak, and which she regarded as the sole cause of her banishment; yet was this poor sufferer the peculiar care of the great and mighty God. He caused the clouds of densest darkness to close around her—from them to bring forth the brightest, most enduring light. He deigned, by His angel, to speak comfort and hope, and even for her human wants provided the necessary aid. He did not guard from sorrow; for it was not until "the water was spent in the bottle, and she cast the child under one of the shrubs, and she went and sat down over against him, a good way off, for she said, Let me not see the death of the child; and she sat over against him, and lifted up her voice and wept"—not till her trial was thus at its height, that the angelic voice descended from heaven in such pitying and sympathizing accents: "What aileth thee, O Hagar? Fear not, for God hath heard the voice of the lad whence he is. Arise, lift up the lad, and hold him in thine hand, for I will make him a great nation." And the promise was fulfilled.

The whole history of Hagar is fraught with the deepest comfort. She was one of the many in individual character; pos sessing alike woman's engaging and faulty characteristics: feeling and affectionate at one time, overbearing and insolent at another—loving Ishmael with impetuous and clinging love, which could not bear to see his supposed heritage become the property of another, though she knew it was the decree of God —reverencing and loving Abraham alike as her master and the father of her child, but unable always to preserve the submission and respect due to Sarah as her mistress and indulgent friend; for, though the mother of Abraham's child, she was still Sarah's maid;—such was Hagar. Neither in character superior, nor in station equal, to the daughters of Israel now; yet was she the peculiar charge of the Most High, and twice did He deign, in closest communion, to instruct and console. Her life had its trials, in no way inferior in severity or in deep suffering to the trials of the present day. Yet God was with her in them all; and, in His own appointed time, permitted them to give place to prosperity and joy. And as He worked then, so He worketh now. It is no proof of His dearest love, when life passes by without a cloud—when sorrow and trial are strangers to our path. His word reveals that those whom He loved the *best*, alike male or female, endured the severest trials—that His love, His guiding word, were not given to the children of joy. To become His servant, His loved, His chosen, was to suffer and to labor. We see this throughout His word; and shall we, dare we, expect their exemption now? Oh! no, no! Would we love the Lord, would we truly be loved by Him, would we pray for and seek His paths, would we struggle on to the goal of immortal love and bliss, we must nerve both heart and frame to *bear;* strengthen and arouse every faculty to *endure* and *suffer;* for so did His chosen, His best beloved, and so too must we. We have still His word to be to us as the angelic whisper was to our ancestors. Their hope is ours, and their *reward.*

Few other events mark the life of Sarah. The Most High had brought her forth from the trials, anxieties, and doubts of previous years. He had, in His infinite mercy, fulfilled His word, and bestowed on her the blessed gift for which, in the midst of happiness, she had pined. Continuing His loving kindness, He lengthened her days much beyond the usual sum of mortality, that she might rear her child to manhood, and receive all the blessed fruit of her maternal care in Isaac's deep love and reverence for herself. In a mere superficial perusal of the life of Sarah, as read in our Sabbath portions, we are likely to overlook much of the consoling proofs of the Eternal's compassionating love for His female children, which it so powerfully reveals. Sarah was ninety years of age when Isaac was born. In the course of nature, ten or twelve years more would either have closed her mortal career, or rendered it, from the infirmities of so great an age, a burden to herself and all around her. There was no need of her preservation to forward the decrees of the Lord. In giving birth to the child of promise, her part was fulfilled, and at the age of ten or twelve the boy might have done without her. But God is LOVE, and the affections of His children are, in their strength and purity, peculiarly acceptable to Him. He never bestoweth happiness to withdraw it; and, therefore, to perfect the felicity of Sarah and her child, His tenderness preserved her in life and vigor seven and thirty years after she had given him birth. In this simple fact we trace the beneficent and tender Father, sympathizing not alone in every grief and pang, but in every joy and affection of His creatures. We feel to our heart's core the truth of the words of Moses, "Who hath God so near to him" as Israel? What nation can so trace, so claim the love of the Eternal?

Nor was the preservation of Sarah the *only* proof of our Father's loving tenderness towards her, and of His condescending sympathy with the love she bore her child. The trial of faith in the sacrifice of his son was given to the *father*; but the *mother* was spared the consuming agony which must have been her portion, even had her faith continued strong. God had compassion on the feebler, weaker nature of His female servant. He demanded not from her that which He knew the mother could not bear. He spared her, in His immeasurable love, the suffering which it pleased Him to inflict upon the father,—suffering and temptation *not* to satisfy the Lord, for His omniscience knew that His faithful servant would not fail; but to prove to future ages the mighty power of spiritual faith and love, even while in the mortal clay.

In the early part of his spiritual career, even Abraham's faith would in all probability have failed. He was *not* supernaturally endowed with divine grace and strength. All through his life we can trace his gradual advance and improvement, till his faith and love arrived at the climax which permitted even the offered and unmurmuring sacrifice of his dearly beloved and now only child. Even in this we trace the guiding and fostering love of the Lord—demanding not more than He knew *could* be given, and measuring the trial of faith according to the advancing strength of His servant, each one more than the last. But this consideration has more to do with Abraham individually and Israel at large. It is His loving kindness manifested towards Sarah that we, her female descendants, must take to our hearts, thence to derive alike strength and consolation. The conviction of the Eternal's love for us *individually* is necessary for woman's happiness, and peculiarly adapted to its bestowal.

It is woman's *nature* to yearn and droop for love—to shrink in agony from a lonely path—to long for some supporting arm on which to rest her weakness; and it is woman's *doom* too often to find *on earth* no loving rest, and therefore is her lot so sad. But when she can once realize that she is the subject of a love as immeasurably superior in consolation, strength, and changeless sympathy, to that of man, as the heaven is above the earth:—when she can once feel she has a friend who will never "leave her nor forsake"—in whose pitying ear she may pour forth trials and griefs, either petty or great, which she would not even if she might confide to man, secure not only of pity but of *healing*—when she is conscious that she is never lonely—never left to her own weakness, but in her every need will have strength *infused*—then, then is she so blessed that she is no more lonely, no more sad! And the word of God will give us this thrice blessed consolation, not in His gracious promises alone, though they in themselves would be sufficient, but in His dealings with his creatures.

As the ancestor of His beloved, we find Sarah's death and age particularly recorded; being the first woman of the Bible whose death and burial are mentioned. The deep grief of her husband and son are simply but touchingly betrayed in the brief words, "And Abraham came to mourn for Sarah, and to weep for her;" and, at a later period, not till his marriage with Rebekah, "and Isaac was comforted after his mother's death." Words that portray the beauty and affection of Sarah's domestic character, and confirm our belief that, although perhaps possessing many of the failings of her sex, she was yet a help meet for Abraham—a tender and judicious parent to her son—and a kind, indulgent friend to the large household of which she was the mistress. Her noble or rather princely rank, received as it had been direct from the Lord, is still more strongly proved by the intercourse between Abraham and the sons of Heth, when seeking from them a place to bury his dead: "Hear us, my lord," is their reply, "thou art a *mighty prince of God* amongst us; in the choicest of our sepulchres bury thy dead;" and it was with difficulty Abraham could elude the offered gift, and procure the cave as a purchase. His princely rank, however, and in consequence that of his wife, we see at once acknowledged, even by strangers, and the promise of the Lord, expressed in changing the name of *Sarai* into *Sarah*, clearly fulfilled.

The grief of Isaac appears to have lasted yet longer than that of his father, and beautifully illustrates the love between the mother and son. Abraham, advanced in years and spiritual experience, felt less keenly the mere emotions of humanity; he was convinced that Sarah had only gone before him to that world in which, from his great age, he would no doubt speedily join her. His many duties—his close communion with the Eternal—enabled him to rouse himself sooner from the grief, which at first was equally severe; but Isaac was, according to the patriarchal reckoning of time, still a very young man, at the age when feeling is keener, less controlled than at any other; and when, though spiritual comfort is great, human emotions will have full vent. Except the three days' journey to Mount Moriah with his father, Isaac does not appear to have been separated a single day from his mother; and her care, her guiding and fostering love, had so entwined her round his heart, that for three years after her death her son could find no comfort. How exalted and lovely must have been that mother's character to demand such a term of mourning from her son; whose youth and sex would, in some, have speedily roused him from sorrow, or urged its forgetfulness in scenes of pleasure!

We have little more to add on the spiritual lesson and divine consolation which Sarah's life presents to her female descendants, than those hints already given. Differently situated as we are, with regard to station, land, and customs, we may yet imitate her faithfulness in all her household duties—her love and reverence to her husband—her tenderness to her child—her quiet, unpretending, domestic, yet dignified fulfilment of all which she was called upon to do. We may learn from her to set no value on personal charms, save as they may enhance the gratification of those who love us best; or of rank and station, save as they demand from us yet deeper gratitude towards God, and more extended usefulness towards man. We may learn too from her history that it is better to wait for the Lord—to leave in HIS hands the fulfilment of our ardent wishes—than to seek to compass them by human means. We may trace and feel that nothing, in truth, is too wonderful for the Lord; that He will do what pleaseth Him, however we may deem it hopeless and in vain. Direct revelations, as vouchsafed to Sarah, indeed we have not, but God has, in His deep mercy, granted us His word—the record of all HE HAS DONE—that we may feel He is still OUR God; and though He worketh now in *secret*—for our sins have hid from us His ways—yet He worketh for us still, and hath compassion and mercy and love for each of us individually, even as He had for Sarah, and her bondwoman Hagar. All these to us, as women, her history reveals: as women of Israel, oh! yet more. It is of no stranger in race, and clime, and faith we read. It is of OUR OWN—of one from whom Israel hath descended in a direct, unshadowed line—of one—the beloved and cherished partner of that chosen servant and beloved friend of the Eternal, for whose sake revelation was given to mankind—Israel made not alone the nation, but the FIRST-BORN of the Lord; and that law bestowed, which revealed a God of "love, long-suffering and gracious, plenteous in mercy and truth;"—instructed us how to tread our earthly path, so as to give happiness to ourselves and fellow-creatures—to be acceptable to Him;—and pointed with an angel-finger to that immortal goal, where man shall live for ever!

Is it nothing to be the lineal descendants of one so favored—nothing to hold in our hands and shrine in our hearts, the record of her life from whom the race of promise sprang? Nothing, to peruse the wonderful manifestations of the Lord's love to her—to feel that from Him direct was Sarah's patent of nobility, and yet possess the privilege of being her descendant? Will the women of Israel feel this as nothing? Will they disdain their princely birth, their heavenly heritage? Will they scorn to look back on Sarah as their ancestor, and yet long for earthly distinctions, earthly rank? No! oh, no!

Let us but think of these things, of those from whom we have descended, and our minds will become ennobled, our hearts enlarged. We shall scorn the false shame which would descend to petty meannesses to hide our faith, and so exalt us in the sight of a Gentile world. Humbled, cast off for a little moment as we are—liable to persecution, scorn, contumely—to be "despised and rejected" of men—to bear the burden of affliction from all who choose to afflict—still, still we cannot lose our blessed heritage unless we cast it off; we cannot be deprived of our birthright unless, like Esau, we exchange it for mere worldly pelf, and momentary (because *earthly*) gratification. We are still Israelites—still the chosen, the beloved, the ARISTOCRACY of the Lord.

CHAPTER III.

REBEKAH.

In the same beautiful country whence, nearly seventy years previous, the son of Terah had been called by the divine command, still dwelt the children of his brother, Nahor. Contrary to the long period of childlessness which had been the portion of Abraham, eight sons were born unto Nahor. And when tidings of his family again reached the patriarch, just after the offered sacrifice of his son, he heard that his brother was also a grandfather—Bethuel, one of his sons having married, and possessing sons and one fair daughter. The many wanderings of Abraham, the distance to which he had removed, and the almost impossibility of obtaining reciprocal intelligence, had, of course, prevented family intercourse. Yet, by the notice taken of Abraham's having unexpectedly received intelligence of his kindred, and also by the momentous events recorded in the xxiv. chapter, it is evident that both Abraham and Nahor retained a vivid recollection of, and continued affection towards each other—an affecting illustration of the doctrine we so earnestly uphold

—that Holy Writ never fails to inculcate—alike by precept, character, and narrative—the *ascendency*, *necessity*, and *beauty* of the natural affections. Though elected to know and serve the Lord, and to promulgate the knowledge of the true religion throughout the world, still, no forgetfulness, no contempt of the less favored of his father's house, actuated Abraham. In simple, questionless obedience to his God, he had departed from all the haunts, the friends of his youth; but to a disposition so strongly affectionate as his own, often and often must the yearnings have returned, to learn somewhat of the brother of his love. The characters of the Bible are all *human:* though we are but too apt to judge them by any and every other test than that of humanity. Religion, instead of *deadening*, ever deepens and strengthens mere human feelings. No one has ever yet truly and devotedly loved God without feeling every natural affection heightened and more precious. Indifference in any one single point is utterly banished. It *cannot* exist with true spirituality; and therefore do we always find in the Bible, the strongest, most affectionate feelings actuating the chosen servants of the Lord.

From a careful consideration of this portion of Bible history, and of Laban's family in the sequel, it appears probable that Abraham had other reasons besides those of kindred for wishing his son to choose a wife from the daughters of Mesopotamia, instead of those of Canaan. Had the patriarch's kindred been merely idolatrous as the other families of the earth, it is not likely that the mere recital of the steward should have called forth Laban and Bethuel's answering exclamation—"The thing proceeded from the Lord, we cannot speak unto thee bad or good!"—nor many years afterwards, in Laban's intercourse with his nephew, his entreaty, "Tarry with me, for I have learned by experience that the Lord hath blessed me for thy sake." It would seem from these simply recorded facts, that though they worshipped images, which are referred to more than once in the sequel, their religion was certainly purer than that of the Canaanites. It was from his father's house Abraham had been elected and called by the Almighty. His firm rejection and abhorrence of idols, his meek and gentle un-upbraiding conduct, his departure in simple obedience to an unknown Being,—all this was probably remembered and so commented upon by his kindred, that his memory had more influence than his presence;

and vague notions of the religion and the God whom he had followed and preached, mingled with the image-worship which they still retained. These notions, very possibly strengthened by the rumors of Abraham's continued communings with this mysterious God, and the many manifestations of a superhuman agency vouchsafed to him, which, by slow degrees, reached even Mesopotamia, prepared them to acknowledge and even believe in Him; though from ignorance as to the manner of worship which could be acceptable to a Being so awful and invisible, they adhered to the worship of their fathers.

Abraham no doubt felt that it would be easy to impart to the daughter of such a race, the true and spiritual religion of which the Patriarch's own family was the only witness. There would be no fear of her retaining and secretly promulgating the impure and idolatrous notions which would undoubtedly have been the case with the daughters of Canaan; and this, acting powerfully on the affecting recollections of kindred and home, appears to me the real cause of Abraham's intense anxiety to take a wife for his son Isaac from the daughters of his father's house.

Meanwhile the daughter of Bethuel had grown into beautiful womanhood, beloved and cherished alike by her parents and brothers, and pursuing with cheerful content and affection the simple routine of domestic life. There is no mention in Scripture of her having ever been sought in marriage before the offer of Isaac. We are rather to suppose, that she was scarcely seen or known beyond the precincts of her father's establishment; and as this was the case also with the daughters of Laban, some years afterwards, the supposition of their superiority to the other heathen nations is confirmed.

The daily employments of the young females of the East appear to have been completely domestic; and in obedience to these daily duties we find Rebekah one evening going as usual to the well with her pitcher on her shoulder to draw water. The group of strangers beside the well must have struck her as something remarkable, but we do not find that she in any way loitered or wavered in the steady performance of her task.

"And the damsel was very fair to look upon, a virgin: *and she went down to the well, and filled her pitcher and came up.* And the servant ran to meet her, and said, Let me, I pray thee, drink a little water of thy pitcher. And she said, Drink, my 'ord: and she let down her pitcher upon her hand, and gave him drink. And when she had done giving him drink, she said, I will draw water for thy camels also, until they have done drinking. And she hasted and emptied her pitcher into the trough, and ran again unto the well to draw water, and drew for all his camels."

Among the many little exquisite touches of artless and gentle nature with which the Bible abounds, none surpass this for truth and beauty. The same unsophisticated nature that led her quietly to pursue her duty, without turning to the right hand or to the left, also prompted the active and cordial kindness to the stranger when he addressed her, and the respectful deference to his age and sex which the words "Drink, my lord," imply. It was the quiet self-possession, the modest ease and frankness, the total disregard of self, alike with regard to personal trouble as to the impression her own beautiful face and form might make, which ever proceed from a proper self-esteem, without which no woman, however situated, can happily or with propriety pass through life. She not only gave refreshment to the steward, but filled the trough for the weary camels to drink also. Many times must she have ascended and descended to the well, burdened with a weighty pitcher—a fair and gentle girl, while so many strong men were standing round—but they were strangers and travellers, and she was in her own land.

Well might Eliezer, "wondering at her, hold his peace, to wit whether the Lord had made his journey prosperous or not." It was difficult to believe that the prayer he had scarcely concluded before Rebekah appeared, should so speedily be answered; and it was, no doubt, with some little trembling he asked, "Whose daughter art thou? Tell me, I pray thee, is there room in thy father's house for us to lodge in?" and how must his heart have bounded with returning confidence at the artless reply: "I am the daughter of Bethuel, the son of Milcah, which she bare unto Nahor. She said moreover unto him, We have both straw and provender enough, and room to lodge in." Our ancient fathers, with much justice, suppose that the splendid presents of the steward *followed* this announcement, and were not given, as we might imagine from the general translations of the Bible, *before* he knew her name. They had been intrusted to him for the bride of Isaac; and therefore, it was not likely he should bestow them on any one, however beautiful and hospitable, unless perfectly convinced that she was the maiden destined so to be. The little conversation between them, and even the steward's fervent ejaculation of thanksgiving, probably took place while the camels were drinking; and it was when they had done, "that the man took a golden earring of half a shekel weight, and the bracelets for her hands of ten shekels weight of gold." Greatly must the maiden have marvelled, not only at the richness of the presents, but that they should be offered at all; and, true to the almost childish nature which the whole narration displays, "she ran and told them of her mother's house these things."

It is by some commentators considered strange, I believe, that in all which follows, Laban, not Bethuel, should be the principal actor. The Bible appears to tell us, that Laban was decidedly the head of his father's house; and, as there is no mention whatever of Rebekah's father, no reference to any relation but her mother and brother, it does not seem probable that she had a father living, the Bethuel who is mentioned being possibly a younger brother, and one of very inferior consequence.

We have already perceived that Rebekah "told them of her *mother's* house." And now, without any notice whatever of a father, we read, that "Rebekah had a brother whose name was Laban." And when he saw the earring and bracelets on his sister's hands, and when he heard her words, he came unto the man who still stood with his camels beside the well, and accosted him, not only as one who was master, with independent authority, but with an exclamation which confirms our previous suggestion, that some vague notions of Abraham's God had reached even Mesopotamia. The hurried narration of his sister would not have been sufficient incentive for such greeting;—"Come in, thou BLESSED OF THE LORD; wherefore standest thou without? for I have prepared the house, and room for the camels. And the man came into the house, and he ungirded his camels. And they gave straw and provender for the camels, and water to wash his feet, and the men's feet who were with him. And they set meat before him to eat: but he said, I will not eat till I have said mine errand. And he (Laban) said, Speak on."

Laban, as the generous, unsuspicious host, had performed his part. And now, the servant of Abraham failed not to perform his. Earnest in his master's cause, his mission occupying alike heart and mind,—convinced that he was in the Lord's hands, he would not wait till hunger was appeased and weariness subdued, but at once spoke; his first words refusing all honor to himself by the simple declaration עֶבֶד אַבְרָהָם אָנֹכִי, "Servant of Abraham am I." It was, indeed, a wondrous tale to which the family of Bethuel listened. By the words of Laban, at its conclusion, "Behold, Rebekah is *before* thee," we may infer, that the maiden and her mother were both present; though, by no word or exclamation did the former interrupt a narrative which concerned her so deeply; yet as a woman, and a very young one, how many feelings must have stirred within her, as the steward spoke!

Eliezer told how his venerable master had grown rich and great by the blessing of the Lord, who had also granted him, in his old age, a son, to whom Abraham had given all that he had:—how anxious he was to guard his son from a connexion with the Canaanites, and to take him a wife from his own kindred; overruling Eliezer's objection—"Peradventure, the woman will not follow me,"—by the solemn assurance that "the Lord, before whom I walk, will send His angel before thee, and prosper thy way;"—how, in obedience, he had set forth, and, arriving that day at the well, had prayed to the Lord God of his master Abraham, to grant that the virgin who, when he wished for a little water from her pitcher, should reply, "Drink thou, and I will draw for the camels also," should be the maiden whom the Lord had appointed for his master's son;—how his prayer had been heard and answered, by the appearance and kindly courtesy of Rebekah;—and he concluded, "I bowed down my head, and worshipped the Lord God of my master Abraham, who had led me in the right way, to take my master's brother's daughter for his son. And now, if you will deal kindly and truly with my master, tell me; and if not, tell me; that I may turn to the right hand, or the left."

Deeply indeed must the simple tale have affected its hearers. The rich, the princely Abraham had remembered and yearned towards his father's house; even those who, perchance, in his youth had reviled and persecuted him for his rejection of their idols; seeking from them, in preference to every other, a wife for his son. "The thing proceedeth from the Lord," was their instant answer. "We cannot speak unto thee bad or good

Behold, Rebekah is before thee, take her, and go, and let her be thy master's son's wife, as the LORD hath spoken."

Blessed thus far, the richest jewels of gold and silver were presented by the steward to the youthful bride, her mother and brother. Surely, if her father had still been living, he would here have been mentioned: but neither here, nor in the 55th and 60th verses following, which are important as relating to her influential kindred, is there any notice taken of his existence.

One night only, the steward accepted the lavish hospitality of his hosts. Anxious to report the success of his mission, he entreated, "Send me away to my master." But natural ties could not be so quickly severed without pain. How could they so suddenly part with the cherished darling of their house—in all probability never to look upon her again? "Let the damsel abide with us a few days," her mother and brother said; "at least ten, after that she shall go." But the steward entreated them to "hinder him not," believing that to loiter, would be "displeasing to the Lord who had prospered his way." And they said, "We will call the damsel, and inquire at her mouth." Young and retiring as she was, her own voice was to decide the matter. They would neither retain nor send her away without her own consent; thus proving that even family authority, in the Bible, was an authority of love. "And calling her, they said, Wilt thou go with this man? And she said, I will go;" —a brief and simple answer, yet suited alike to her character and the occasion. No doubt, there will be some to exclaim against the reply as abrupt and unmaidenly; but have they quite considered all the circumstances of the case? Rebekah's character, at this period of her life, was a beautiful blending of simplicity and truth. Sought by Abraham for his son, of whom, in all probability, she had already favorably heard; selected by God himself, every *natural* feeling of woman was satisfied and soothed. Perhaps, now, in this period of ultra refinement, such simplicity will scarcely be understood. Yet, *then*, her meek assent was in perfect accordance with all that had passed before. Is it not ordained, even by God himself—that woman, even as man, should leave father, mother, and home, to cleave unto her husband? Besides, this was no engagement of mere human devising. She was, unconsciously, the instrument in the Eternal's hand to further His decrees.

And her brief assent was his inspiration, as certainly as all the previous incidents. Nor can we doubt for a moment, even while she declared her willingness to go, that natural affections were busy within her. Have not our readers themselves felt, at times, two completely opposing feelings filling their hearts at once? And oh! how blessed would it be at such times, if we could but realize that the words, fraught with a pain and anxiety unknown, unthought of, when we spoke them, proceed alone, as Rebekah's "I will go," from the guidance of the Lord, and that therefore, spite of all the sufferings which may gather round us, they will in the end be blessed.

Rebekah had accepted the presents of betrothal, and was therefore already of the family of Abraham. How then might his steward go without her? It was not her part to detain him on his way. We may imagine the tears of affection with which the fond blessing was pronounced by her brothers. The mother, though still present, is not mentioned; for her prayers were in her heart. "And they blessed Rebekah, and said unto her, Thou art our sister; be thou the mother of thousands of millions, and let thy seed possess the gates of those which hate them." And Rebekah arose (probably from the detaining arms of her kindred), and with her nurse, and attendant damsels, sought their camels, and accompanied the steward on his homeward way.

How many thoughts must have crowded the heart and mind of the young daughter of Bethuel during this journey—the home she had left, and the home she was about to seek—the friends of her childhood, and those unknown; yet towards whom she turned with the yearning to love and be beloved: probably hearing from the lips of the steward so much of his young master, as to render him in her mind no longer a stranger.

Simply and beautifully is the last touch to this portion of her history given by the inspired historian. Canaan was reached; the tents of the patriarch in sight. And lifting up her eyes, Rebekah beheld a man walking forth in the fertile fields; bearing in his pensive mind and measured tread, the aspect of one in holy meditation. It was eventide, that still solemn hour of holy musing, sought only by those who have no thought from which to shrink, who can call up sweet dreamy visions of the past—sad, yet how inexpressibly soothing. That holy hour, when the soul of the departed comes back to the spirit of the bereaved, holding such commune as *must* proclaim our union with the invisible world, and confirm our immortality. The maiden probably guessed who it was on whom she gazed. But when the question was asked and answered by her guide, modesty, refinement, simplicity, and that respect which ever springs from the heart, all impelled her to "light off her camel," and "to take a veil and cover herself."

This was true humility, for she knew her own dignity. She demanded no more respect than she paid herself. She waited no ceremonious introduction, but alighting from the camel, completely shrouded in her veil, she proved by the one action, the respect due to the son of Abraham, her destined husband, and by the other retained her own gentle dignity, by concealing every charm, till the servant's tale was told, and Isaac claimed her as his bride. Personal beauty was in this case as nothing, though she possessed it in no ordinary degree. Her conduct proceeded from an artless, unsophisticated nature, timidly shrinking from the eyes of him whom she most wished to please—a desire to conceal the very beauty which she must have yet ardently hoped that he might prize; and her hope was fulfilled, for "Isaac brought her into his mother Sarah's tent, and he took Rebekah, and she became his wife, and he loved her, and Isaac was comforted after his mother's death." How beautifully do those few words illustrate the extent of his love both towards his mother and wife! Though three years had passed since the death of his mother, he yet mourned for her. Not even the affections of his father could satisfy that painful yearning;—not even religion, with her host of soothing thoughts and blessed images, could wholly *comfort* him, though she gave him strength to endure, and spiritual love to bless the hand which smote. Nor is this a contradictory assertion. Religion leads us to Him who alone can heal, in deep and most fervid prayer;—that prayer brings us, from Him whose deep mercy hears and answers, support and consolation, by the conviction that we are not lonely—that we shall meet again those whom we love in His presence, who is love itself; and this is comfort. The comfort here alluded to was for the yearnings of the mortal; the *immortal* could realize consolation, the *mortal* could not. Though it be in very truth the *invisible soul* we love, yet we become so knit with the *mortal* habitation of that soul, that we cannot feel it has perished from our sight for ever, without an agony of heart that time and prayer, and constant communings with the *invisible* Spirit alone, can in any way assuage. Nor is there one portion in the Holy Bible which would tell us that God condemns such grief. If with the whole fervor of our immortal being, we can bow in much submission, faith, and love, unto His will, He condemns not, nay, feels compassionate, and in His own good time heals the agony which our *human* nature feels through the human agency of wife, or friend, or child. And so it was with Isaac. Wedded as he was to the memory of his mother, no ordinary woman could have so gained his love as to give him comfort, and fill up the aching void which had existed three long years. He must have seen in Rebekah when she first became his wife, a reflection of Sarah's endearing qualities; and united as these were to youth and beauty, inspired still deeper and dearer emotions than he had ever experienced before.

To some dispositions, this sudden elevation in a social and domestic position would have been a dangerous ordeal; but neither presumption, arrogance, nor pride, appears to have marked the conduct of Rebekah. The same steady performance of household duty manifested in her girlhood, probably continued in her higher and more responsible station; and year after year found her calmly following the quiet routine of daily duty happily to herself and to her household. And here, for a brief while, we would pause to gather the sweet blossoms of instruction and guidance proffered by a Father's love, which Rebekah's history, thus far considered, can impart. We would linger a moment on the past ere we go forward, for the picture must be changed. Yet it is no marvellous or incomprehensible change—it is no history of woman in an era so long past that we wonder, and scarce believe—the picture is too perfect even now;—it is woman *then*, and woman *now*, as we shall see hereafter.

Although from the wide distinction between patriarchal and modern times, our position and duties as daughters of Israel can never resemble those of Rebecca, we have, like her, domestic duties to perform, and a station not only to fulfil but to adorn, so as to excite towards us respect and love. The women of the Bible are forcibly portrayed, not for us to follow them exactly, for that we could not do, but from their conduct in their respective spheres to guide us in ours; from the approval or reproof bestowed directly or indirectly upon them, to teach their descendants what is acceptable in the sight of our heavenly

Father and what is not; and of this we may rest assured there is no contradiction to puzzle us in the Word of God. The *precepts* of His law are proved by the *practice* of His servants. "Whatsoever thy hand findeth to do, do it with all thy might," was said centuries after by the sage monarch, who, in obedience to the command of God relating to Kings, must have been acquainted with the whole of His law; and that precept was exemplified in Rebecca's conduct at the well. She had every temptation to turn aside a few moments in her simple task. Had she ever accustomed herself to encourage wandering thoughts in her different employents, to turn from them for every frivolous pretence, she would never have withstood the temptation of idling away her time with the goodly looking strangers, and thus demonstrated a character totally unfit to be the ancestress of God's chosen race. But as she went down to the well and filled her pitcher, and came up, "neither turning to the right nor to the left," so it behoves us to follow our daily duties, would we, like her, receive the blessing of the Lord. It is said to be woman's nature ever to be unsteady—to be caught by the glare of every new object, every new face—to become frivolous from allowing herself in youth to flutter from one employment to another, seeking but sweets, and terrified at the first sight of all that may seem more harsh or stern. But such frivolity is incompatible with the regenerate and spiritual woman whose guidance is her Bible, whose sustainer is her God. She feels too deeply responsible to Him for every hour of her time to squander its smallest portion needlessly away. She seeks to love Him too earnestly, too continually, not to associate the hope of His approval with her every employment, and so associated it is impossible for them to be frivolously followed or lightly interrupted; and if domestic duties were thus performed by the young daughter of a house who knew not by direct revelation the Lord, how much more devolves upon us her descendants, to whom the Lord himself has vouchsafed, through His holy Word, both guidance and example! O! let us then, in our every pursuit, first ponder well if we may lay it before our God, and upon it ask His blessing; and if we truly can, let us pursue it with all our heart, and soul, and might, if we would indeed seek the loving tenderness of our God, the respect of the world, and of ourselves.

Nor is her steadiness the only portion of Rebecca's early

character demanding our admiration. The winning and obliging gentleness with which she met the stranger's address proceeded from the genuine kindness, the real politeness of an utterly unselfish heart. The request was not only granted, but granted with such sweetness of manner and respectful words as threefold to enhance the kindness of the deed. The beautiful laws contained in the 32d, 33d, and 34th verses of the 19th chapter of Leviticus had not then been issued, yet the conduct of Rebecca was a practical illustration of the *spirit* which they teach. She paid respect to age, and did unto the stranger even as if he had been one born in the land; and this we may all do. It is not enough that we *act kindly*, and *mean kindly*, in our intercourse either with friends or strangers. We must make manifest kindly *feeling* by a kindly and conciliating *manner*. At a period when the drift of education sometimes appears to condemn, conquer, and entirely annihilate feeling, this will be difficult, for widely different is the manner which is *taught*, however perfect may be its propriety, its gentleness, its suavity, to that which springs from the heart, and has its origin in overflowing and unselfish feeling. But has the heart—has feeling anything to do with our behavior to a perfect stranger, and acquaintance of the hour, whom in the whole course of our life we may never meet again? It has, and it may be productive of good, both to ourselves and others. The great, the good, the mighty and most merciful Creator of heaven and earth disdained not, even in the midst of this stupendous creation, to bid the earth bring forth her *flowers*, not to serve as food, or shelter, or absolute use in the common meaning of the word, but simply to beautify, to enliven, to rejoice, to fling a gladness and a sunshine on the desert waste and weary wilderness, and add beauty and rejoicing even where all around is joy; and as flowers to the earth, so is kindliness to man. It will not remove grief, nor give him what perchance he needs, but it may cause a flower to spring up in the lonely recess or careworn furrow of his heart, whose memory may linger long after the flower itself has perished. And shall we scorn the power that will do this? Shall we think a flower of half an hour's growth too worthless to be given, too trifling to be gathered? Oh! let us not encourage such a thought. We may know, indeed, nothing of the stranger with whom, for a brief hour, we may be thrown; but that very ignorance should urge us to courtesy and kindliness. His course may have been one of care, his present lot a waste, and a gentle tone and kind manner may be to him as the flower in the desert wiling him a brief while from his own sad thoughts. Or it may be his lot has been and is all joy; and yet will kindliness be sweet, even as the flower in the festive hall, or in the pathway of the bride; its form scarce noticed at the time, yet so blending with its associated images as in memory to be called up again and yet again. We are not placed here to live for ourselves alone, and more powerfully than aught else, *if it spring from the heart, and has its birth in feeling*, will a kind and gentle manner rivet the links of brotherhood, bid us feel we are all children of our common Father, and so strengthen our love in Him, and for each other.

On us more especially, aliens and exiles from our own land, is manner, as the mirror of the heart, incumbent. There was a time, but lately passed away, when to perform this duty was impossible, and therefore supposed to be unnecessary. When scorned, persecuted, condemned as the very scum of the earth, hated and reproached, it was as utterly impossible for us to manifest courtesy and kindness, as to receive them. Hatred begets hatred, as scorn begets scorn, more especially when neither emotion may be avowed. What did the cringing manner, the abject tone of the persecuted, tortured Jew conceal? Was it marvel it should be hatred as strong, if not stronger, because utterly powerless, than that of his cruel, his tyrannical oppressor? But now that in some enlightened and blessed realms these fearful times are past, and the right hand of fellowship extended to us, shall the exile and oppressed refuse to meet in amity and confidence, the sons of the land which gives them protection and home? We were commanded to show kindness to a stranger, as to one born amongst us. That blessed privilege is no longer ours, for we are strangers in a strange land; yet may we still obey the *spirit* of the law, and in the cultivation of a kindly heart, and manifestation of a kindly feeling, let us remember we have not only an *individual*, but a *national* character to support—that a brief half hour's intercourse with a stranger is endowed with power to *exalt* or to *lower* the cause of Israel; and as Rebekah's kindly cordiality was blessed to her, by making her the wife of Isaac, and so revealing to her the glorious tidings of a God of love, so may the kindly manner of the youngest daughter of Israel be blessed to her, by making her the unconscious instrument, in God's hand, to exalt His holy faith, and proclaim His truth in the heart and mind of the Gentiles amongst whom she dwells.

Yet, Rebekah's courtesy to the steward demonstrates neither presumption nor forwardness incompatible with her age or sex. We find her, directly her brother Laban comes forth, retiring to her own modest station in her mother's tent, and claiming no further notice. We see, therefore, that to act kindly demands not the forsaking our natural sphere. We are not to *look abroad* for opportunities to act as Rebekah did; but, like her, we shall find them without leaving our home, in the domestic and social intercourse of daily life. Let us ponder well upon these things, and, as daughters of Israel, make it our glory and our pride to do our simplest duty "with all our might;" our pleasure, to scatter flowers on the path of all with whom we may be thrown; and dwelling with meek and loving contentment in our appointed sphere, remember that the cause of Israel is our own, and it is in our power to exalt or degrade it.

For twenty years, the lives of Rebekah and Isaac appear to have passed in all the quiet felicity of domestic love and peace. Abraham was still living, happy in the happiness of his son Isaac; for to his other sons "Abraham gave gifts, and sent them away from Isaac his son, while he yet lived, eastward unto the east country." He gave them, in all probability, a knowledge of the Lord enough to recognise and worship him; but in Isaac, Abraham knew was the promised seed, and therefore by him was the aged patriarch's home. Anxiously he, too, must have anticipated the birth that would prolong his line, but from his personal experience in "waiting for the Lord," his feelings must have been less anxious than those of Isaac. In these twenty years, we hear of no temporal disturbance nor divine interference, as in the earlier life of Abraham; but that spiritual communing with the Lord, and improvement in knowledge of and faith in Him, in no ways slackened or diminished, we are called upon to believe by the simple fact of Isaac going to "entreat the Lord for his wife," and the instant answer to his prayer. Again we see divine interference, not what is called *natural causes*, operating for the fulfilment of the Eternal's promise of a chosen seed. Jacob, the father of the twelve tribes, from one or other of whom the wandering Hebrew can still trace descent and claim the promises vouchsafed unto his fathers—Jacob, even as Isaac, was the child, not alone of promise, but of PRAYER.

Those twenty years saw Rebekah as we last beheld her, only matured in the graces of womanhood, and so grafted on the house of Abraham, as like him to worship and know the great God alone. She had had, as yet, no temptation to swerve aside from the straight path of duty. A beloved and cherished wife, daughter, and mistress, her life passed by so smoothly, her affection so devoted to one first object, and thence calmly emanating on all under her influence, that she was, as every other woman in a similar position must have been, still entirely ignorant of the shoals and quicksands in her heart, which might lead to sin, and end in sorrow.

Yet her first action, after proof was given of the Eternal's gracious answer to her husband's prayer, was one of such child-like simple confidence in the power and wisdom of the Lord to answer all of doubt and fear, that to reconcile her conduct afterwards becomes more difficult. Unusual and incomprehensible suffering so oppressed her as to raise a doubt of the promise being then about to be fulfilled. "If it be so," she thought, "why am I thus?"—and without pause or hesitation, went directly "to inquire of the Lord." She asked no advice, demanded no human aid—but in heartfelt prayer—for in prayer only could she so inquire—laid before Him her every emotion, and from him implored reply. We would humbly ask those, if indeed there can be such, who deny to woman an immortal soul, refuse her the blessed privilege of individual and secret commune with her Creator, and believe man's prayer alone omnipotent, how they would interpret this very simple narration? They may assert, as I believe some commentators do, that it was through Abraham she inquired of the Lord, and received reply—but, as we have no warrant whatever in Scripture, by direct word or implied inference, to confirm this assertion, we must reject it altogether. The long years which Rebekah had passed in the household of Abraham, had not flown by unused and spiritually unimproved. She had seen the Great and Invisible Being acknowledged and adored. She had been taught by example; and we may be scripturally certain, though the fact itself is not mentioned, by precept also. The natural impulse of humanity, under all difficulties and suffering, is to pray—and in the beautiful simplicity of the patriarchal ages, no artificial coldness, no appalling scepticism, no disheartening doubt, could have crowded round her, whispering that the prayer was vain, that the Creator of heaven and earth was a Being too far removed from woman's petty griefs to listen and give reply. In the simple trusting confidence of a child, she sought the Parent whose love was omnipotent not only to understand the doubt and pain, but to give relief, and her confidence was answered. How that gracious answer was vouchsafed, whether through Abraham, or directly to herself, is I believe, an argument—but Scripture bids us believe, without hesitation, the latter—"And the Lord said *unto her*," clear simple words, banishing at once all necessity for mediation either of man or angel; words almost impossible, even wilfully to be misunderstood. The *how* she received this answer, whether through the medium of the ear, or by an impression on the mind—can be of very little consequence; and is one of those cavilling inquiries which we could wish banished, ere formed into words; tending as they do to fill up the mind with vain and idle speculations, instead of the pure simple truths of Scripture. It is enough, and a most blessed enough for us, that the "Lord said unto her," the direct answer to her inquiring prayer. The words were mysterious—that she was already the mother of two opposing nations, one of whom should be stronger than the other—and the elder should serve the younger." Yet, mysterious as they must have been, they came from the Lord. He had graciously vouchsafed to explain the cause of her unusual sufferings, and Rebekah was satisfied; for we find not another word from her of either wonderment or complaint.

And oh! what a blessed incentive have we from this simple narrative, in all our griefs and sufferings, bodily or mental, to inquire of the Lord—to come to Him as our ancestress, in guileless faith and simple-minded prayer. He is our God as He was hers—yea, ours—exiles, wanderers, WOMEN as we are, and who, with the holy word of God within his hand, shall dare to refuse to us, as women, as Israelitish women, the power, the purity, the privilege of prayer? Who shall dare assert that we are powerless to pray, or need the mediation of man, to bear up our petitions to the throne of grace? Mothers, wives, daughters of Israel, you alone must prove the utter falsity of this charge! Before the law, under the law, during the captivity, we shall still find the Hebrew woman seeking her God in prayer and receiving from him direct reply. Oh! shall we not thus prove that we have a soul immortal as that of man—that the very breath of our being, the light of our path, the support of strength, is prayer—that prayer which brings us daily, nay hourly, in commune with a loving Father, whose tender sympathy is endless as His love. Let us prove we need not Christianity either to teach, or direct us how to pray—but, turning to the blessed pages of our own Bible, make manifest that to look further is not needed. That there we have indeed sufficient for encouragement and hope; for confidence and faith. As Rebekah prayed, so too may we; and as our Father answered her, so will He us. Not indeed with word direct, but with that blessed calm, and hope, and faith, which prayer only can bestow; and with that heavenly patience which will enable us to "wait for the Lord," in the firm belief that whatever He may will is best. It is worthy of remark that Rebekah is the first recorded instance of woman's immediate appeal to God, and the condescending reply.

At the appointed time Isaac and Rebekah became parents of twin sons, who grew and flourished; and in early youth displayed a contrariety of disposition and pursuits which must have appeared strange, in such nearly allied relations, had it not been rendered clearly intelligible, at least to their mother by the previous words of the Lord. But yet these words do not appear to me sufficient for Rebekah always to have regarded Jacob as the promised seed. The promise, or rather explanation, given in answer to her prayer, was simply, "the one people shall be stronger than the other, and the elder shall serve the younger;" not as was the case with Abraham, when the promised seed was specifically *named.* And in the very next revelation which was vouchsafed to Isaac, a few years afterwards, we read, "Sojourn in this land and I will be with thee, and will bless thee; for unto thee, and unto *thy seed,* will I give all these countries, and I will perform the oath which I sware unto Abraham thy father. And I will make *thy seed* to multiply as the stars of heaven, and will give unto *thy seed* all the countries; and in *thy seed* shall all the nations of the earth be blessed;" and again, the last verse of this same xxvii. chapter—the Lord appeared unto him the same night, and said, "I am the God of Abraham, thy father; fear not, for I am with thee, and will bless thee, and multiply *thy seed* for my servant Abraham's sake."

The Eternal expressly says "thy seed." Isaac might be justified in supposing that *both* his sons were concerned in the promises, until Esau's reckless disregard of his birthright, and other spiritual blessings, in addition to his intermarrying with the daughters of Canaan, must have convinced his father that not from him could spring the chosen seed. The revelation that "the elder should serve the younger," must have occasioned Rebekah many mental inquiries; but even if she herself supposed that Jacob was the destined inheritor of Abraham's line, it is evident that she did not impart it to her husband.

Isaac's love for the reckless and able hunter, Esau, is one of those contradictions of the heart, unaccountable indeed, but very often found. He loved Esau best, because in every respect he was completely his opposite. Isaac was meek, affectionate, faithful, quietly and contentedly dwelling in one spot, moving thence only at the command of the Lord: satisfied with the temporal blessings around him, and the spiritual blessings of promise. Esau, bold, enterprising, ever roving in search of active pursuit; heeding naught but the present; scorning his home and home ties; rude and rough, yet, when excited, deeply and warmly affectionate to his aged father. And Isaac loved him better than his younger son, who, more like himself, "was a plain or upright man dwelling in tents." But Rebekah loved Jacob. Sacred history does not say why—and we are therefore permitted to infer, that it was simply because it is in woman's nature to love him best who is least loved by his father. But Rebekah's favoritism, as we shall see in the sequel, was stronger and more culpable than that of Isaac. All such emotions are stronger in woman's heart than in man's—because, with the former, *feeling* is the most powerful, and with the latter, *reason*. Partiality must always occasion injustice, and more particularly in a parent; for no task demands more control and feeling, more complete conquest of self, than that of parental affection. The dispositions, the characters of the divers members of one family are so varied, that it is impossible to guide all by one and the same training. An impartial mother will know every light and shadow of every disposition, and guide and act accordingly. A partial mother sees but the virtues and qualities of *one*, and from want of sympathy and proper management of the other in early years, makes him in reality all that she believed him. Jacob was domestic, because a mother's doting love made his home one of enjoyment, and administered to every want.

It was not till after Sarah's death that Isaac even sought a wife, and not till he was parted from his mother that Jacob loved, proofs all convincing of the strength, the beauty, the fulness of the love which in those simple ages united the mother and the son.

To Esau this soothing and blessed love was not given as it was to Jacob; and while his hasty and inconsiderate marriage with the daughters of the Hittite was a grief of mind to Isaac and Rebekah, the latter's neglect might have been in part their cause. Esau had no kindly woman's heart to turn to, as had his brother, yet we have proof that his affections were as strong —perchance, from his ruder character, yet stronger—and the very want of female love at home might have first urged him to seek it from the stranger. Oh! it is sad when partiality and its concomitant, injustice, obtains entrance into a mother's heart. It steals in so silently, so disguisedly, that unless every avenue be guarded, its advances are utterly unknown, till it has gained a strength and substance which hold us chained. Mere human love, omnipotent as in a mother's breast it is, is not sufficient to guard us from such weakness—no, nor former strength and stability of character. Rebekah had all this, and yet as a mother she fell. It can only be that close communion with the universal Father, who alone knows and feels every secret throbbing of a mother's heart, and from whose hand alone can come the strength, not only to *guide* aright her treasures, but to *feel* aright herself.

During the growth of his sons, Isaac's temporal riches very greatly increased. Abraham's death did not take place till his grandsons were fifteen. He who had believed it next to impossible in his old age to have a son, lived not only to bless his son, but his son's seed. A famine had sent Isaac and his family, by direction of the Eternal, to Gerar, and there he dwelt until he became so rich and great that the "Philistines envied him;" and their king, Abimelech, said unto him, "Depart from us, for thou art much mightier than we." And he did so, and after some wanderings, fixed his tent at Beersheba; and there again the Lord appeared unto him, bidding him "fear not, for He was with him." Beersheba, therefore, appears to have been the scene of all the domestic events which followed—Esau selling his unvalued birthright—his subsequent marriage—the vexations thence proceeding to Isaac and Rebekah—and those bodily infirmities of the former, which occasioned his anxious desire to "bless his son before he died."

Rebekah heard the words of her husband. She had seen him call his firstborn to his couch, and bid him seek venison, and bring the savory meat that he loved, that his soul might bless him before he died; and her heart swelled tremblingly within her. Esau? Was Esau to have his father's blessing? He who had sold his birthright, and so spurned his privileges as heir; and if he had it, how could the Lord's word be fulfilled, and the "elder serve the younger?" Why could she not prevent it, and secure to him whom the Lord before his birth had chosen as the mightiest, the blessing of his father? It was easy to be accomplished; and surely, as the Lord had said it, she was justified in using any means to bring it to pass. Such was weak, finite reasoning—such the baneful whisper of our earthly nature, urged on by the rushing torrent of human affections. In that dread moment of temptation, how might she realize the unquestioning faith which would bid her feel, "The Lord hath spoken, and will he not do it?" That His will needed no human aid for its fulfilment; that He would do His pleasure in the very face of those contradictory events, which human will and finite wisdom might so weave as to render its fulfilment seemingly impossible. If Rebekah had but "inquired of the Lord" in this perplexity, as on a former one, the whole train of deceit and its subsequent suffering would have been averted. But she was still a woman, weak, wavering, a very reed in her mortal nature, and liable, as every child of Adam, to temptation and to sin.

Had she even waited but one brief hour, all would have been well—the evil impulse would have been conquered in her pious heart, by a train of thought as above, but there was no time either to wait or think again; and, acting on the impulse, she called Jacob, and after informing him of his father's directions to his brother, continued in a strain that would lead us to believe, that even at that moment she feared Jacob's upright nature would shrink from the task she imposed. "Now, therefore, my son, OBEY my voice, according to that which I command thee." She claimed his unquestioning obedience, ere imparting that which she desired, and then proceeded. Surely her heart must have reproached her, when her own son ventured to suggest, though guardedly and respectfully, that it was a fraud, and might bring upon him a curse instead of a blessing. Yet still she enforces the command, "Upon me be the curse, my son, only obey my voice." And he did obey her, weakly and mistakenly; for had he resisted, had he submissively, yet firmly braved her momentary wrath, the evil temptation must have been subdued, and the mother saved by the unscrupulous honesty of the son.

But this was not to be. To make manifest His ways, that suffering *must* attend deceit, however for the moment it may seem to succeed, the Eternal permitted the plans of finite forming uninterruptedly to proceed, working out indeed His will through them, but punishing even in success. The kid was procured and dressed—the very hands and neck of Jacob disguised, lest their smoothness should betray him; and thus attired by a mother to deceive, he approached the bed-side of his blind father. How fearfully must the heart of Rebekah have throbbed at every word uttered by her husband and son! How terrified at the words of the unsuspecting, yet half doubting Isaac! "Come near, I pray thee, that I may feel thee, my son, whether thou be my very son Esau or not." And Jacob went near unto Isaac his father, and he felt him, and said, "The voice is Jacob's voice, but the hands are the hands of Esau." And, again, as doubting still, he asks, "Art thou my very son Esau? and Jacob answered, I am." The inspired historian might not interrupt his brief, yet how deeply impressive detail, to dilate on a woman's feelings; yet we, her descendants, are surely justified in judging for a moment of Rebekah's emotions during this interview, by what our own would be. She could have had no support, no stay, for she had wilfully banished TRUTH, and how, then, might she PRAY? Her whole heart and mind must have been troubled and tossed by every trifling word; discovery and shame, perhaps the very loss or estrangement of her husband's love, were as likely as the longed for success. How often, during that interim, must she have longed once more to tread the path of truth, for Rebekah was a mere novice in deceit! Her nature, as we have seen, was guileless and open as the day; the mere temptation of the moment, and its consequent anxious and impelling feelings, could not have so changed that nature, as to make her an unmoved witness of that which followed—the very falsehood repeated and insisted upon by those lips which she had taught from infancy to lisp forth truth. But when the blessing was obtained, when she saw her plan had in truth succeeded, we may suppose, judging still by human nature, that these agonizing doubts and fears were for the moment calmed in the triumph of success—conscience was hushed again, in the thought that she had compassed by stratagem that which she believed impossible to have been obtained else—that it must have been right and good so to have acted, or it would not have been permitted to succeed. Alas! how often do we so deceive ourselves! Could we but glance a little, a very little, further on, we should know, and feel (how bitterly!) that the very deceit we believed innocent, because it brought success, has been our first step in the paths of woe.

And so it was with Rebekah, though as yet she knew it not. Her feelings of triumph could not, however, have lasted long: "And it came to pass, as soon as Isaac had made an end of blessing Jacob, and Jacob was yet scarce gone out from the presence of his father, that Esau, his brother, came in from hunting;" and that interview followed, which, for simple and touching pathos, is not surpassed by any incident in the Bible.

Rebekah was a partial, but not a weak or unkind mother. She loved Jacob better than his brother, but Esau was still her son, her first-born, and oh! how painfully must her heart have yearned towards him, when she heard his "great and exceeding bitter cry!"—"Hast thou but one blessing, my father—bless me, even me also, O my father—and Esau lifted up his voice and wept." Esau, the rude, the careless hunter, who had seemed to care for naught but his own pleasures; the chase, the field, the wild! He bowed down by his blind father like an infant, and wept; beseeching the blessing of which a mother and a brother's subtlety had deprived him. Could Rebekah have been a witness, or even hearer of this scene, without losing all the triumph of success, in sympathy with the anguish of her first-born? It is impossible to ponder on her previous character, without being convinced of this. It is not from one act, one unresisted temptation, that we ought to pronounce judgment on a fellow-creature: yet, from our unhappy proneness to condemn, we generally do so. The character of Rebekah is thus too often supposed to be evil alone, and her unfortunate deception in favor of her best beloved son is the only part of her life brought strongly forward: whereas, if we look and think on all that sacred history has recorded of her, that there is also perfect silence as to any other fault (which, had she committed, we may be sure would have been told for our warning)—it becomes evident that this guilty action proceeded, not from *forethought*, which would have manifested a naturally evil disposition, but from *impulse;* the thought, the temptation of a moment, overbalancing by its force the rectitude of years. As forethought, we must condemn both the sin and the sinner. As impulse, we must abhor the sin—but only grief and trembling for the weakness of human nature must attend our reflections on the sinner. Nor are we justified in denying her those emotions of grief and doubt, which must have succeeded the triumphant success of her momentarily formed plan.

But self-accusation was not to be her only punishment. Did the blessed word of the All-Just relate the deception alone, we might well hesitate to affirm that her conscience brought reproach, and believe that the deed was not as guilty as it seems. But we are not thus left to our own imaginations. The events which followed, so prove, without doubt or question, the displeasure of the Eternal against the deed, that we can have no hesitation whatever in believing that conscience, "the angel of the Lord," was busy within her, ere the bolt of justice fell.

"And Esau hated Jacob, because of the blessing wherewith his father blessed him. And Esau said in his heart, The days of mourning for my father are at hand;—then will I slay my brother Jacob. And these words of Esau her elder son were told to Rebekah." What fearful tidings for a mother! How must her thoughts have returned, with agonizing forebodings, to the *first death* which had marred this beautiful world. Had not that been *fratricide* and for envy, the same feeling which now actuated Esau? And was not she, as Eve had been, the cause? Still nearer cause; for she it was, who, by leading Jacob to deceive, had armed a brother's hand against him. How Esau's intentions could have been revealed to her, when the sacred historian expressly tells us that Esau but spake them *in his heart*, must remain unsolved, unless, as appears most probable, it was Rebekah's own fears which betrayed them; con firmed by the manner of Esau towards his brother, and by her own knowledge of his character. His strong love for his father, which to me is the redeeming beauty of Esau's character, might restrain him awhile—but were the death which Isaac himself appeared to anticipate, speedily to take place, the mother's forebodings well imagined that the haughty Esau would never submit to bow to his brother, and call him heir. Painfully she must have felt, that not for her would Esau restrain his purpose, though the wildest ebullition of his natural anger was subdued by the deep loving reverence he bore his father. Might not she too have claimed that love, had she lavished on his youthful years the same affection she had given to his brother? Was it not her own fault, that in this wild wish for vengeance, the death of the offender, he thought not of the suffering which such a deed would inflict on her? That such thoughts were ascendant, and the voice of self-reproach more loud and thrilling than any anger against Esau for his fearful design, is proved by her counsel to Jacob—when calling him to her, she said, "Behold thy brother Esau, as touching thee, doth comfort himself, purposing to kill thee. Now, therefore, my son, obey my voice and arise, and flee thou to my brother Laban, in Haran. And tarry with him a few days, until thy brother's fury turn away, and he forget that which thou hast done to him; then I will send, and fetch thee from thence. Why should I also be deprived of you both in one day?"

There is not one word of invective against Esau. If she still supposed that her act was justified, inasmuch as it seemed to further the designs of the Eternal, Esau's intention to slay his brother must have seemed too sinful, too horrible, to be passed without some comment either of anger or fear. But far otherwise is the spirit of her words. They breathe but a mother's anxious agony—a consciousness that Esau's wrath was but too just. Jacob had no defence to plead, and so avert the threatened wrath. Nothing could save him but flight, till the hasty but not placable Esau was appeased; and from *her* lips the mandate of exile went forth:—"Why should I also be deprived of you both in one day?" How affectingly do those simple words betray, not alone the love she bore to *both* her sons, but that her thoughts turned to the history of the past—foreboding Eve's awful trial for herself! There is no wailing, no complaint, but in those brief words, what a volume of woman's deepest feeling is revealed!

Her real emotions having thus had vent to Jacob, Rebekah was better able to control them before her husband; and she said unto him, "I am weary of my life, because of the daughters of Heth. If Jacob take a wife of the daughters of Heth, such as these which are of the daughters of the land, what good shall my life do me?"

It would have been the extreme of cruelty to have increased the grief of the infirm Isaac, by a narration of Esau's evil intentions towards his brother—when Esau himself had controlled his fierce passion for his father's sake. Nor could Rebekah's confession of her fault now in any way redeem it. It would but have excited against her the anger of her husband, as being the primary cause of the dissensions between his sons—and have occasioned him increased affliction. It was, in this instance, wiser and better to hide from Isaac the sad cause of Jacob's departure; and urge him to do that for *his son* of promise, which Abraham had done for him; and the mother's fearful anxiety was calmed by the paternal command, coupled with a reiterated blessing, for her younger son "to go to Padan-Aram, the house of Bethuel, thy mother's father, and take thee a wife from one of the daughters of Laban, thy mother's brother." "And Isaac sent away Jacob."

And thus was the mother parted from the son, for whose beloved sake she had been tempted to turn aside from the straight line of probity and truth which in such guilelessness and beauty she had trodden so changelessly before. And is it not ever thus? When we once turn from the one straight path, can we say, thus far shall we go and no further? Can we set a boundary to the rushing flood of pain and sorrow which, when we have removed the barrier of truth, obtains dominion, dashing our fairest dreams to earth, and bringing misery in the very garments of success? And well is it for those whom the Lord so graciously compassionates as to reveal these fatal companions of deception ere it be too late, and the charmed path be trodden till there is no turning back.

Who can peruse the history of Rebekah, and yet believe she was not punished for her sin? Wherefore had she pursued such fatal measures for the obtaining of the blessing for her favorite Jacob, save to keep him for ever by her side, even as Isaac had never quitted the tents of his father? As a younger son, his lot would in all probability have been to seek his own fortune. As the inheritor of the blessings vouchsafed to Abraham, there could be no need for him to leave her; and what was the issue? Banishment from his mother's home, or exposure to his brother's wrath,—the sword of vengeance ever hanging above his head. Was this nothing to a fond mother's heart? Let a parent ponder for one moment on the idea of one beloved child falling by the hand of another, and his heart will give the answer. Parting itself was preferable to such ever present dread, yet what agony must have been that parting!

Not then, as now, might the absent ones be united by mutual intelligence. Neither post nor traveller passed between Beersheba and Padan-Aram. Long weary wastes of country stretched between, and though Rebekah's command was, "Tarry there a *few days*," she knew it must be long months ere they met again. Nor will the vague thought of the hour of meeting ever lessen the pang of parting. It is the pang itself which is felt, the looking in vain for the beloved form in its accustomed haunts, the wild yearning to list once more the voice which sounds in memory alone, to feel the fond pressure of the hand, the kiss which welcomed morning and evening, without which day seemed scarce begun, and night came unobserved. The pictured hardships of the lonely wanderer which no mother's hand may soften, the woe unsoothed, the pain unhealed, the tired frame untended,—these, and a hundred other fears, and thoughts of suffering, haunt a mother's waking dreams, and nightly pillow,—felt not, dreamed not by the wanderer, yet clinging to woman's breast with a tenacity and anguish time only can dispel. And because Rebekah lived so many thousand years ago, shall we deny to her these feelings when the hour came, and her beloved one departed—departed and alone, with no manifestation of the fruit of that blessing which she had lured him to obtain?

With the departure of Jacob, the history of Rebekah concludes, for her name is no more mentioned.—Even on her death Holy Writ is silent. We only know that she was buried in the cave of Machpelah, by the words of Jacob in Gen. xlix. 31. And from there being no mention whatever of her on

Jacob's return to Hebron, we must infer that she died before his arrival, and never had the happiness of folding him to her heart again. How sad and lonely must her declining years have seemed without him who had been so long her stay; even though her long dormant affection for Esau may have been aroused from the injustice she had done him—and he evidently sought, with a softened spirit, to gratify his parents, by a union with a daughter of his uncle Ishmael,—he could never have been to her as Jacob; and painfully and sadly must she have yearned for the absent, as the "few days," which she had pictured, widened into long months and yet longer years. How changed must her life have seemed, and changed from the impulse of a moment; and as death neared—as she felt it might no longer be averted, and she had waited and prayed in vain to behold her son on earth once more—must she not have felt to the full, that, though the deception had been successful, though the blessing had been given, the *means* of its bestowal could not have been "acceptable to the Lord?" and had she, as we are privileged to do, beheld the life of trial and disappointment, and *retributive deception*, which marked the earthly course of her favorite son, this solemn truth would have been impressed still more.

Yet the death of Rebekah was in all probability one of peace, and calm holy reliance on the infinite mercy of her God. He had chastised, but in the midst of chastisement had mercy; the fury of Esau had been turned aside, Jacob been saved, and peace preserved in the household of Isaac. Her earthly idol removed from her sight, we may well believe that Rebekah returned to her domestic duties with that singleness of purpose and uprightness of heart which had marked her earlier years. The temptation to turn aside, the loving mercy of the Eternal had removed, and the mother, even while her heart bled, must have pronounced the mandate just. If in her youth, before the knowledge of the God of Abraham had been imparted, she had felt with her brother, "It is the Lord, we cannot speak unto thee bad or good," would she not—now that long years had been passed in his service—have felt even in her affliction "it is the Lord," and, without murmur or complaint, submit herself to His will?

Are we then, it may be asked, to give Rebekah the meed of unmixed admiration? to rest only on the good points of her character? No. Like all human nature, it was a blending of the good and evil. Had Rebekah been told that, ere her life closed, she should have acted as she did, she would in all probability have felt it impossible; nay, ere her children were born, would have shrunk with horror from the idea of loving one more than the other. All we would urge is simply, that we are not to condemn her, as if the unfortunate propensity of woman, "to compass by stratagem," were the marked failing of her character, and that therefore the *evil* not the *good* was ever the ascendant. This is the common error into which superficial thinkers fall; and from such have arisen questions as to the morality of the Bible, that its holiness would be more confirmed were there no such faults recorded. If indeed those, of whom it so impartially writes, were thus faultless, it would be destined for the use of Angels, not of man. But not such was the design of the Eternal. He inspired holy men to write that which would comfort and sustain man, when his immediate presence and guidance were veiled from mortal eyes; and His faithful servants alike, male and female, were depictured in their virtues and their failures, with an impartiality and truth which were to be our hope in our lowly efforts after virtue, and our consolation in our weakness and our sin. Rebekah's fault was one, her virtues many; and therefore, while we abhor and pray against the *sin*, we can only grieve and lament that human weakness which triumphed in one moment of strong temptation over the virtuous strength of years. We dare not condemn and scorn that weakness; for did we so, we scorn, and condemn, and pronounce judgment on ourselves. How may we assert that, had we been placed as Rebekah in that dread moment, we too should not have done as she did? Can we assert that the promise of the Eternal would have been so strongly impressed within us, that we could have left its fulfilment in His hands, without one effort by our own agency to forward it? Can we say that we should have gone to Him in prayer, beseeching Him to counteract the design of Isaac in favor of his firstborn, and rest contented that the prayer would be heard and answered?

There may be some too, loudly and reproachfully to condemn that weak partiality which was the real origin of the evil,—yet let such take heed, lest they too should fall by the same weakness, for they know not how their affections may equally be tried. Oh! not in *condemnation* of our meek and gentle ancestress shall we reap the benefit of her example, and turn aside from her faults. If, even in her, the weakness of human nature once triumphed over the immortal spirit, what may save us from the same fault? Will the purity of youth, the piety of early womanhood, the truth and virtue of long years? Will these obtain such sway as always to be our safeguard and our strength? Alas! not these: it must be the grace of God alone, sought by constant prayer and utter dependence upon Him,—the constant watch over ourselves,—the knowledge of our own weakness,—that which most exposes us to fall beneath temptation,—the consciousness that there is not a domestic duty,—not a home affection,—not an hour's employment,—not a daily path or nightly thought, in which sin may not creep in and obtain dominion, unless effectually guarded against by unceasing watchfulness and prayer. And to us, yet more than any other nation in the world, is this watchful care and daily petition needed. To ISRAEL IS INTRUSTED THE HONOR OF THE LORD; His chosen, His beloved, His witnesses, the recorders of His ways unto man, the promulgators of His eternal love. How may we be lukewarm in His cause, when we are so called upon to exalt His glory? We are scattered among the nations as witnesses of the PAST and pledges of the FUTURE, and shall we with indifference permit others to claim the privileges which are ours, and assert that, until the epoch of Christianity, God had no witnesses upon earth? No, O no! Surely, individually and nationally, we shall use our every effort to proclaim our high and glorious descent amid the nations!

One point more, and we must conclude this memoir, already so much longer than we intended. It has been said, that as the Eternal ordained that Jacob was to receive the promised blessing, and that the "elder should serve the younger," it must have been obtained in some way; and therefore the *means* of its accomplishment were of little consequence, thus endeavoring to remove all that was reprehensible in the conduct of Jacob and his mother. Nay, some commentators try to make her conduct proceed from a belief that her course of "acting was in such conformity with the divine prediction, that she determined at all risks, and by any means, to secure the blessing for her younger and more worthy son." *

This species of reasoning appears as mistaken as the too violent condemnation of Rebekah, and so completely at variance with the simple, trusting piety of the patriarchs and their families, that we cannot at all suppose it actuating the mother's feelings. Besides which, to think thus, supposes a *pre-determination* to deceive her husband, whereas the narrative of the Bible clearly marks it the *impulse* of the moment.

Isaac, before his birth, was the child of promise to Abraham: the Lord had promised he should be the father of a multitude, and in him and his seed all nations should be blessed. Yet that very child, Abraham was commanded to sacrifice, and without hesitation he prepared to obey, feeling convinced, that though to him the means of accomplishing the divine promise were plunged in darkest mystery—if indeed his child must die—yet still that the promise *would be* fulfilled without any intervention of man; his duty was simply to obey, and the promise *was* fulfilled.

As the command of the Lord to slay his son was the trial of Abraham's faith, so were the words of Isaac to Esau the trial of Rebekah's. She ought to have known, from that very incident in the early life of her husband, that whatever the Lord has once said, He WILL perform, however mysterious may seem the means of its accomplishment—that though Isaac might intend to give the blessing to his first-born, his words would have been overruled, and the blessing reserved for Jacob, without any strife between the brothers or their consequent separation. But her *faith* was not strong enough for that most difficult duty—to "wait for the Lord." Woman-like, *feeling* was her *weakness*, *impulse* her guide, faith succumbed before these, and so left her unguarded, when its invulnerable defence was more needed than it had ever been before.

Rebekah had perhaps some excuse for her momentary fancy that her course of acting was, from its *success*, acceptable to the Lord; but we have NONE. The idea that human means are necessary to forward any intention of the Most High, cannot be entertained a single moment without verging on impiety, when we have the whole Word of God to prove by

* Philippson:—See Notes to Mr. De Sola's Bible.

precept and example that He is as omnipotent to *do* as to *will*. Man is a free agent. Rebekah had equal power to "wait for the Lord" as to urge her son to deception. That she chose the latter was human frailty, no pre-ordainment. He indeed permitted the fraud in appearance to succeed, because He had already ordained that Jacob should be the promised seed, and His changeless and all-wise decree might not be turned aside even to annul, and so punish the designs of sin. But that in no way exculpates the fraud. Had no deceit whatever been practised, the blessing would still have been Jacob's. It matters not how; it is enough to know that the ways of the Eternal are not our ways, and that His decrees require no aid of man.

That human designs, however sinful, however contrary to the pleasure of the Lord, are overruled to further His divine economy—no one who attentively studies and believes God's Word can for a single moment doubt; but this truth in not one tittle renders us less responsible beings. That the Eternal ever bringeth forth and worketh universal good from partial evil, proves His loving kindness, His beneficence, His all-wise, ever acting mercy alone. Not that man is in any point acquitted, or that evil is a necessary adjunct to the bringing forth of good. The workers and the designers of evil are, individually, objects of displeasure, and will suffer the burden of their guilt. The *doers* of evil the God of Love abhors, even while His compassion overrules the *deeds*, and turns them in His hand to the furtherance of good.

We are earnestly and heartily anxious to impress this important truth on the minds of our younger readers, who, in their early perusal of God's Holy Word, may and will feel startled, that human weakness should not only be recorded, but its actions be permitted to succeed. Success is not always a proof of the Eternal's approbation. The history of both Rebekah and Jacob proves the displeasure of the Lord *towards themselves individually*, though their action was overruled to the accomplishment of His previous will. Rebekah never saw her son again; and Jacob, though *spiritually blessed*, was in his earthly career more unfortunate than any of his family before or after him.

This narrative alone, then, ought to bid us eschew a wandering from the one straight path of single-hearted truth that we never can do so without exciting the displeasure of our Heavenly Father, even though our plans may seem crowned with unmerited success. The attribute of our God is TRUTH: how then dare we believe that He smiles upon those who depart from it, or requires human deception to forward His almighty will? As His children, His own, His first-born, oh! let our watchword be TRUTH! Let our upright, single-minded, straightforward adherence to truth in every thought, word, and deed, proclaim WHOSE WITNESSES we are, and compel the nations to acknowledge that we are "Israelites indeed!"

CHAPTER IV.

LEAH AND RACHEL.

It was on the same spot, in the land of the East, where nearly a century previous Abraham's steward had bowed himself to the earth in prayer, that several shepherds and their flocks were assembled, grouped by the side of a well, from whose mouth the great stone covering had not yet been rolled aside. It was high noon, when a stranger approached, and courteously addressing the shepherds, inquired: "My brethren, whence be ye? And they said, Of Haran are we. And he said unto them, Know ye Laban, the son of Nahor? And they said, We know him. And he said unto them, Is he well? And they said, He is well, and behold Rachel his daughter cometh with the sheep. And while he yet spake with them Rachel came with her father's sheep, for she kept them. And it came to pass when Jacob saw Rachel, the daughter of Laban his mother's brother, and the sheep of Laban his mother's brother, that Jacob went near, and rolled the stone from the well's mouth, and watered the sheep; and Jacob kissed Rachel, and lifted up his voice and wept, and Jacob told Rachel that he was her father's brother, and that he was Rebekah's son. And she ran and told her father."

Such, in the simple yet impressive language of Holy Writ, was the first meeting of Jacob and his beautiful cousin.

Lonely and sad the exiled Jacob had turned from the home of his childhood and the parents of his love. The child of promise and of prayer—the inheritor of God's especial blessing—the ancestor of kings—was compelled to make his bed on the cold earth, with nothing but stones for his pillow. How must his thoughts have clung to his mother and his home! That his heart was once more fitted for the reception and comprehension of holy things, is proved by the dream which Infinite Wisdom vouchsafed, to strengthen and encourage him. The promise would not have been revealed to one unworthy to receive it. Though human weakness may sully and darken even the choicest servants of the Lord, yet not unto the impure, the unholy, the unrepentant, would the Holy One impart the blessing of His spirit and His guidance. Acknowledgment of his fault must have brought Jacob once more to the feet of his Heavenly Father, or the confirmation of the blessed promise would have still been delayed.

On the beautiful, the most consoling vision vouchsafed to Jacob, consoling, not only to him but to us, we may not linger. Yet, though so spiritually consoled, strengthened, and refreshed, the mortal nature of the wanderer must often have obtained ascendency during his journey, and have rendered it at the very least dreary and sad. Jacob had never been tried till his departure from his father's house; and, therefore, though awe-struck and "afraid" at the glorious revelation when its impression was vividly before him, his very vow supposes a slight degree of doubt, natural to one only just called upon to believe: "If the Lord will be with me, and will keep me in this way that I go, *give me bread to eat and raiment to put on*, so that I come again to my father's house in peace, then the LORD shall be my God." "Bread to eat and raiment to put on." Even for these petty cares and trials he was dependent on the Lord alone; yet that he did not possess even these—that he had literally left the tent of his father with his staff for his sole possession, may give us some idea of the *human trials* of our forefathers, even of those whom the Lord most blessed. Their greatness, their influence, their riches, were to come *from God alone*, not from man; their *lives* were to bear witness to His providence, even as their descendants are witnesses of the fulfilment of His word.

As Jacob was subject to all the inconveniences, fatigue, and suffering of travelling through a strange and often hostile country, as any other wanderer—his feelings, on nearing the abode of his uncle, may more easily be imagined than described. In his conversation with the shepherds, and then in his actively rolling aside the stone and watering the sheep, we may read the manly effort to restrain emotion, which, however, spurned all control when, in the simple and beautiful affection of the patriarchal age, "he kissed Rachel, and lifted up his voice and wept." Wept, that God had in His loving mercy guided him thus far, and seemed to promise that newly known, yet instinctively loved, relations should fill up the aching void in his heart, which the sudden separation from his mother must have caused.

"And it came to pass, when Laban heard the tidings of Jacob, his sister's son, that he ran to meet him, and embraced him, and kissed him, and brought him to his house. And he told Laban all these things. And Laban said, Surely thou art my bone and my flesh. And he abode with him the space of a month." Again is family affection vividly brought before us.

If the reckoning of some commentators be true, and Jacob was seventy-six when he entered the household of Laban, nearly one hundred years must have elapsed since Rebekah had quitted her maiden home. Yet how closely and fondly must her memory have been enshrined in the heart of her brother, and through him cherished by his children, that Jacob was thus so warmly and delightedly welcomed, simply because he was "Rebekah's son."

Youth in Laban had changed to manhood, manhood to age. He had nearer and dearer calls upon his heart in his character of husband and father; yet still the memory of the "hand-in-hand companion of his childhood" remained pure, and beautiful, and strong, as if absence had never come between them. Will not this fact reveal how acceptable in the Lord's sight is the encouragement of those affections which His love has given to his children? And how sad, how wrong it is to permit coldness and indifference to steal in between the members of one family. Would Laban have entertained such fond recollections of Rebekah, had their early youth been passed in that utter want of cordiality and confidence, faithfulness and affection, which but too often mar the unity and beauty of modern fashionable homes? Oh! not to be expended only on the stranger, hath the God of love stored our hearts with affection, with reverence, with all that can make home an earthly heaven! Would we truly love and seek to please Him, our first duty must be, to love and make those happy with whom our daily lot is cast.

Two daughters blessed the house of Laban; the elder Leah, the younger Rachel. Now "Leah was tender-eyed, and Rachel beautiful and well-favored." As the sacred historian disdains not to mention this, we may be permitted to pause one moment upon the characteristics of the two sisters. That Leah was much less beautiful than her sister is evident from the words of the text, but it does not appear that she was as plain and homely as some commentators declare her. The Hebrew word translated "tender," "And the eyes of Leah were tender (וְעֵינֵי לֵאָה רַכּוֹת)," does not signify *weak* only, as is generally supposed, but soft and delicate, and leads me to suppose that the soft and tender eyes of Leah were her only good feature, whereas her younger sister was "very beautiful and of exceeding beauty," which is the literal meaning of the Hebrew expression תֹּאַר וִיפַת מַרְאֶה וְרָחֵל הָיְתָה יְפַת, though even such translation is far from possessing the force of the original. This difference of appearance occasioned, as would appear by the sequel, a complete difference of character.

One month Jacob abode with his uncle, evidently doing him active service in return for the hospitality which he had received. That he did so, tells well for the real character of the wanderer; for in his father's house Jacob had never been accustomed to active service, and it must have demanded some little exertion of will over inclination, to have permitted its steady and active performance. Laban, however, at this period of their intimacy, felt too kindly and generously towards his nephew to permit him to work without wages. "And he said unto him, Because thou art my brother, shouldst thou therefore serve me for naught? Tell me what shall thy wages be? And Jacob loved Rachel, and said, I will serve thee seven years for Rachel thy younger daughter. And Laban said, It is better I give her unto thee than to another man. Abide with me. And Jacob served seven years for Rachel; *and they seemed unto him but a few days, for the love he had to her.*"

We think much of those tales of chivalry where man performs some great and striking deed—conquers his own passions—becomes a voluntary wanderer—all to win the smile and love of woman. And we do right, for the motive is pure and the moral good. But such high-wrought volumes should not blind our hearts and eyes to this exquisite narration, wherein the same truth, the same moral is impressed, with equal force and beauty, only in the simple language of the Bible. Jacob's servitude was a more convincing proof of his love and constancy than those exciting deeds of heroism which chivalry records. His was no service to call upon distant lands and far-off ages to admire. Nothing for FAME, that brilliant meteor, which, equally with love, divided the warrior's heart in the middle ages. Nothing to vary the routine of seven years' domestic duty, the wearisome nature of which we find in the 38th and 39th verses of chapter xxxi. Yet these "seven years seemed but *as a few days for the love he had to her*." A brief yet most emphatic sentence, revealing the purest, the holiest, the most unselfish love, unrestrained by one fleeting thought of worldly aggrandizement, or a hope beyond making that beloved one his own. "Consumed by the draught by day, chilled by the frost at night," still he never wavered. Love was his upholder—his sustainer. And it was for this end love was so mercifully given.

As the word of God disdains not to portray the extent of love borne by one mortal for another, we trust we may be pardoned if we linger a moment on that emotion, the very name of which is generally banished from the education of young females, as if to feel or excite it were a crime, forgetting that, in banishing all idea of its *influence*, we banish also the proper means of regulating that influence, and subject our young charge unguarded to the very evil that we dread.

God gave not love to bind to earth, but to raise to heaven: not to make us earthly idols, but, on the very love we bear each other, to lift up the soul to Him—to lighten toil and soften grief, to heighten joy and bless our earthly sojourn with a bright ray from that exhaustless fount of love which waits for us above. Without some emotion powerful enough to draw us out of ourselves for an earthly brother, how could we ever subject our selfish hearts to the will of our God? how perform those self-sacrifices most acceptable to Him? Stronger than pain and toil, and even death, it is the very essence of our being, the spiritual essence, which marks more powerfully than aught else our immortal destiny; and from the reflection of that destiny lends a glow to earth. "Thou shalt love the Lord thy God with all thy heart, and soul, and might," is the command of the Eternal—an important command—yet not given till after His word had revealed to us that it was possible, nay, that it was a necessary consequence, for those who served and loved Him best, to love and cleave unto each other. Had not the heart been created with full capacity to love, this command would not have been given; and He who has placed us in a world of beauty, who has gathered around us objects to excite every feeling, demands not that those feelings are to be devoted to Him alone in utter neglect of our fellows.

It is not passion to which we allude, though but too often the words are deemed synonymous. Nor do we mean passion when we say that love is the handmaid of religion. No, it is a spiritual, not an earthly feeling; spiritual even when it relates to man, not God. And if, indeed, it be so, and the more we reflect upon it the more we feel it is, or *ought to be*, why should it be a subject, as it too often is, of jest, of scorn, and those under its influence deemed not far removed from folly and romance? Why should education never allude to it save as a dreadful and unlikely thing, and the sage lesson so often conned, that *reason*, not affection, is to be our guide? Were the word *religion* substituted for reason in such educational codes, the young heart would be so trained as to eschew all fear of mere earthly love; it would know itself, its own impulses, its own feelings, and so set a strong guard upon those most likely to lead to error, while it encouraged all that would urge to good. It would feel that love was of God, and therefore not a subject for levity or jest; —that it was sent to lift up the spirit to Him, and therefore not so to expend its force on an earthly idol as to lead to extravagance and folly;—that it was to last for ever, not unto *death, but beyond it*, and therefore not to be given to one whose future was of earth, and who sought in its possession but the gratification of a few fleeting years;—that it was to endure through sorrow and sickness, and trial and woe, not to be the mere harbinger of gaiety and joy, to shine in a ball-room and glitter in a bridal robe;—but to bear with occasional irritability or even with unkindness and apparent neglect· with faults which we must never breathe; with intervals of an utter want of sympathy, even of depreciation, which we must endure, solace, and forgive:—not to suppose that we shall ever be as when that love is first called forth, our wishes granted ere told, our every feeling answered, our every virtue appreciated, our very failings loved. And to be prepared for this—to love thus with a strength, a purity that will bear all this, aye, and more painful still, the very sacrifices of self which love impels, unfelt, unknown, uncared for, or if seen, but deemed our duty, and coldly passed uncheered—will aught but that love which is spiritual sustain us? and will such emotion come to the young heart without some preparatory training? Oh! not while love is deemed romance, not while it is made a jest, or shunned as something guilty or derogatory, will it, can it ever be as the God of love ordained, the purest, dearest blessing earth can know, the loveliest type of heaven.

Something more than Rachel's beauty, marvellous as that was, must have so retained Jacob's love for her in those seven years of domestic intercourse, as to make the time appear but a few days. Beauty may attract and win if the time of courtship be too brief to require no other charm, but it is not sufficient of itself to *retain* affection. Gift from God, as it is, how may it be abused, and how may it be wasted in caring only for the lovely shape *without*, and leaving the rich invisible gems *within* uncared for and unused! Oh! if there be one among my youthful readers, of beauty exceeding as that of Rachel, who holdeth in her possession this rich gift of God, let her remember that He will demand of her how she hath used it,—that its abuse, its *pretended* neglect, yet in reality proud value, will pass not unnoticed by its beneficent Giver. It has been granted for some end,—for if to look on a beautiful flower will excite emotions of admiration and love, and consequently enjoyment, how much more deeply would such feelings be called forth by a beautiful face, could we but behold it as the hands of God had formed it, unshaded by the impress of those emotions of pride, contempt, or self-sufficiency, or that utter void of intellect, which are but too often its concomitants, from the mistaken notion that outward beauty is omnipotent, and needs no help within.

To hide from a young girl that she is beautiful is the extreme of folly, for her mirror will tell her that she is being deceived, and the influence of such informers will be lost at once No—

let the real value and consequent *responsibility* of beauty be inculcated, and there will be no fear of its abuse.

That Rachel had many most endearing qualities we may quite infer from Jacob's devoted love to her even to her death. The spirit most impatient under contradiction, and loving its own will, is often united to a manner so engaging, and qualities so calculated to win regard, that trivial faults of temper and will are literally engendered from the difficulty it is to reprove a being so beautiful and so beloved; and this would seem the case with Rachel. Young, joyous, and loving, we may fancy her the very star of her father's home, valuing her beauty as it gave her power to obtain whatever she willed uncontradicted, but using it only in the sphere of home.

But though Jacob's affections were devoted to one alone, those seven years of intimate association must have been fraught with suffering and sadness to Laban's elder daughter, whose strong affection for Jacob the sequel will reveal. Her compelled agency in her father's fraud must have been fraught with absolute horror to a heart that loved secretly and unreturned, as herself, and heightened the trial of unrequited affection in no ordinary degree.

We will not linger on the affairs narrated in Genesis xxix., from the 21st to the 30th verse, because they belong so strictly to the manners and customs of the Eastern nations, that it is quite impossible to comment upon them with any justice, prejudiced, as birth and education cannot fail to make us, in favor of the manners and customs of modern Europe. Yet the customs of the East have undergone little or no change; and repeatedly we find that, which in the narratives of the Bible may startle our modern European notions, as strange and improbable, confirmed by events passing in the East at this very day, so that those very narratives would there be scarcely considered a history of the past.

Though beguiled into another seven years' servitude for his much-loved Rachel, it is evident that she had become his wife *first*, Jacob honorably performing the word he had pledged, *after* the wished-for prize had been obtained; and not till those seven years were completed, do we hear him utter one word of complaint or one wish to provide for "his own house also."

"And when the Lord saw that Leah was hated (lit. less

loved), He gave her children, but Rachel had none. And she called the name of her eldest son Reuben: for, she said, "Surely the Lord hath looked upon my affliction; now therefore my husband will love me." What a volume of woman's deepest feelings and the compassionating love of the Eternal do these brief lines reveal! He who had, in His inscrutable wisdom, ordained that Leah should be tried in the fiery ordeal of woman's saddest loneliness, unrequited affection, yet deigned to grant a compensating blessing in all the sweet, pure feelings of a mother's love. Who that reads but this one verse can uphold that woman is less an object of tender love and compassion to her God than man? Who can say that the Mosaic records are silent on this head? The words of *man* to point out the proper station and value of woman we need not, for the children of Israel have the WORD OF THEIR GOD. And do we not still recognise the God of Leah? His ear has not become heavy that it cannot hear, nor His arm shortened that it cannot save. And though He may not bestow on us a *visible* and audible manifestation of His tender compassion as on Leah, yet we may be certain that He will grant us some compensating blessing for every joy of which he may think fit to deprive us. And even for those bitter griefs, which from their nature, their seeming selfishness, woman shrinks in trembling from bringing before her God, and buries them in her own heart till it bleeds at every pore,—Leah's history proves that He will grant peace and healing. It may be that a wiser and kinder will than her own has flung an insuperable barrier between woman's heart and its dearest object; and impelled her by all that is refined and delicate in her character, to hide deep from every eye the anguish which is her burden. How blessed then that even for such a grief there is the fount of healing waters still in the word of God—that she may come there and read, not only the abundance, the fulness of his love, but that He has especial tenderness for those by earth *unloved!* And as He gave Leah children because she was not loved, so will He grant such sufferers a peace, and calm, and joy in the consciousness of His unfailing tenderness, far surpassing even the rich and glowing, but too transient happiness of sympathy on earth.

Leah must have known and loved the Lord long before the event recorded, else she had not thus welcomed the birth of her first child. Eight years of Jacob's sojourn in her father's household would scarcely have been sufficient for her to know and love her cousin's invisible God, had she not had some vague yet true notions of Him before.

That Jacob should often have alluded to the God of his fathers, and narrated the wonderful manifestations of His providence, and that such solemn themes should have fallen with peculiar impressiveness on the heart of Leah, and but lightly on the buoyant impetuous Rachel, may be inferred from the history of both. After the gods of her father, Leah has no hankering whatever; her reference, in both her griefs and joys, is to Jacob's God alone.

By her exclamation at the birth of her second son, we may suppose that the fond hope expressed the year previous, "Now therefore my husband will love me," was still not realized. "Because the Lord hath heard that I am not loved, He hath therefore given me this son also." To many the repetition of a blessing renders it invaluable, and, in the imperfection of our earthly nature, the continued disappointment of our dearest wishes would have rendered the heart callous, perhaps repining, at the very blessing which had before brought joy. But not thus was it with Leah: gratefully she received a second little treasure from the hand of her God; and, bearing again the pang of ever-blighted hope, she utters no wish of an earthly kind, but simply feels she has still the love of God. Another year, and another son is granted; and we may trace a ray beaming even through her earthly darkness, in the new upspringing of buoyant hope—"Now will my husband be joined unto me, for I have borne him three sons."

Whether, indeed, the fond wish was realized, and Jacob's heart was softened towards her, must be but conjecture; yet it would almost appear so, for, at the birth of her fourth son, her pious heart is satisfied with the fervent ejaculation, "Now will I praise the Lord." Drawn closer and closer unto her God, with His every precious gift, she, who gave her first-born a name signifying "the son of affliction," gave her fourth the beautiful appellation of "praise unto the Lord." It was not only a gift of children, then, His love bestowed. He had brought light from darkness, He had turned her mourning into praise, and returned with tenfold blessing her meek enduring confidence in Him. Shall we then, who may be in the darkness of sorrow and heavy care, shrink from walking in her steps, and dwell only on the *afflic tion* which is ours? Shall we not also look and strive for some blessing which can bid us too "praise the Lord," and lead us to behold *light* where all was heaviness? There is no lot so desolate which, if we seek Him, the Lord will not bless: not, perhaps, by the removal of our present sorrow, but by some compensating mercy. We must not suppose that seeking Him and loving Him will exempt us from affliction. No, for, if it did, where would be that heavenly exercise which alone can fit us for heaven? Nor are we, as some enthusiasts would urge, to regard *trials* as *joys*, and welcome them with gladness. When a tender loving parent chastises a beloved child to keep him from the paths of sin, would he feel that the chastisement had done its work if the little being received it with smiles and rejoicing? Surely the parent would be more hopeful if the child were serious, and even sad. And is it not so with the afflictions sent from our eternal and most tender Father? We may think that we surely need them not; and our lives may even be, in the sight of man, as we ourselves suppose them. Nay, they may be numbered amongst those whom the Bible gives us promise shall be accounted the righteous in the sight of God; yet how know we what we might have been *without* such affliction? How know we but those very sorrows, lasting but a *time*, are preparing us to be of those whom the Lord writeth in His book for eternity, who shall be His when He maketh up His jewels? Of this only are we certain, that the Lord *loveth* whom He correcteth. Then, while like Leah we *feel* affliction, let us hope on, pray on, with undoubting faith, that one day we too shall cry aloud, "Now will I praise the Lord."

Very different to the meek submissiveness and gentle disposition of her elder sister, is the impetuous temper and sinful feeling of envy which urged Rachel angrily to exclaim, even to her doting husband, "Give me children, or else I die. And Jacob's anger was kindled against Rachel: and he said, Am I in God's stead, who hath withheld children from thee?

We have been previously told,—"And when Rachel saw that she bare Jacob no children, she envied her sister." Envied whom? even the homely, the unloved Leah. It was not enough that God had endowed her with most surpassing beauty, and given her the perfect love of a husband who had proved, was still proving his devoted attachment to herself alone, by fourteen years' hard servitude. It signified little that Leah *had but her children*, and that her own cup of blessings was filled to flowing over.

In glancing over the history of the two sisters, must we not feel that Rachel *ought* to be the happier, as she was the more blessed? Yet it was not so. Leah, with her heavy burden of affliction, was the happier, for she neither envied nor complained, but leaned upon her God—and in consequence, from Him received consolation. Rachel could have had no such stay. "Give me children, or else I die!" was the exclamation of a querulous, self-willed spirit, looking only to man, and depending upon him. Yet the knowledge of the Lord must have been equally revealed to Rachel as to her sister. Daughters of the same household, cousins of the same witness of God,—Jacob's religious education and experience must have been imparted to her also. She may have even listened during the time for Jacob's sake, banishing its recollection entirely afterwards, as a theme much too solemn and grave for her present joyous days. And are there not such even now, deeming religion and her rich train of holy and blessed thoughts, quite incompatible with youth and beauty, and who believe age is time enough to think of such serious things?

That her feeling and its expression were both wrong we perceive by Jacob's anger and reproof. Loving Rachel as he did, it must have been something very blamable to call severity from his lips. Ignorance may excite our pity, but not our blame. Had Rachel been ignorant who had blessed her sister with children, Jacob would have answered differently—but her impatient words caused his "anger to be kindled against her," because he felt and knew that they must have come from a spirit as impatient as rebellious, and were therefore likely to excite the displeasure of the Lord. "Am I in God's stead?" meaning, can I give you children if God hath withheld them. Words brief, but impressively proving Jacob's individual dependence on and trust in his God, and which ought to have subdued and humbled the discontent and envy of his wife. But though they checked the querulous *words*, they had no power to change the inward *feelings*, and determined at all risks, all sacrifices, to obtain children also, she followed the example of Sarah, and forced her husband, by increasing the number of his wives, to undergo all the miseries of a divided household.

Yet, when Bilhah had a son, we find Rachel welcoming him

with such a joyful thanksgiving, and as a gift from God—that we might wonder at her former impatience—did we not know, that there are many who trace the hand of the Lord, and think they love and serve Him, when all of life is smooth and smiling, yet act, at the first trial, for the first cross, as if they knew Him not at all, and denied His power to help and save. "God hath judged me, and hath also heard my voice, and hath given me a son." Had she then prayed—and did she recognise in thoughtfulness the answer *to her prayer?* Or was her exclamation at the birth of Dan but a presumptuous supposition from a presumptuous spirit—believing without due authority that she had prevailed with God? We have not sufficient authority in Scripture, to pronounce judgment one way or the other on this point, and must therefore leave it to the consideration of our readers.

Once only do words of sorrowing reproach escape Leah's lips towards her sister. "Is it a small matter that thou hast taken my husband?" Words simply expressive of the natural pang which must sometimes have entered her heart—when year after year passed, and still beheld her deep affections less valued than the lighter love of Rachel.

Two other sons were born unto the elder sister; and one daughter, a blessing which had never before been vouchsafed the patriarchs. Then it was, "that God remembered Rachel; and God hearkened to her and gave her children." "God remembered Rachel." Had He forgotten? no, neither forgetfulness nor memory dwelleth with God—for He is omniscient as omnipotent, knowing and perceiving all. But when speaking of Him, His dealings with His children must be expressed in language, and by images suited to their finite conception,—not according to the adorable and glorious, but unfathomable infinity surrounding Him. He *thought* upon and *hearkened* to her—for such is, equally with *remember*, the meaning of the term—אֱלֹהִים אֶת-רָחֵל וַיִּזְכֹּר אֱלֹהִים אֵלֶיהָ וַיִּשְׁמַע—words, how full of consolation and encouragement to Rachel's female descendants! Man would have condemned, and sentenced her to a chastisement of perpetual childlessness—for the tenderest mercies of humanity are cruel compared to the tender mercies of the Most High! but He whom she had offended by mistrust, forgetfulness, impatience, angry emotions towards her sister, had compassion, and not only "remembered" that she was a weak and yearning woman, but "hearkened" to her supplications, and gave reply.

"God hath taken away my reproach," Rachel gratefully exclaimed. "And she called his name Joseph, and said, the Lord shall add unto her another son." Could she have penetrated futurity—well indeed might she have felt that God had removed her reproach; for who that reflects on the angelic beauty and faultlessness of Joseph, can recall his mother without bestowing on her a portion of the love and veneration we lavish on her son!

It is when bowed down by inward remorse for a consciousness of innate sinfulness, by the impossibility of realizing that perfect holiness which would guard us from approach to wrong either in act and thought towards our fellow creatures, or in mistrust and forgetfulness of God, that we should remember the history of Rachel and take comfort. There are some, who, unable to bear the sting of an awakened conscience, drown it altogether, by fleeing from every holy exercise of prayer and self-examination, and believe that as in this life we must be liable to occasional faults, it is perfectly useless striving, much less praying against them, as such prayer can be of no service, and is but a mockery before God. Some minds may bear this awful state—to others, the young, the deeper feeling, and more yearning hearts, it is a period of absolute anguish—which, without some spiritual help, is impossible to be sustained; and so religion is cast off as a subject of terror, of suffering, and the world and the world's panaceas substituted in its place. To such, more especially if they be women, we would say, Come but to the word of God—and even for such griefs there is all we need. There the Eternal not only proclaims "Himself a God full of compassion, long suffering, abundant in goodness and mercy, forgiving iniquity, transgression, and sin," but *proves* these consoling and most blessed attributes, not only *after*, but *before* they were proclaimed. Rachel was more faulty than many of her sex, yet her prayers were heard, her affliction compassionated, her wish fulfilled. How may we then despair, or think that the infirmities of our mortal frame and the sinfulness they bring, can throw a barrier between us and our God? It is not to the righteous alone He awardeth mercy and love, but to the contrite and humble spirit, with whom the "High and Holy One who inhabiteth eternity delighteth to dwell." With such proofs we may not despair, we *dare not* doubt, but we are called to Him as little children sorrowing to be *forgiven*, in the full consciousness how deeply we are *loved*.

It was after the birth of Joseph, that Jacob's fourteen years of servitude being completed, he said unto Laban, "Send me away unto mine own place, and to my country. Give me my wives and children for whom I have served thee, and let me go, for thou knowest the service which I have done thee. And Laban said unto him, I pray thee, if I have found favor in thine eyes, tarry; for I have learned by experience, that the LORD hath blessed me for thy sake: and he said appoint me thy wages, and I will give it. And he said unto him, thou knowest how I have served thee, and how thy cattle was with me—for it was little before I came, and now it is increased into a multitude, and the Lord has blessed thee since my coming; now when shall I provide for mine own house also. And he said, what shall I give thee? And Jacob said thou shalt not give me anything."

And that agreement followed which has most unjustly exposed Jacob to the accusation of duplicity and fraud. It is supposed that his plan of placing the peeled rods in the drinking troughs occasioned the greater number of the cattle to be "ring-straked, speckled, and spotted;" and in that manner Laban was defrauded, and Jacob received much more than his due. That Jacob refused all *gifts* from Laban, appears to me to originate in the same feeling which actuated Abraham to refuse gifts from the king of Sodom, "lest he should say, I have made Abraham rich." Depending upon Him who had promised, "I will not leave thee until I have done that which I have spoken to thee of," Jacob neither could nor would accept gifts from man, preferring to work himself, and leave the issue in the hands of God. And this he did, and God blessed him with riches sufficient for his need.

Can it be supposed for one moment, after mature consideration, that the cattle could have become ring-straked, speckled, and spotted, without the immediate agency of God, who had determined thus to provide for His believing servant? Can it be believed that it was in the power of man, by however subtle a scheme in appearance, to create a variety in the cattle, unless the Lord also had so willed it? Laban had not behaved as generously or even as fairly by his nephew as his first affectionate welcome might lead us to suppose. We know from the vows of Jacob himself, which Laban *does not contradict*, that, "except the God of my fathers had been with me, surely thou hadst now sent me away empty." And we may, therefore, rest perfectly content, that in the affair of the cattle no blame can be attached to Jacob. He was but a secondary cause, whose scheme would have been entirely vain had it not been blessed by the Eternal.

Increasing exceedingly in much cattle, and maid-servants and men-servants, and camels, and asses, the wrath and envy of Laban's sons were excited towards him. And he saw that Laban's own countenance was not towards him as before—circumstances which must have excited much human anxiety and fear. And then it was the Lord said unto him, "Return unto the land of thy fathers and thy kindred, and I will be with thee."

"And Jacob sent and called Rachel and Leah to the field unto his flock." And in the perfect confidence of love and respect, imparted all to them. "I see your father's countenance is not towards us as before; but the God of my fathers has been with me. And ye know that with all my power I have served your father; and your father has deceived me, and changed my wages ten times; but God suffered him not to hurt me. If he said thus, The speckled shall be thy wages, then all the cattle bare speckled; and if he said thus, The ring-straked shall be thy hire, then all the cattle bare ring-straked. *Thus God hath taken away the cattle of your father, and given them to me.*"

There is something to me peculiarly beautiful in this simple address of Jacob, spoken as it is to his wives. Not a word of reproach on their father, but the simple truth—infinitely more expressive of the wrong he has suffered than any violence or invective. All that has blessed him, he traces unfailingly to God. The whole of his address, from the 5th to the 13th verse of Gen. xxxi., demands attention from its revealing so much more concerning Laban's real conduct to his nephew, and in what manner that conduct was regarded and overruled by the Eternal, than we can learn by the bare narration of the previous chapter. Our present subject forbids our lingering on it, except to say, it completely absolves Jacob from all fraudulent dealings with his uncle, while it reveals that he himself was the victim of deceit.

The mandate of God was in Jacob's ear, and every emotion of humanity was urging him to tarry not, but to flee at once. He had dominion over all his household, yet he waits to impart his wishes and his fears to his wives: he will make no step in advance without their concurrence; thus at once proving his love and their equality. And, without a moment's hesitation, Rachel and Leah answered and said unto him, "Is there yet any portion or inheritance for us in our father's house? Are we not accounted of him as strangers? for he hath sold us, and has quite devoured our money For all the riches which God has taken from our father, that is ours and our children's. Now then, whatsoever God hath said unto thee do."

Different as the sisters were in disposition, and placed in a situation most likely to create discord and disunion, yet when the interests of a beloved husband are at stake, they act in perfect unity and love. There is no "mine and thine"—words how often fraught with discord—but simply "*ours* and *our* children's." Seeking even to reconcile him yet more to his flight—enriched as he was—by stating the simple fact, that Laban had failed in his duty towards them, by giving them neither portion nor inheritance; and by having *sold* them to Jacob for fourteen years of labor. That which God then had marked as Jacob's share of the flocks and herds, was but their right and their children's.

Yet it must have been a trial to both sisters to remove so hastily and unexpectedly with their young children from the home of their earliest years, without even bidding farewell to the parent they had loved so long, to their brothers and their friends, to venture on a strange and dangerous track to a land they knew not, save that it was far away from their childhood's home. We already know where Leah's affliction always led her, and are, therefore, justified in believing that now, as before, prayer was the soother of her natural sorrows, and her confidence, that even if her father pursued them, he would not be permitted to work them harm. But Rachel could not thus realize the ever present, ever protecting arm of the Eternal; and, as before she had sought human means to further her impatient wishes, so now does she bear away with her secretly "the images which were her father's;" superstitiously believing, according to some commentators, that by consulting them, Laban would discover their route, and so be enabled to follow and arrest them. It is scarcely possible to peruse the history of these two sisters without being struck with the beautiful unity and harmony displayed in their two characters—distinct from first to last, and each preserving her individual peculiarities. Thrown back upon herself, from wanting the attractions of beauty and vivacity granted to her younger sister, Leah's graces expanded inwardly and spiritually; her yearning affections always strongest from never finding vent by being called for and appreciated by man. Rejoicingly and gratefully acknowledging and believing the blessed religion which told her of an unchanging Friend and most tender loving Father, she found in such belief enough, and could realize content in the midst of trial, happiness in the midst of grief. Such a character as Leah's, from the time she is revealed to us, so perfectly free from all wrong feelings in a situation so likely to excite them, is not natural to woman; and we may, therefore, infer that her youth had had its trials, which the grace of God had blessed, in making her rise from them the gentle, enduring, lovable being which His word reveals.

The faults of Rachel originated in the very cause which had been a chastening to her sister. Her own surpassing loveliness, while ever the theme of admiration to her fellows, so raised her in her own estimation, that it was difficult to look beyond this world, where she reigned pre-eminent, to another, where she, in all her beauty, was but an atom—a creature of the dust. What to her was the love and protection of an Invisible Being, when she was so surrounded by the love and care of man? What to her needed the tale of future happiness? Was she not joyous and laughter-loving the livelong day? With power in herself to bend all hearts, and direct all circumstances to the furtherance of her own impetuous will? Such we must believe the youth of Rachel, when we see her repining that children were granted to her sister and not to her. We behold her secretly bearing away the gods of her father—whether from the reason mentioned above, or from her own lingering belief in their efficacy and power, still equally reprehensible in the wife of Jacob.

If, indeed, Rachel supposed that in removing the images she prevented her father from discovering their route, she very speedily found herself mistaken. Jacob had stolen "away unawares from Laban the Syrian, in that he told him not that he fled; so he fled with all that he had, and he rose up, and passed over the river, and set his face toward the mount Gilead." And there, seven days after their hasty flight, Laban overtook him with all his kindred, and sufficient followers "to do them hurt," "Had not the God of your father," he said, "spake unto me yesternight, saying, Take thou heed that thou speak not to Jacob good or bad."

Anxiously and fearfully, according to their different characters, must Leah and Rachel have awaited the issue of the conference. The number of followers argued ill; yet the words of Laban were at first but mild reproach. "Wherefore didst thou flee away secretly, and steal away from me, and didst not tell me, that I might have sent thee away with mirth and with songs, with tabret and with harp: and hast not suffered me to kiss my sons and daughters? Thou hast done foolishly in so doing."

We may well suppose words as these, being fraught with self-reproach to affectionate daughters, that they had indeed so left their father. To Leah his next words, alluding to the "God of thy father," must have been particularly and gratefully soothing. He to whom she prayed was indeed ever around them, turning aside the wrath of men, forbidding him to arouse wrath by "speaking either bad or good." Holy writ does not indeed tell us, that Leah prayed in this instance; but she who welcomed the birth of every child with prayer and thanksgiving—who in no instance had recourse to her father's gods—was not likely to forget her husband's God when his protection was so needed We may be permitted to believe she prayed; and can we not imagine the fervor of her grateful thanksgiving when she heard such words from her father? And we may all experience this. There is not one who has addressed the Lord in prayer—the daily prayer for all things, who can say he has had no answer. And oh! who would not realize the glowing of the heart—the burst of thanksgiving which fills it—when we trace his hand in the daily events of life, and feel that that which we have asked for He has given? But to realize this, we must come to Him in all things. We must pray to Him in our hearts as well as with our lips; we must *think* individual prayer as well as those public petitions framed for us. We must be in the constant habit of tracing all things to His almighty hand, and believe that his love is as deep, as pitying, for us individually, as his bounty is shown throughout the world. We must so commune with Him, that the hours of prayer will feel but the *continuation*, not the commencement and end of devotion. Did we but do this—bring before Him every care, and thought, and grief, and joy, and doubt, and thankfulness—how many, many instances of *answered* prayer would the briefest life recall. Then, oh how can we keep Him far from us, by withholding from Him the wishes which He alone has power to grant, the sorrows which He alone has compassion sufficient to heal?

On Rachel's ear, the words which filled her sister's heart with deepest thankfulness must have fallen little heeded, while those which followed them, utterly meaningless to Leah, must have been fraught to her with wildest terror, fearfully increased by the instant answer of her husband:—"And now, though thou wouldst needs be gone, because thou sore longedst after thy father's house, yet wherefore hast thou stolen my gods? And Jacob answered and said (in reply to Laban's previous words of reproach), Because I was afraid, for I said, peradventure thou wouldst take by force thy daughters from me." And then, with regard to the last accusation: "With whomsoever thou findest thy gods let him not live. Before our brethren discover what is thine, and take it to thee. For Jacob knew not that Rachel had stolen them."

That she had concealed the theft from her husband proves at once that she knew the feelings dictating it were wrong, yet had not sufficient moral courage to resist them. And now what must have been her terrors? Not only was the plan which she had adopted to prevent a hostile meeting between her father and husband, apparently about to be the very means of dissension, but if discovered, Jacob's own lips had pronounced her death-doom. We know not if in the patriarchal times death was usually the punishment awarded to criminals convicted of theft; but it is evident that Jacob fully intended the criminal in his household to suffer even death for his offence, by the sacred historian so expressly declaring that "Jacob knew not that Rachel had stolen them." How could he suspect the wife of his bosom—his best beloved—of such theft as might almost convict her of idolatry!

Little did he dream whom he was condemning, or the misery he would have drawn upon himself, had not the God who had promised to bring him to his father's home in peace, here interposed, and saved both him, and for his sake, and the sake of His own great name, the faulty Rachel.

Yet during the period of Laban's search for the images, till the danger of discovery was quite past, how terrible must have been her alarm, and how painful her emotions! How different from the meek quietude of a holy spirit, at peace with itself and its God, which throughout this interview was Leah's! Yet no doubt, true to the contrarieties of imperfect humanity, when discovery was averted, and Laban found not the gods, Rachel only felt penetrated with pious gratitude, and resolved to keep her fault more strictly secret from her husband than ever. Some commentators, I believe, accuse her of an inclination to, if not of direct, idolatry; but we do not think that Holy Writ sufficiently authorizes such a charge. Superstition, the remains of childhood's tales, which urged her to the course of acting with regard to the images already dilated upon, is not in the least incompatible with her recognition of, and belief in, Jacob's God, even though the images remained with her until Jacob bade them "put away the strange gods that were amongst them," nearly seven years afterwards. As his household consisted only of those who had lived with Laban he might easily have supposed the strange gods theirs, and Rachel had thus an opportunity of resigning them, without causing her husband the suffering it would have been, to suspect her of having either stolen them at first, or harbored them so long.

There is something very beautiful in Laban's parting care of his daughters, when the somewhat warm recrimination between himself and Jacob was at an end. The heap of stones was raised by all who had met in wrath, proving their reunion by their united labor, and the feast which all shared in harmony when the work was concluded. "And Laban said, This heap is a witness between thee and me. Therefore was the name of it called Gilead and Mizpah, for he said, the LORD watch between me and thee when we are absent one from another. *If thou shalt afflict my daughters, or if thou shalt take wives beside my daughters* (though no man is with us), see God is witness betwixt thee and me. This heap be my witness, and this pillar be my witness, that I will not pass over this heap to thee, and thou shalt not pass over this heap and this pillar unto me for harm. The God of Abraham, and the God of Nahor, and the God of thy father judge betwixt us. And Jacob swore by the fear of his father Isaac. And Jacob offered sacrifices on the mount, and called his brethren to eat bread; and they did eat bread, and tarried all night in the mount. And early in the morning Laban rose up, and kissed his sons (i. e. grandsons) and daughters, and blessed them; and Laban departed, and returned unto his place."

Thus were angry feelings calmed and soothed by a mutual covenant of love. While to the wives of the one, and the daughters of the other, how thrice blessed must have been the reconciliation which gave them again the dear privilege of a father's loving kiss and parting blessing! We learn too, from this simple narrative, that even in the East, a multiplicity of wives was decidedly *not* lawful, and that Laban considered the rights of his daughters would be infringed, and so call upon him to come forward in their defence, even to break the covenant of peace, did Jacob take any other wives. Human nature is indeed the same in all ages—for as Laban spake to Jacob thousands and thousands of years ago, so would a father now. As truly as the Bible reveals the truth, the beneficence, the tenderness of God—so truly does it reveal and answer every emotion of the human heart.

As our task is a record only of Leah the wife of Jacob, we must pass lightly over the events of the xxxii. and xxxiii. chapters of Genesis, which belong exclusively to the history of the patriarch himself. The wrath of man was again turned aside, and the blessing of the Lord made Jacob at peace even with his brother Esau. His doubts and fears, which must have extended painfully to the weaker nature of his wives, at news of Esau's armed approach, were subdued by the influence of his prayer, and the long separated brothers met in mutual tenderness and love. They did not, however, long remain together. Jacob and his family proceeded to Succoth, and then to Shechem, where he "bought a parcel of a field," after erecting his tents, and "built there an altar," and there remained, till commanded by the Lord to "arise and go to Bethel."

The period of these sojournings between his departure from Padan-Aram, to his proceeding to Bethel, must have been full seven years. The then tender ages of his younger children, and the number of his flocks and herds, in all probability prompted him to settle his residence in the first convenient spot in the land of Canaan. It appears strange that he did not pursue his way without any pause to his father's house; but it is one of those subjects on which the word of God gives us no information, and therefore may be dismissed without wasting time and thought on what can be only speculation. At Shechem, Leah must have encountered indeed a fiery trial in the insult offered to her daughter, and the guilty conduct of her sons—Simeon and Levi. Here, as elsewhere, Jacob was punished by *deception*, causing fear and trouble, as he justly says: "Ye have troubled me to make me to stink among the inhabitants of the land, among the Canaanites and Perizzites, and I being few in number, they shall gather themselves against me, and slay me, and I shall be destroyed, I and my household."

But though punished for the sin of his youth by mortal anxieties and fears continually darkening around him—the God of his father Abraham, mindful of His gracious promise to that holy man, still watched over Jacob, and relieved him from threatening danger by commanding him to go to Bethel and build an altar there. The patriarch without hesitation obeyed—first purifying his household of all strange gods;—and when "they journeyed, the terror of God was upon the cities that were round about them, and they did not pursue after the sons of Jacob." Then, as now, punishment fell not at once upon the sinning ones. They were preserved to work out their own chastisement in furthering the will of their God.

At Bethel, God again appeared unto the patriarch, and not only reiterated the promise made to his fathers and to himself, but confirmed the change of name from Jacob to Israel; that holy and blessed name which was to descend through thousands and thousands of ages, associated for ever with the mercy and the love and the glory of the Lord—given by the Eternal; a mark of especial favor from the King of kings, expressing that as a Prince our father Jacob had power with God and with man, and had prevailed. Is there, can there be one amongst the descendants of this prince of God's creating, ashamed of the name he bears? Should it not be our glory, our pride—of which no persecution, no injury, no wrong can rob us? Does not its very sound teem with the wondrous mercies of the past—with the truth, the unanswerable truth of revelation? What scorner, what sceptic can point the finger of doubt or denial at the Bible—while that name is yet heard in every corner of the globe, borne by the very descendants of him, on whom by God himself it was bestowed? The watchword, the banner of our cause, recognised as such in every nation, every land—the man or woman who feels ashamed to call himself of ISRAEL, flings scorn upon his God. Cheered and consoled by this renewed blessing of God, Jacob proceeded on his journey, advancing southward in the direction of Mamre, where Isaac his father then was.

Ephrah was nearly reached, when the sudden illness of Rachel compelled the whole cavalcade to halt—and Jacob must have beheld with inexpressible anguish his best beloved wife torn from him, at the very moment she had increased his joy and her own by giving birth to a second son. When in the midst of bodily and mental anguish, she called his name Benoni, son of my sorrow, did she think of her own impatient words—"Give me children, or else I die!" and feel that it would have been better for her to have waited for the Lord? How may we answer? Enough for us to benefit by the record vouchsafed, and feel His will is better than our own—and in impatient restless longings for blessings granted to another, we may know, that even in the very fulfilment of the wish, the punishment may fall.

Rachel committed no fault in wishing for a child—her fault had been envy and its subsequent discontent. Years had passed, the very recollection of her restless discontent may have faded from her mind, but not from His whom she had by want of faith and gratitude offended. In His infinite mercy He forgave, He blessed, for He called her to Himself ere the evil days came, and her beloved one was sold by his brethren, and reported for long long years as dead. He saved the mother this deep suffering, but, in His justice towards her and love to her descendants, He chastised by an early and painful death, the most trying separation of soul and body which human nature (so to speak) may know. Her husband, her Joseph—her new-born—suddenly and fearfully the silver links of love, binding her to all of these, were snapt asunder, and she might know her place on earth no more. "Give me children, or else I die." Alas! the too impatient cry was heard and answered; children *were* bestowed, and with them death. How little knew she what she asked! In all her surpassing loveliness, in the full possession of most faithful love, the destroying angel came and snatched her from this world. Oh! will not this teach us to be content with what God has given, and restrain us from looking with secret envy on the richer (in seeming) blessings of another? Will it not bid us beware of seeking aught of good only because it belongs to a companion, or because we fancy we have equal right to its possession, by the lesson that, even were it ours, we might have no power to enjoy it? Death, indeed, may not come between us and its enjoyment; but that which we have coveted loses its value the moment we possess it. Will not the warm young heart shrink from the very anticipation of the sin towards God and man which discontent may bring? Let us think *more* of our sorrowing and afflicted fellow-creatures, and *less* of those more blessed in outward seeming. Did we think on the bereaved, the physically afflicted, the poor, how could we still retain discontent of our own lot, or envy of our fellow-creatures? And oh! if no other reasoning will avail, let us remember, our God is not only a merciful, tender Father, but a just and jealous God, who will one day, we know not when or how, call upon us to render an account of the blessings He has given; and if we know them not, how may we answer? Long years had passed since Rachel's offence, yet He who slumbereth not nor sleepeth, chastised it in the very hour that the wish which caused it was fulfilled.

It may be asked (as in similar cases of bereavement it, alas! too often is), Why, granting that the lot of the departed is blessedness, does the God of love so afflict the survivors? Why did He cause such deep grief to His favored servant Jacob? Because God loved him; because His omniscience had seen that Rachel might come between Jacob's heart and his God; because He would demonstrate to futurity that, to possess His favor, His blessing, does not in any manner emancipate us from trial and suffering in this world; because He would lift up our affections from the narrow limits of this world, He would make His heaven a dearer home than our earth, He would people it with the immortal spirits of those we have loved on earth, that we may look upon it no longer as a strange land; but as the beautiful country where our beloved are gone, and where we shall follow. This is wherefore He bereaves, and therefore even in the bereavement there is love.

There is no mention of Jacob's grief; yet in the very silence of Scripture, in some points, there is eloquence, borne out, as in this case it is, by the deep love he bore towards Joseph and Benjamin. What can more exquisitely express the intensity of that love, than when entreated by his sons to let Benjamin accompany them to Egypt, he answered, "My son shall not go down with you; for his brother is dead, and he is left alone: if mischief befal him in the way which ye go, then shall ye bring my grey hairs with sorrow to the grave." "He is left alone," and yet he had ten brethren—alone of his mother, the patriarch felt —sole record of that beloved one whom he had lost, and how might he let him depart? It is impossible to reflect on Jacob's intense love for Joseph and Benjamin, without fully imagining the suffering of their mother's loss. Silent he was, for who might question the decrees of the Most High? but faith and love for our Father in heaven do not forbid us to mourn. We are placed here to love each other; and if we love not those with whom we are in daily, hourly intercourse, how may we love God? Without love, earth would be a desert and heaven a void.

The death of Leah is not recorded; we only know that she did not accompany the patriarch and his family to Egypt, and that she was buried with Abraham and Sarah, Isaac and Rebekah, in the cave of Machpelah. Left dependent on her tenderness and love, the extent of which we know, Jacob no doubt lavished warmer affection upon her, after the death of Rachel than before. How gratefully her pious heart must have traced this tranquil calm, which probably closed her days, to her God, we may infer from the thanksgiving with which every previous blessing had been received. But, as her future life can only be suggestion, much as imagination may love to dwell upon it, our present task must be concluded. We have dilated already at so much length upon the characters of the sisters, and the instruction and consolation therein developed, that we need add little further now, except to notice what has always appeared a remarkable manifestation of the perfect equality of the sisters in their position as mothers of that race which is to last for ever. Ten tribes are lost—not to be discovered till the day which will behold the glorious and stupendous miracle of our restoration. The two which remain to bear witness to the mercy and justice of the Eternal, and the truth of His word, are JUDAH, the descendants of LEAH, and BENJAMIN, the descendants of RACHEL, from one or other of which every Israelite (except the representatives of the Levites, who were accounted the priests of the Lord, not of the twelve tribes) traces his descent.

Shall we then dismiss the beautiful record of Leah and Rachel, which the word of God contains, as a mere relation, concerning an age so long past as to appear almost fabulous and obsolete? Shall we not rather take it to our hearts, and, as women of

Israel, feel it is of *our own ancestry* we read? Shall we not emulate the much enduring piety of Leah; and in all our afflictions—even in that of a lone and unloved heart—turn to her God, and emulate her rejoicing acknowledgment of blessings at His hand? Shall we not take warning of the loved and lovely Rachel, and feel that neither beauty nor love—the dearest love of man—can afford us happiness and joy, unless both are traced to, and held from the grace of God? That not in outward attraction—not even in human love—can blessedness exist, unless the vital spark, to give them rest and life and continuance, hath dwelling *within*, to lift up the whole soul to God. O better—far better—homeliness of form and face, with a guileless contented heart. Better—far better—a heart desolate of earthly sympathy, with the love of our Father in heaven, than beauty and grace and human love, the fullest, dearest, combined with every worldly blessing—if these be sufficient for our need, and we pass through life without one thought of God.

END OF THE FIRST PERIOD.

SECOND PERIOD

CHAPTER I.

EGYPTIAN CAPTIVITY AND JOCHEBED.

We are now to commence the second period of our history—an interval, differing materially from that which went before, and from that which will succeed it, yet of vital importance to the women of Israel. Their station is no longer to depend upon the changes of time and states. The protection, tenderness, reverence, and support, which in their varied relations of life they so imperatively need, no longer rest on the will of man alone: the God of Abraham proclaims Himself their Guardian and their Father, and, by innumerable statutes in His Holy Law, provides for their temporal and eternal welfare equally with that of man.

The mother, the wife, the daughter, the maid-servant, the widow, and the fatherless—for each and all, His love and mercy so provided, that every social and domestic duty became obedience unto Him, and woman was thus raised to that rank in the scale of intellectual and immortal beings, by the ordinance of God, from which her weakness of frame and gentle delicacy of mind would, had she depended on man's judgment alone, have entirely deprived her.

For the women of Israel were those laws issued which were to guard the innocence, purity, honor, and well-doing of woman in general throughout the world; for, however other revelations may profess to be the first and purest, however the smile of scorn and unbelief may attend the mention of the Jewish dispensation in conjunction with woman, the truth remains the same, that as from that law every other sprang, so from that law does woman in every age, clime, rank, and race, receive her guardianship on earth, and hope of heaven.

That this assertion will meet with scorn and denial on all sides, we believe—perchance even from those whom nationality and duty both, should arouse to its defence. Yet firmly and unhesitatingly we retain the position we have advanced, prepared to defend it from the same blessed Book on which it is founded—the Word of God. Much has been said of the wide distinction between ancient and modern Judaism, of Talmudical perversions of Holy Writ, of Jewish degradation of woman, and a melancholy list of similar accusations. With them we neither have nor intend to have anything to do, save boldly to assert, that IF there be this wide distinction between ancient and modern Judaism—IF customs and laws derogatory to God's changeless truth, and contrary to His holy Word, have crept in amongst us,—the dark and bloody eras of persecution are at fault, not the ancient fathers, who knew how to *die* for their faith, but not to sully or degrade it. And it behoves us, in this blessed age of peace and this land of freedom, to prove the falsity of the charge, to awake and manifest to all men, that the religion of the Jew is the religion of Moses, as given by the Lord; and that *if* laws have crept in *contrary* to the spirit and the ordinances of his word, they are *not* Judaism, but the remnants of an age of barbarism and darkness, when that pure and holy word was almost death to read. Oh! why has not Israel joined heart and hand in this holy cause? Why has he not borne, in charity and patience, with those who differ from him in minor points, and thought only how, by union, harmony, and love, he could exalt his nation and his faith in the sight of the Gentile world, and *prove* that, however close and binding may be the casket, the jewel it enshrines is still the revelation of the Lord, the religion of the Bible?

But our present task has not to do with the nation and Judaism at large; it is simply to prove to the women of Israel their position in the sight of God, and their duties towards man. The intricacies of the law, as commented upon and explained by our ancient fathers, are not for us. Woman needs only comfort, strength, and guidance, so simply yet so clearly given, that a little child may read and understand them; and these are ours, alike in the records of our female ancestors and in the precepts of the Lord.

Hitherto we have been regarding His love, mercy, and justice, as manifested to individuals; deriving lessons from exam ple, and guidance from the Eternal's dealings with His creatures. Recorded in His book, we know that their lives are now intended for our instruction and benefit, or they would not have been written. But God knew that something yet more was needed, for the religious training and well doing of His elected people; something more than the mere history of the past, bright as that was with the wonderful manifestations of His presence in direct communings with His saints;—and for the love He bore His faithful servant Abraham, it pleased Him to bring from the deepest darkness the purest light, and vouchsafed a law which was to last for ever, and through which not alone His chosen but every nation should be blessed.

From the death of Joseph to a short time preceding the birth of Moses, Holy Writ is silent as to the history of the Israelites, both individually and nationally, except the important truth that "they were fruitful and increased abundantly, and multiplied and waxed exceeding mighty, and the land was filled with them." Though no law had been given, they were still, it is evident, a completely distinct people, retaining a pure religion in the midst of barbarous idolatry. With no ordained worship—no revealed ordinances—no appointed sacrifice, or priest; still they were the elect and beloved of the Lord, requiring no mediator, either angelic or human, to bring up their prayers before God, and render them acceptable. Yet God not only "heard their cry, but had respect unto them." This is a point in our history too important to be overlooked, though it concerns Israel generally, not the women of Israel alone. It is very often brought forward as a proof, that we must now be wholly rejected by the Lord, because the daily sacrifice has ceased, and many parts of the law, obligatory upon us in our own land, are scarcely possible to be observed in our captivity—the cessation of sacrifices and atonement offerings especially are perpetually insisted upon, as proving that unless we acknowledge the atoning sacrifice of Jesus, and regard him as our High Priest, we are lost temporally and eternally.

The simple fact that the Israelites in Egypt had neither sacrifice nor high priest, though the former was already ordained, yet were still a distinct people, still the first-born of the Lord, and had power to lift up their cry to Him, and be heard, compassionated, and answered, is a sufficiently convincing answer. Israel is now, and has been for eighteen hundred years, as he was in Egypt, with the sole difference that there we were not the captives of the Lord as we are now; nor had we then a law to guide us, and by obedience prove repentance. We are now fulfilling the prophecy, that "Israel shall abide many days without priest or sacrifice," etc. (Hosea iii. 4): but the same blessed word which foretells this, says not one word of our being utterly cast off, but repeatedly enforces the divine consolation, that we have but to cry unto the Lord, even from the lands of our captivity, to be heard and compassionated as we were in Egypt. We have no need of sacrifice, when God Himself ordained that it should cease; nor can we have the head of the nation, alike of its religious, civil, and even military divisions, while scattered in every quarter of the globe. Were we to accept Jesus, in his blended character of sacrifice, atoner, and high priest, the prophecies would all remain *un*fulfilled; as we should still possess all these, instead of being, as the prophet so expressly declared, deprived during our captivity of "king, prince, sacrifice, image, ephod, and terephim," Hosea iii. 4.

To Israel in Egypt they were not given; to Israel in her lengthened captivity they have ceased, until she be purified and chastened sufficiently to receive once again the visible manifestation of the Lord's acceptance, their constant attendant, and which was forfeited by our rebellion. Yet still, even as in Egypt, we are the first-born of the Lord, and have nationally and individually, equal access to His compassionating love.

A new king had arisen in Egypt; one who knew not Joseph, and saw only in the Israelites, a people harmless indeed in employments and pursuits, but sufficiently mighty in numbers to arouse the jealous fears of tyranny: and the commandment went forth to afflict them, by weighty tasks and heavy burdens. But the more they afflicted them, the more they multiplied and grew; and, in consequence, heavier and heavier grew their afflictions, till at length the fatal command was given to destroy every male child at its birth. Yet even this was overruled by a merciful God. The hearts of the women designed for this barbarous office were in His hand, and he so softened them into tenderness and compassion that the innocent babes were saved by the very means adopted for their destruction. Finding this scheme unavailing, Pharaoh issued another command more fatal than the first, for it seemed not in the power of man to evade or counteract it. And in the power of man it was not;

God alone could bring forth delivery; and therefore did He permit the deepest darkness to close around his people, that both they and the Egyptians might know the power to redeem, and the love to accomplish it, were in Him alone.

The situation of the women of Israel, at this period, must have been terrible indeed. Their infants, born in the midst of sorrow, yet hailed, perhaps, as the sole blessing which they could call their own, snatched from them by ruthless murderers, and flung into the Nile. And where were they to look for redress—for pity? Where but to their God—and "He heard their groaning;" and from this very desolation raised up His own.

The family of Amram, a son of Levi, already consisted of himself, his wife, a little son of three years old, and an elder daughter. The birth of Aaron must have been attended with heavy sorrow from the tyrannical oppression under which his father and the other Israelites labored; but dark as was that hour, it must have been almost joyous compared with the awful trial awaiting his mother now. About to add another little one to their family, how agonizingly must the shriek of torture, wrung from her sisters in Israel—marking every fresh assault of the Egyptians within their houses, in search of their babes—have sounded in her ears? Day after day, night after night, one or other dwelling of the miserable Hebrews was searched; and ransacked, if no child were found. Voices of cursing and mockery mingled with the wild entreaties for mercy—the scream of agony—the wailing moan of impotent suffering—the feeble wail of helpless infancy—the sullen splash, that told the work of butchery done;—such must have been the sight and sounds around the home of Jochebed, as she awaited in trembling horror that day which must expose her to the same. It came at length, and a fair lovely babe was born—a boy—whose first wailing cry, if it reached the ears of the Egyptian butchers, would be his death-knell. But the prayers of the mother had not been in vain. Her God was with her, endowing her with wisdom and energy sufficiently effectual to conceal her boy three months. But then, danger once more approached. Suspicions had either been excited, or the increasing age and size of the child rendered the task of concealment no longer possible. Fearful must have been the struggle of natural terrors and spiritual confidence, filling the mother's mind, ere the plan she eventually followed was matured and executed. Faith alone in a God of infinite compassion could have inspired a mode of proceeding apparently so fraught with danger, as herself to expose her babe to the deep and dangerous current of the river; but even while faith impelled, and at times soothed, by the firm conviction that her God would save, natural affections and human fears must often have had the ascendant, breathing but of danger and of death. The future was veiled in impenetrable darkness. The fate of her child, even if his slender ark bore him in safety on the waters, must be one of suffering, or perhaps of starvation—for who would give him food? Did she do right to expose him thus? If he were to be saved, would not the Eternal equally accomplish it without this fearful venture? Such would be mere human reasoning in woman's feeble heart. But prayer gave her the needful grace and strength to listen only to the immortal spirit, and trust undoubtingly in God. Can we not picture the anxious throbbings of maternal affection as her own hand weaved the ark or basket of bulrushes, in which her babe was to be exposed? Would not merely earthly natures have smiled in scorn on this feeble invention, and pronounced it futile? But the mother of Moses had not such to increase the difficulty of her task. Her husband's name is never mentioned in this proceeding; for Amram, as the remainder of his miserable brethren, was in all probability too much weighed down and spirit-broken by their multiplied afflictions, to think of the inmates of his home, save with increased affliction and despondency; nay, had perchance closed his heart against all love for his new-born, believing it was destined, as every other, for immediate death. He could have had no time to watch over it, and share his wife's anxieties. To his mother alone, therefore, under the especial providence of God, did Moses owe his preservation.

The ark was completed. Gifted with unusual foresight and wisdom for the task, Jochebed carefully daubed it with slime and pitch, that no water should penetrate within; and with trembling yet still trusting spirit, placed her babe therein, and laid it on the flags by the river's brink. To watch what would be done with it—whether it would rest there till some compassionating passer-by should behold and save him, or be indeed launched on the waters and carried from her sight—was indeed a task too fearful for maternal love. We may picture, with perfect truth and justice, her last lingering kiss pressed upon the lips, cheek, and brow of the unconscious babe; her waiting till sleep closed those beauteous eyes, which, in their pleading gaze, seemed to her fond heart beseeching her not so cruelly to aban don him—waiting till slumber, light, pure, beautiful, as only infancy can know, lay upon those sweet features, those rounded limbs—making them seem like some folded flower, waiting but the return of day to brighten into renewed and still lovelier existence. Would that day ever dawn for that sweet unconscious slumberer on earth? Alas! how may she answer? Her look deepens in its silent anguish—its immeasurable love. Faith seems departing in that intensity of human feeling; she will look no more, lest indeed it fail. The light lid closes softly over the sleeping babe. She lays it amidst the flowering flags—looks once, once more. Does the infant moan or weep? How may she leave it, if it does? No: all is silent, voiceless—the boy still sleeps—and she hurries from the spot—bids Miriam stand "afar off," yet near enough "to know what would be done with him." And for herself?—where, where shall she find rest, from the anxiety and suffering of that fearful hour? Where, but at the footstool of her God, in whose gracious hand she has placed her babe? What could calm that heart but prayer? And how can we doubt one moment that to the MOTHER of MOSES prayer was her whole support, strength, and life?

Holy writ is silent as to the length of time which elapsed ere Pharaoh's daughter "came down to wash at the river; and her maidens walked along by the river's side, and when she saw the ark among the flags, she sent her maid to fetch it. And when she had opened it, she saw the child: and, behold, the babe wept. And she had compassion on him, and said, This is one of the Hebrews' children." How exquisitely true and touching is this picture of human nature! The simple words, "and, behold, the babe wept," even in reading, seem to fill woman's heart with a gush of tears. The utter helplessness, the innocence, the beauty of the poor babe, seem to cling to our affections, as if he were entwined with them by stronger ties than mere narration. And is he not? What woman of Israel can read this touching narrative unmoved? "The babe wept;" and, true to nature, Pharaoh's daughter had compassion on him. Cold, terrified, hungry, the poor infant might have been weeping long in his bulrush prison; but those tears, sad as they were to him, obtained his human preservation.

The compassion of the princess emboldened Miriam to go forward, and respectfully to ask, "Shall I go and call to thee a nurse of the Hebrew women, that she may nurse the child for thee?" An address which would almost make us believe that the compassionate and gentle character of the tyrant's daughter must have been known to the Hebrews, or the young Miriam would scarcely have had sufficient courage so to have spoken. This, however, must be suggestion; the inspired narrative only enforces upon us the hand of God throughout. The same God who inspired Rebekah unconsciously to speak those words which answered the steward's prayer, and elected her for Isaac's wife, also inspired the youthful daughter of Amram to come forward and speak such words to the princess of Egypt, as, at another time, she would have trembled to utter even in thought.

"And Pharaoh's daughter said to her, Go. And the maid went and called the child's mother. And Pharaoh's daughter said unto her, Take this child away, and nurse it for me, and I will give thee thy wages. And the woman took the child and nursed it."

What must have been the emotions of Jochebed, thus to clasp again to her heart her rescued treasure! Not alone saved from present death, but future suffering and labor—restored to her maternal bosom, to receive thence not only his necessary infant nourishment, but such lessons of his father's God and his brethren's faith as would render him invulnerable to the temptations and idolatry of the Egyptian court. Her emotions in parting from her child we might try to picture; but on those which must have attended his rescue, his restoration, silence is most eloquent. How had not her simple trusting faith been rewarded! How clearly, how startlingly had the hand of the Eternal been displayed! And how could she prove the grateful devotedness of her overflowing heart, save by devoting the child His love had saved unto His service? Not even poverty and privation had she to encounter. While her brethren were enduring the heaviest burdens from cruel taskmasters, she was receiving wages from the princess of Egypt for the nurture of her own child; and well may we believe those wages were devoted to the needy and the suffering—from her who in the midst of natural sorrow must have felt herself individually so blessed.

"And the child grew, and she brought him unto Pharaoh's daughter, and he became her son." But it was in those years he had passed with his own mother his character had been formed; his principles were fixed; his religion obtained living and breathing, and ever-actuating influence. We know not the age at which he left his mother, but we must infer, from all that is narrated of him, that *her* influence, not that of his adopted parent, made him what he was. No lessons of Pharaoh's daughter could have endowed him with that feeling of patriotism which bade him rise up against the Egyptian who was smiting an Israelite, or interfere between the two Israelites, endeavoring meekly to restore peace. Had his early instruction been confined to Pharaoh's palace, his very birth and race would have been unknown; he would have imbibed only such principles as actuated the Egyptians, and could not fail to have bowed down to their idols. Some very powerful influence must have been at work counteracting these evils; and what influence is so great over the susceptible age of infancy as that of mother or nurse? and Jochebed combined both these endearing relations. Even after the actual task of nursing was accomplished, "and the child grew, and she brought him unto Pharaoh's daughter," it appears to me more than probable that she was still retained near the person of her child, tending him even after he was called the princess's son; and thus had frequent opportunities of inculcating those divine truths which, though no law was yet given, the past history of his people so vividly revealed.

That Moses makes no further mention of his parents is no proof of such idea being but fancy. Of everything concerning himself he writes so slightly, so evidently imagining his personal history of no possible consequence, compared with the mighty and solemn matters intrusted to him, that it was not likely the days of his childhood should be recalled and dwelt upon. Nay, he himself might have been perfectly unconscious to what influence he actually owed his peculiar feelings as an Israelite, his gentle lovely virtues as a man. The work of a mother is silent and unseen as dew upon the earth:—the seed must be planted, watched, watered, but unless spared to behold it springing into flower, the hand of the planter may for ever rest unknown.

Jochebed was parted from her son, years before this blessed reward could have been given; his *childhood* alone was hers. His youth, his manhood, when the seed she had sown might have repaid her with abundant harvest, were passed, the one in all the temptations, the luxuries of an Egyptian court; the other in exile—the lowly shepherd of his father-in-law, a priest of Midian,—apart even from his countrymen. It does not appear that his parents were among those who left Egypt, or their names would have been mentioned with the other relatives of Moses. Jochebed had not the privilege of beholding the spiritual and temporal greatness of her rescued boy; but had the seed of her sowing withered? Were her counsels vain? Can we not trace in the peculiarly gentle, much-forgiving character of our lawgiver, the moulding of a *woman's* hand? Is there aught to prove the minion of a court, the favorite of a princess? No, O no. The whole character of Moses displays a mother's guidance. A mother's love watching over childhood, and inculcating those high and glowing principles of virtue and patriotism, which the blessing of the Eternal ripened into such a beautiful maturity, as to render Moses a fit instrument in His hand to lead His chosen people from the land of bondage, and to reveal His changeless law.

And what will not this beautiful narrative teach us? As Jochebed, we too are in a land of bondage; indeed, in free and happy England, not a bondage of suffering and persecution, but yet as exiles from our own land, and, alas! too often, exiles from our God. We too are in a land of strangers, whose faith is not ours; a faith which, though it be not idolatry, is fraught with yet more temptation and danger. In this blessed land, no cruel taskmaster afflicts us with heavy burdens; yet there are some to look upon us with scorn and hate, who would strew our daily path with the thorns and briers of contempt, calumny, and abuse; and others again who, with kindly yet mistaken zeal, would appal us by the vivid recital of the fearful precipice on which we stand, telling us that but one escape is left us, one only way, or we are temporally and eternally lost; and that way no Israelite can recognise. Yet fearful are the temptations to seek it, and few, too few, his weapons of defence. Worldly rank and worldly honors are closed to the believing Hebrew, and wherever he turns he feels himself a stranger.

Blest in this land with peace and freedom, yet, ever and

anon, the low growl of the tempest of persecution reaches him from distant shores; sometimes sinking into silence, ere more than the heart's quick throbbing is aroused; at others waxing louder and more loud, till the wailings of thousands, and the shrieks of torture, are borne on the heavy air, breathing that Israel is afflicted still. And wherefore? To bid us still feel we are the captives of the Lord—that Jerusalem lieth desolate and waste for our sins—that the awful prophecy of the twenty-eighth chapter of Deuteronomy has been, and in many lands still is, in actual fulfilment—that we are now, as we were in Egypt, afflicted and oppressed—"despised and rejected of men—a man of sorrows and acquainted with grief"—"as one that gropeth at noon-day, as the blind gropeth in darkness, that shall not prosper in his ways, that shall only be spoiled and oppressed evermore, and whom no man shall save."

And if it be so (and who shall say it is not?), oh! does it not devolve on the mothers of Israel to do even as Jochebed, and so influence the childhood of their sons, as to render them indeed faithful to their God, meek and forgiving towards man, and invulnerable to every temptation held forth by the opposers of their faith?

The very safety we enjoy, the habits of friendly intimacy which it is right and happy we should cultivate, all call upon the Hebrew mother to instil those principles in the heart of her son which shall guide him through life, and, while they raise him in the estimation of the nations around him, inspire him individually to glory in his own.

We have enlarged, in a former work, on the duty of mothers regarding religion generally. We would here conjure them to follow the example of the mother of Moses, and make their sons the receivers, and in their turn the promulgators, of that holy law which is their glorious inheritance. Their faith, in England, may not be tried as that of Jochebed—they may not be called upon to expose their innocent babes to the dangers of the river, to save them from the cruelties of man—but they are called upon to provide a suit of defence for riper years. They must so instruct, so guide, the first ten or twelve years of boyhood, that even then they may leave their maternal homes as Israelites rejoicing in their faith. They must infuse some balsam to heal, or some invulnerable shield to eject, the arrows of contempt or pity which, ere they pass through life, they must encounter.

They must so lead, that graver years may conduct them to that only study, the blessed word of God, which alone can give peace to their spirits, rest to their minds, and conviction to their hearts —alike in their private hours and their communings with the Nazarene world. This is now the Hebrew mother's task, which may be blessed to their offspring as Jochebed's was to Moses. It is for this they must have faith, must trust that God will perfect that which is imperfect, fill up every deficiency, and bring the seed to flower, or vain and hopeless will be their task. They must impress upon their offspring their SPIRITUAL ARISTOCRACY, and so not only remove all temptation to barter their heavenly heritage for earthly rank, but infuse their minds and hearts with that nobility of thought, word, and action, which should be the heir-loom, the glory of every Hebrew, be he of what rank, profession, or even trade, he may. Persecution and barbarity in our opposers, and their consequent ignorance and superstition in ourselves, have for long ages so crushed and trampled on this innate nobility, that in all but a very few instances, it seems, and has long seemed, departed from us; its banishment stigmatizing us as degraded to the lowest and vilest of mankind. Can we now then, in those blessed lands where the Jew may walk in freedom, with "none to molest or make him afraid," permit this stigma to remain? Shall we not rather wake every energy, string every nerve, to prove that it is not Judaism, but persecution at fault; and that wherever the Hebrew is FREE, he is NOBLE? That the princely blood of Abraham, Moses, and David still flows within his veins, and incites him to thoughts and deeds as far removed from ignorance and degradation as the sun is from the earth?

But not when arrived at manhood can this nobility be infused. It must be imbibed with the mother's milk, and form the very atmosphere of childhood and youth. Let every mother in Israel look upon her infant treasure as direct from the hand of God, and believe that He saith to her, as the princess of Egypt said to Jochebed,—"Nurse this child for ME, and I will give thee thy wages;" for HIM, for the LORD, who in every age, clime, and position, calleth Israel His CHILDREN. And let her indeed so nurse him, that whenever he may be called to his Father in Heaven he may be fit to go. Let her, weak and feeble of herself as she is, remember that with the Lord all things are possible, and that as He blessed Jochebed in the preservation and nurture of her child, so if we will but blend effort with prayer, perseverance with faith, He will equally bless us—and though it may not be ours to rear a deliverer from Egyptian bondage, yet how will the mothers in Israel rejoice and glory, to receive "their wages" in the elevation of their nation by their sons?

To do this, they must be NOBLE; and to become so, let the Hebrew mother teach her boy, from his earliest years, to think of his heavenly heritage, his spiritual election, his eternal life, and leave the interests and ambition of earth till riper years, when even these dull sordid cares shall become ennobled and spiritualized, by the purer atmosphere which he has in his boyhood breathed. We are not, indeed, while denizens of earth, to think so exclusively of heaven as to unfit us for the life of trial and temptation which, in our mortal career, we are commanded to tread; but we are to infuse earth with Heaven, time with Eternity, the soul with GOD. As Israelites, we *cannot* sever our temporal from our eternal interests, we *cannot* fling off the memory of, and obedience to, the Eternal, for with every single relation, duty, ordinance, and habit of daily life His commands are blended. We *are* not Israelites, if we think to live apart from Him, or to do aught in which we cannot associate Him by the entreaty for His blessing, and the looking to Him throughout. We are not Israelites, if we do not feel our every domestic duty and loving tie sanctified by Him, and bringing us nearer, closer, more lovingly to Him, with every passing month. This is to be an Israelite—this is to be the aristocracy of the Lord; for did we so associate our religion with our lives, we must be NOBLE. But how can we attain this, how dare we hope it, if the pursuit of gold, the vain longing for wealth, the idle dream of worldly aggrandizement, the empty rivalship with those richer and higher than ourselves, be the sole end, aim, and being of the Israelite? We look with loud condemnation and scorn on the worshippers of the golden calf—we contemn the worshippers, more than we tremble at the awful chastisement from the hand of the Lord—yet let us beware, lest our sons too bow before the golden idol. It may take no form, we may not approach it with forms of worship, and priests, and incense, but if it fill up our hearts to the exclusion of all other and nobler thoughts, if its pursuit drag us from the house of God, from our own hearths, deaden us to the love of home ties, prevent the spiritual and enlarged education of our children, what is it to us but as the golden calf to the Israelites of old? And how dare *we* hope to be exempt from the chastisement of God, when it fell upon our brethren? Oh! let us not case up our hearts, and pursue our way in confident security, because it is deferred. God works not now as He did then. Israel, in his redemption from Egypt, needed constant, visible, and palpable evidences of the providence and the justice of the Lord. *We* have them not to guide us now, but their *record* is ours, in which to learn our duty, and the effects of its neglect or disobedience. That which was displeasing to Him *then*, is displeasing to Him *now;* but, scattered as we are among the nations, deprived through our iniquities of the visible manifestation of His presence, His approval, and His wrath, not on earth may our judgment be known; nor can we "discern between him that serveth God, and him that serveth Him not," till that day when "the Lord shall make up His jewels, and spare those that love Him, as a man spareth his own son that serveth him."

That the long dark ages of persecution originated that fearful indifference to all ennobling pursuits, of which the Hebrew is accused, we quite acknowledge. Deprived of all honorable and elevating employment, of every profession, of every trade, which, bringing them into friendly contact with their fellow-men, would have enlarged their minds, and awakened social affections; cowed, crushed, hunted down, and often persecuted for the sake of their wealth; deadened, stupefied, to all spiritual elevation, even as the Israelites in Egypt; was it marvel they should cling to gold, and seek its increase, as their sole rank and privilege? For them God had compassion, for He knew how they were tried. It was natural too, that, even when in lands of comparative freedom and peace, the habits and associations of past years should cling pertinaciously to them still. But their encouragement is no longer guiltless—prosperity, peace, friendly intercourse with some of the nations, are granted us, that we may come back with heart and soul unto our holy law, and strive with all our might against every idol which comes between us and our God. In England, France, Belgium, and America, it is no longer persecution and intolerance that degrade and pronounce us vile. If such feelings do find entrance, it is the prejudice arising from what we *were*. They, as is natural, see not the *cause* of that past degradation, but let *us* make it manifest—let us evince, more and more, that gold is no longer our sole pursuit; that fraud and cunning, which to the ignorant Gentile are synonymous with the word Jew, are as far from us as from them—that when free we too are noble, honorable, and spiritual to an extent that, if we adhere to our blessed law, only Israelites can be—and prejudice *must* pass away, and Israel be acknowledged the witnesses of the Lord.

It is this noble, this spiritual feeling of independence we would beseech every Hebrew mother to instil into her boy; and which we now humbly, yet earnestly, prayerfully, and heartfully conjure every Hebrew father to aid and confirm. Let not the ears of the infant Israelite be polluted by reference to earthly gain and worldly rivalship, but let him hear often from his father's lips those sweet lessons of heaven and God—of self-denial and its blessed reward—of those purer pleasures of intellect and heart, which, if not infused into his infancy, can never find entrance and dominion in after years. Ably and delightfully would such paternal lessons assist the mother's task, and lighten the blessed yet exquisitely anxious labor of teaching their offspring their proper station in the sight of God and man, and so ennoble, purify, and spiritualize heart and mind, as to render them fit descendants of the princes, priests, and prophets from whom they spring.

And let not such parents fear for their sons' earthly welfare. Such training will not unfit them for the necessary cares and toils of life. It will but render them less engrossing, less worldly, and annihilate every feeling which they would blush to acknowledge before God and man. It will take from life its dross, its stagnating care, teaching them that their duty indeed is to work and persevere, alike for their families and themselves, but that in the hand of the Lord is their portion, and that He will order their daily lot as will be most fitted for their eternal welfare. It will remove every temptation to turn aside, for lucre or ambition, from their father's faith. It will open heart and hand towards the suffering and the poor, and, removing every selfish feeling and grovelling thought, prepare them for that day when the Lord again shall call them His, and bid them resume that kingly station in the sight of the nations, of which for "a little moment" only they are deprived.

The suffering Israelites, under the terrible oppression of Pharaoh, imagined not the rank to which they would be called by the word of the Lord. While groaning under their heavy burdens, toiling day and night, with neither relief nor relaxation, could they have imagined that, in their persecuted offspring, princes should arise;—that, in a brief interval, Chiefs of their tribes, Heads of families, Captains of well-appointed squadrons—Priests, sacred in the sight of all the people, and acknowledged by the Eternal—Workers in every elegant art, which was needed in the building and embellishment of the Tabernacle—Warriors, dauntless in bravery, and skilful in the art of war—Judges, gifted to decide causes, award sentences, and keep civil peace and order amid a disorderly multitude—Princes, of such wealth and consequence as to make the splendid offerings enumerated in the seventh chapter of Numbers—could they have imagined that such would be? Yet such WAS, and such WILL BE. We know not when, we know not how—we only know that the word of God has said it, and that He is a God of truth. Shall we not remember this in the education of our sons, and infuse such feelings as will render them indeed but sojourners in the land of the captivity, watchers, as it were, on the frontiers, prepared to arise, and fall into their appointed stations, the moment the Lord shall call? Let us welcome in them the inclination for the liberal professions, all that will enlarge the mind and ennoble the heart, and bid them prove, in the sight of the whole Gentile world, that where the Hebrew is FREE, he his brave, enterprising, self-denying, gifted, wise, magnanimous, as the noblest of the nations around him. Let the Hebrew mother give her boy the solid foundation of his glorious faith, and he may go forth in the Nazarene world unharmed; and in other professions, other lines than that of merchant, in which alone till now the Jew has been known, he will honor the name of Israelite.

And if such be the fruit of nursing her child for God, oh! will not every Hebrew mother feel, that she has indeed received "her wages?"

CHAPTER II.

THE EXODUS.—LAWS FOR THE MOTHERS OF ISRAEL.

We have seen quoted in a Jewish periodical, "that it was for the sake of the righteous women the Lord delivered our ancestors from Egypt." Scriptural authority for this assertion we certainly cannot find, as it is expressly said, "the Lord remembered the promises which he had made to Abraham, Isaac, and Jacob." We only quote it as a proof that the ancient fathers from whom we believe it taken, could not have had the low idea of women with which they are charged, to have put such an opinion forth, even in suggestion; but must have imagined the righteousness of women of no little importance towards the well-doing of the state. That so, in fact, it is, we have direct scriptural authority to believe; as not only a review of the law will make manifest, but the consequences of the sins of the women in a more distant period. Were not woman an equally responsible agent in the sight of God—were He not in His infinite mercy tenderly careful of her innocence, her honor, her well-doing, her protection by man—no law for her in particular need have been issued, nor such especial care taken to cleanse her from impurity and guilt, to free her from false charges and an unjust husband, to permit and sanctify her singular vow, and give her every incentive for a chaste, virtuous, and modest life. This need not have been—would not have been—if the Eternal had not, in His compassionating love, regarded His frailer, weaker children with even more tenderness than He looked on man, and resolved on fixing her station and her privileges, and so bringing her forward as an object at once of tenderness and respect—of cherishing, as a wife and daughter—of the deepest veneration, as a mother—the especial object of national as well as individual love and protection, as widowed and fatherless—and of the kindest, most fatherly care and gentleness, as the maid-servant. Nay, even the female captive was marked out for fostering and healing kindness, and allowed time for mourning, instead of, as in the case of other nations, aye, even those of later days who called themselves followers of Jesus, being hurried to the bed of the brutal conqueror, who was often still reeking with the blood of her relations. How then can it be said, that in every other religion save that of the Nazarene, woman's station is degraded, even as the heathen and the slave?

With a mighty arm the Lord had brought forth Israel from the land of bondage, enriched by the spoil, which they did not *borrow* from the Egyptians, as the usual translation renders it, but had *demanded*, as their right from weary years of unpaid labor, and which, terrified at the awful plagues which had befallen them, was granted them at once. "The Lord gave the people favor in the sight of the Egyptians," are words twice repeated, thus doing away at once all idea of the Eternal having favored fraud, even against His enemies and the enemies of His people. They demanded the long arrears of payment, and they were given, in jewels of silver, and jewels of gold; and so, not by deceit, but in justice, they, to use the Bible language, "spoiled the Egyptians."

The powers of Nature herself succumbed before the mighty will of her Creator. Fire, earth, air, and water, had departed from what is called their natural course, to bring forth Israel from bondage, and to falsify at once the awful denial of a God, in the vain dream of necessity and nature. The sea itself—as the final seal to the stupendous manifestations of Almighty Power displayed in the ten plagues—divided at the word of its Creator, and the host of Israel—men, women, and little children—passed through on dry land, with a watery wall, seeming to unite earth to heaven, on either side. And when the unbelieving scoffers followed—when, denying still the sanctity of Israel, the wonders of Israel's God, the chariots and hosts of Pharaoh dashed on in vain defiance of the Lord—down tumbled the overwhelming mass of mighty waters, and the proud hosts of Pharaoh lay dead before their slaves. And when the song of thanksgiving, of adoration, rose from the hearts and lips of the redeemed, the voice not only of man but of *woman* prolonged the strain. "And Miriam the prophetess, the sister of Aaron, took a timbrel in her hand; and all the women went after her with timbrels and with dances. And Miriam answered them, Sing ye to the Lord! for He hath triumphed gloriously. The horse and his rider hath He thrown into the sea."

Woman is not gifted with a silvery voice and an ear for harmony, to devote to the pleasure of man alone. Let her devote them sometimes to the praises of the Lord, and bid the psalm of thanksgiving filling the sanctuary of the Lord be answered from her lips; and the sweet sanctuary of home, at morning and evening prayer, behold her leading infant lips to tune their first song in thanksgiving to their Father and their God.

As a general view of the beautiful laws constituting the Mosaic religion does not enter into the plan of this work, we shall throw together those portions on which, as they regard woman, we shall somewhat lengthily treat, without any reference to their probable dates. We know that all the laws forming our religion were given between their departure from Egypt and arrival in the promised land, and are contained principally in chapters 19, 20, 21, 22, 23, and 29 of Exodus—in the whole book of Leviticus—in chapters 5, 6, 8, 9, 15, 16, 17, 27, 28, 29, 30, 35, and 36 of Numbers—and in the whole book of Deuteronomy. From these we select and examine all that can give weight to, and throw light upon, the six divisions of our present subject.

As the first and most beautiful relationship in which woman is undeniably necessary to man—the object of his first affections, to whom he owes all of cherishing, happiness, and health, from infancy to boyhood, and often from boyhood to youth; and who, in consequence, must be entwined with every fond remembrance of childhood, the recollection of which is often the only soother, the only light, in the darker heart of man—it is but just that we should examine, first, how the holy relationship of a MOTHER in Israel is guarded and noticed by our law.

The very first command relative to the duties of man towards man, marks out the position of children with regard to their parents, male and *female*, the representatives of God on earth. It was not enough that such position should be left to the natural impulses of gratitude and affection—not enough that the love and reverence of a child to his parent should be left to his own heart, although in the cases of both Isaac and Jacob such had been so distinctly manifested. No; the same tremendous voice which bade the very earth quake, and the fast rooted mountain reel—which spoke in the midst of thunders and lightnings,

"Thou shalt have no other gods but me,"—also said, "Honor thy father and thy MOTHER," and added unto its obedience a promise of reward, the only command to which recompense is annexed, that its obedience might indeed be an obedience of love. And lest there should be some natures so stubborn and obtuse that the fear of punishment only could affect, we read in the repetition, and, as it were, enlargement on the ten commandments, "And he that smiteth his father or his MOTHER shall surely be put to death, and he that curseth or revileth his father or his MOTHER shall surely be put to death" (Exodus xxi. 15—17). "Ye shall *fear* every man his MOTHER and his father, and keep my sabbaths; I am the Lord" (Levit. xix. 3). "For every one that curseth his father or his MOTHER, shall surely be put to death. He that cursed his father or his MOTHER, his blood shall be upon him." And again, in Deuteronomy v. 16, we have the repetition of the fifth commandment, the reward attending its obedience still more vividly enforced: "Honor thy father and thy MOTHER, as the Lord thy God hath commanded thee, that thy days may be prolonged, and that it may go well with thee in the land which the Lord thy God giveth thee."

With laws like these, bearing on every one of them the stamp of divine truth, of a sacred solemnity which could come from God alone, how can any one believe in, much less assert, the Jewish degradation of woman, or call that Judaism which upholds it!

How could these solemn and often reiterated commands be obeyed, if the son of Israel beheld his mother merely the ignorant bond-slave of his father? How could he honor her? What could have such influence upon his moments of passion as to restrain him, when so tempted, from smiting, reviling, or cursing her? How could he *fear* her, when he beheld her trembling before his father, not as her husband, but as her master? But such he saw not. Weaker in frame, from her position and her duties; less mighty in mental powers, yet possessing every attribute to make home blessed, and her children holy followers of God, virtuous and patriotic citizens of their land; shrined in his heart with every memory of his infancy;—such was the Hebrew mother to her son. Were the laws obeyed, there could be no neglectful or sinning mother. Not even suspicion could attack her. The law guarded her even from her own relatives, if they falsely wronged her, compelled her, even under the fear of death, to be chaste, holy, virtuous, and faithful in every duty of domestic and public life; and, therefore, it was a labor of love for her children to obey their God in honoring her, and a crime worthy of death, if indeed there could be found any sufficiently hardened and rebellious as to disobey.

Again, we find in Deut. xxi. 18, "If a man have a stubborn and rebellious son, which will not obey the voice of his father or the voice of his MOTHER, and who, when they have chastened him, will not hearken unto them, then shall his father and his MOTHER lay hold of him, and bring him to the elders of the city, and unto the gate of his place. And they shall say unto the elders of the city, This our son is stubborn and rebellious; he will not obey our voice. And all the men of his city shall stone him with stones that he die. So shalt thou put away evil from among you, that all Israel shall hear and fear."

We here find at length a practical commentary or example, as it were, of the briefer laws on the same subject, given previously. To modern ears, and present notions of false refinement, such commands seem unnaturally harsh and terrible. In those times, they must have been needed, or they would not have been given. And beautifully, even in their harshness, do they demonstrate the reverential duty of Israelitish children to their parents. Still more powerfully do they illustrate the perfect equality of father and mother in respect to their children. It was not only that disobedience to the latter was equally punishable as to the former, but that the voice of the MOTHER was also to condemn her son, or he could not be proved guilty; a peculiarly just law in a nation where more than one wife was allowed. Without it, how often might the more favored work upon the husband to believe false tales of the offspring of her rival! How often might innocence have been condemned, injustice and cruelty permitted, in a man's own household! Evils effectually prevented by the father's witness being unavailable without that of the accused's own mother—one, we must feel, not at all likely to come forward against her own child, unless his crimes had been so heinous as to prevent the possibility of her shielding him any longer. We have no recorded instance of such a fearful evil in Israel; but the severe law given in case of such, should never be forgotten by us, marking, as it does, the wrath and justice of the Lord against all those of His chosen people who could forget, neglect, or wilfully abuse, in any one point, their duty to their earthly parents.

Although mothers are not individually commanded to instruct their children in the knowledge of God and His Law, they are certainly joined with the fathers in the performance of that sacred duty. Every statute, every ordinance, given by the Lord to Moses, was always introduced by the command, "Speak ye to the *Children of Israel;*" "Say ye to the children of Israel;" or, "Hear, O Israel;" words including the *whole* congregation, male and FEMALE. Had *man* only been included, Moses would have addressed them as sons, or as fathers of tribes, as we find Aaron and his sons, and the priests or Levites, in some few instances particularly specified. That woman is intimately joined with man in the religious instruction of her children, is also proved by the fact that the *mothers* of the kings of Israel and Judah are always mentioned by name, as if to them, yet more than to their fathers, they owed their early impressions of good or evil which their after lives displayed. The very commands regarding parents are strong confirmation. A son could not honor, and fear, and love his mother, if he only owed her his first nourishment, and received nothing at her hand but the same instinctive care as the brute creation display towards their young. The immortal mind and soul of man must have something more to reverence and fear, even if the natural links binding mother and son were sufficient (which we much doubt) to call for love. In commanding reverence and obedience from children, God knew that He had so gifted the Hebrew mother, and so marked her duties and position, as to render such emotions merely her due. To her, then, as well as to the father, are those important injunctions contained in Deut. vi. 20—25, emphatically addressed; and according to the measure of her obedience to them, so will be the measure of her children's reverence and love.

The same chapter, but a few verses previous, had solemnly commanded Israel to love the Lord his God with heart, and soul, and might—to lay his words upon his own heart, and teach them diligently to his children. And, after demanding obedience and righteousness in other statutes, proceeds: "And when thy son asketh thee in time to come, saying, What mean these testimonies, and statutes, and judgments which the Lord our God hath commanded you? Then thou shalt say unto thy son, We were Pharaoh's bondmen in Egypt, and the Lord brought us out of Egypt with a mighty hand; and the Lord showed signs and wonders, great and sore, upon Egypt, upon Pharaoh, and upon all his household before our eyes; and He brought us out from thence that he might bring us in, to give us the land which He sware unto our fathers. And the Lord commanded us to do all these statutes, to fear the Lord our God, for our good always, that He might preserve us alive, as it is at this day. And it is our righteousness if we observe to do all these commandments before the Lord our God, as He hath commanded us.

On the weighty *all*, which to Hebrew parents is comprised in these emphatic verses, we must not at present linger, save to observe, that much as was required from parents, when the law was given, and in Jerusalem, still more is needed now. We have to add to the history of our bondage and redemption, that of our glory and our sins—of our first captivity and our partial restoration—our renewed and increased iniquities—of the long suffering, long forbearance of an infinitely merciful God—of His averted, yet at length falling wrath—of our exile, our persecution, and misery—all which Moses himself foretold; and yet our never-dying hope, our incentive for constancy, even through the flames of martyrdom, or the more lingering martyrdom of a crushed spirit and broken heart; the imperative necessity of a return unto the Lord through humility and righteousness, trusting in Him to purify and save.

All this must now be added to the parental instruction enforced by Moses: and all this is equally demanded from the mother as from the father, would they receive to its full extent the reverence ordained by God Himself. For not by *precept* alone must this instruction be given. The young spirit must be led by example as well as exhortation. Let him see that the instructions of his parents come from the heart as well as lips—influence their thoughts, words, and actions—nay, their very being—and never need they despair. However long it may be before the fruit they have sown appear, it will spring into beautiful maturity at last, and shed its purest fragrance in that hour when the faithful mother watches the rapid approach of that last struggle which shall wing her spirit to the footstool of her God.

Will, then, the Hebrew mother rest content with the station assigned her by the ignorant and the prejudiced, and not strain every nerve, rouse every energy, to make the command of the Eternal for her children to honor and fear her, easy, and joyous to obey?

She has done, and she does this! Not a slur, not a stigma, not a shadow can be flung upon the conduct of Hebrew mothers to their offspring. Neglect, injustice, partiality, want of affection, harshness, coldness flung by fashion between mother and child, that littleness and jealousy which would keep back youthful loveliness for a longer individual reign,—such things may be known—may be common—among other nations, but to the Hebrew they are utterly unknown. It is easy to assert that the woman of Israel is degraded and a slave; but did such false accusers visit a domestic circle—did they but see a Hebrew mother and her children—they would find it difficult to *prove* it. Then let every son of Israel receive such religious training from his mother, in addition, or rather closely twined, to the moral and intellectual education she has so long given, that he may be ready, from his very boyhood, indignantly to repudiate the charge, and prove, by his whole conduct—alike in public career, as well as his domestic reverence and love—that his mother is as free in the sight of man, as responsible in the sight of God, and as much the possessor of an immortal spirit as his father and himself.

To the Mosaic religion, then, and to no other, does not only Israel, but every other nation by whom the Bible is acknowledged divine, owe the elevation, the dignity, the holiness of woman as a MOTHER, a position marked out by God Himself, and proclaimed and held sacred, not only by the awful threat of punishment, but by the solemn promise of divine reward. How sacred then to every son and daughter of Israel must be their duty to their parents! Disobedience, neglect, scorn, are no longer capital offences according to the justice of man; but, oh! let us not for one moment forget, that the same God who commanded that such they should be, is watching over Israel still, will demand from every child if His command has been obeyed—from every parent if they have done their duty, and taught their children from earliest years, that *disobedience to them is disobedience to their God, and in His eyes, and in His law, a capital offence.* Were this truth more constantly, more impressively enforced, the reciprocal duties of parent and child would be more easily and more happily fulfilled, and the heart-burnings, the anguish, occasioned to parents by neglect and unkindness, and the rebellion and constant struggles of their offspring to fling off an authority which has never been exerted in infancy, and so must gall in youth, alike be at an end, and Israel's homes, as well as Israel's law, proclaim the guiding spirit and loving mercy of the Lord.

CHAPTER III

LAWS FOR THE WIVES OF ISRAEL

The laws instituted for the protection, the position, the duties, of the wives of Israel, were more peculiar to the manners and customs of the East only, than those relative to mothers, which can be obeyed and attended to in every age and clime. Still much was instituted, even with regard to wives, which marked and fixed their position, and decidedly elevated woman in the scale of being, and proved that, though, as was just and wise, "her desires must bow to her husband, and he should rule over her," yet that this rule was to be one of perfect confidence and love.

It has always appeared a mystery, how any person, even among the Gentiles, who has seriously reflected on, and studied the word of God, can assert that it was *only* through the preaching of Jesus and his apostles that woman took her proper station, and those ordinances were given, which restrained the passions of men, and made marriage a pure and holy tie. Centuries before the advent of Christianity, those laws were given, which, regarding and prohibiting too near consanguinity in marriage, are acknowledged and obeyed by the whole civilized world. Where do we find, amid the Gentile nations, the purity, the chastity, the stainless virtue of woman, to the extent which is still the glory of Israel, and which owes its origin simply to the laws which were issued by the Lord through Moses; seeming, indeed, most terribly severe, but blessed in their very severity by the beautiful purity in Israel which they wrought? Were the law of Moses universally received, how different would be the aspect of the world!

Polygamy was permitted in Israel, at the period of the delivery of the law, simply because the Eternal's mercy would not interfere with an immemorial usage, which his wisdom knew, from local customs and long-indulged habit, would demand violence to be relinquished. The laws He instituted in no way interfered with those habits of His people which custom had endeared; His prescience leaving to time that improvement and greater refinement of the human race, which demands ages to accomplish, but which would at length fling aside of itself every fetter that once had linked it to the customs of less enlightened nations. The Eternal never works by superhuman agency, when His gracious plans can be accomplished without it. "A thousand years in His sight are but as yesterday when passed, and as a watch in the night;" but His infinite wisdom knew, that, to finite man, that period is ever fraught with progression, and His omniscience leaves to time, according to the reckoning of humanity, the effect of His law in the amelioration and improvement of the human race. Our very banishment amid the nations, a banishment occasioned by Israel's sinful abuse of the tender mercies of the Lord—by his *retrogression* instead of *advancement*, in the glorious career to which he was destined—by his indulgence of every guilty passion, and utter forgetfulness of his fathers' God to bow down before the idols of his idolatrous wives—this very banishment will purify Israel from the grosser part of his Eastern nature, and render him fitted, by increase of purity and refinement, to become once more the first born of the Lord, from whose beautiful land those laws shall issue once again, to emanate in reviving light and gladness over the whole world.

But, though *permitted* by the Mosaic law, polygamy was so restricted, that the protection, happiness, and well-doing of both wives were provided for; no partiality could permit injustice; the man that did so was punishable by law. "If a man have two wives, the one beloved and the other hated, and they have borne him children, both the beloved and the hated, and if the first-born son be hers that is hated, then it shall be, when he maketh his sons to inherit all that he hath, that he may not make the son of the beloved first born before the son of the hated, which is indeed the first born, but he shall acknowledge the son of the hated for the first born, by giving him a double portion of all that he hath."

The Hebrew term translated *hated* here, as in the case of Leah, does not signify so strong a feeling, but simply the one *less beloved* than the other. And, as had already been practically illustrated in the wives of the Patriarch Jacob, this law provides for, and fixes the perfect equality of both; guarding the less beloved from all the evil effects of indiscriminate partiality, and utterly preventing the father from doing injustice to her offspring. The care taken of every member of a Jewish family—from the strongest to the weakest—by the law of God, would, had that law been obeyed, have effectually prevented that fearful abuse of the Lord's mercy in not interfering with the ancient customs of His people, which in the time of the monarchy so disgraced and desecrated Israel. But let not the scoffer cast the odium of such abuse on the Jewish Law. That law was pure—infused with the love, the compassion, the fostering care, the justice, and the severity of the God from whom it came. Its OBEDIENCE would have wrought "the days of heaven upon the earth." Its DISOBEDIENCE, springing from the innate sinfulness of man, wrought evil from the good, and plunged the whole nation of Israel into that fearful abyss of crime, which could only be expiated by ages of misery and blood.

But though *allowed* to exist without being considered a crime at the period of the redemption from Egypt, for the reasons stated above, the laws of Moses, relating to conjugal duties, provided for *one wife alone*, thus proving the superior and holier purity of such unions in the sight of God, and thus forcibly marking the distinction between those customs which were to last for ever, through every age, and race, and clime, and those which were merely nationalized from previous habit and association.

The *oneness* of heart and feeling, of purpose and obedience, which was ordained by God Himself, from the very beginning, to exist between husband and wife, and which could only spring from perfect equality, is most beautifully *infused* throughout the law. Inferred from the simple fact, that in every recorded instance of enumeration at festivals, eating of holy meats, obedience to commandments, &c., the wife is *not* distinctly mentioned, although every other domestic relation is expressly stated. As *one* with her husband, the wife was included in the emphatic *thou*, to whom the command or ordinance was addressed. The children and servants of a household might have rebelliously turned aside from the precepts of the Lord, but the wife's duty and happiness were *one* with her husband's. Her will was his, when that will was guided and sanctified by the will of God. That she could require the divine command individually to keep holy the Sabbath day, to share the feast of the offerings, &c., was a supposition too utterly at variance with her duty as a daughter and wife in Israel, to demand a distinct law; being counted amongst those to whom Moses proclaimed, "When *all* Israel is come to appear before the Lord thy God, in the place which He shall choose, thou shalt read this law before *all* Israel in their hearing; Gather the people together, men, *women*, and children, and the stranger that is within thy gates, that they may hear, and that they may learn, and fear the Lord your God, and observe to do all the words of this law," no Hebrew wife could have needed more, for she, as well as her husband—*one* with him—was the recipient, the obeyer, and the promulgator of every law in which there was no specified dis tinction of individual duties.

That the omission of wife in the commandments and ordinances which specify other members of the family, cannot be taken in any other light, is proved by the fact, that wherever there was a possibility of her occupying a distinct position, or being engaged in any devices or employments contrary to the will of her husband, she is expressly named.

"Thou shalt not covet thy neighbor's *wife*," is emphatically commanded by the same Divine Voice which omitted her, or rather included her in the "*thou*" to whom the fourth of the same precepts, whence the line we have quoted was the tenth, was given. Thus guarding her safety, and prohibiting the very first thought towards her which could have led to sin.

Again, "if thy brother, the son of thy mother, or thy son, or thy daughter, or the *wife of thy bosom*, or the friend whom thou lovest as thine own soul, entice thee secretly, saying, 'Let us go and serve other gods, whom thou hast not known, thou nor thy fathers,' &c., thou shalt not consent unto him, nor hearken unto him; neither shall thine eye pity, neither shalt thou spare, neither shalt thou conceal him." Here, in intimate conjunction with the preceding commandment, is a positive mention of the wife, supposing her to be actuated by feelings and principles so distinct from her husband, as to tempt him to sin. The omission of wives in ordinances where every other member of the household is named, is not then in any way whatever to suppose her a nonentity, a mere name in Israel, but simply to mark her *oneness* with her husband, in every duty to her God, and in every command and restriction of His law addressed to the CHILDREN of Isräel, and, therefore, binding on them BOTH.

"When a man has taken a wife, he shall not go out to war; neither shall he be charged with any business, but he shall be free at home for one year." Were this the whole law, we might justly suppose that the happiness of *man* was alone regarded; but it is not so. Why was this year of release granted him? For his own enjoyment? his own pleasure? No! but to "cheer up"—or, in other words, to make happy—the wife which he had taken. Words how exquisitely descriptive of the Eternal's tender sympathy in the *earthly* happiness of his children! He condescended to enter into the minute details of domestic life; He guarded even their earthly happiness from all contingencies, and proved that he demanded not His love to be realized *only* in sorrow, but that joy, chastened, spiritualized by gratitude and love, was equally acceptable and blessed.

Man might find happiness apart from his wife, even in the first year of his marriage. The exciting call of war, or the grosser and more engrossing claims of business, might easily obtain such dominion as to render him less careful of his home, less anxious for the happiness of his wife, than were he free. Woman has no such claims to share her heart with her husband. Almost more than any other time in her young existence does she need the protecting care and fostering tenderness of man, in the first year of her wedded life. She has left the home of her youth, the fond parents who had lavished on her such love and care, that it seems strange how she can possibly exist without them. She has turned from her occupations, the amusements of her early years, dear from long association, to enter into an entirely new scene, new feelings, new duties, new responsibilities: and for guidance and support, under her God, looks with justice to her husband alone. She may be called upon to battle with sickness and with pain, and she has no longer a mother beside her to give her the fond cares of a tender nurse, and take from her all household duties. She has turned from all for the love of One! And how may she be happy if that one be torn from her by the call to war, perhaps never to return, or by civil duties, which, though the lesser evil, might yet check the daily intercourse of mutual love and confidence for which she pines?

But, left "free for one year," how much of felicity, not only for the present, but the future, would that single ordinance bring to both. And must not we, the lineal descendants of those to whom such a revelation of God's love was given, feel, to our heart's core, that God is indeed the God of love which he proclaimed Himself to Moses? Surely no woman of Israel can fear to approach Him, deeming Him a being too awfully holy to look on such as her, when that unapproachable holiness is veiled by such a flood of irradiating love towards her individually, that she is more than weak, is guilty, if she keep aloof, and refuse, under the mistaken plea of too great unworthiness, to clasp the mercy proffered, and fold its healing balsam to her heart. God would not bid us love Him, if we were too unworthy so to do. He would not in His every law, His every promise, demonstrate His compassionating care, His appealing love, His long-suffering mercy, did He deem us too unworthy to receive them. Can the flower that gems the grass give back the loving care that there hath placed, guards, and will renew it? Can the bird give back the fostering love which guards its fragile form, teaches the construction of its tiny nest, and guards its helpless young? Can the insect know and return the Father's love that guards its gossamer life, blesses it with acute sensation, and endows it with such wisdom in the construction of its web, nest, or cell, as to excite man's envy? Yet, has not the Eternal care for these? and will not therefore all Nature confirm His precious word, and tell us He has equal care and equal love for us? True, we have sinned—we do sin—and, alas! will sin again, till that blessed day when the "stony heart shall be replaced with a heart of flesh," which will, unsullied by mortal frailties, cleave unto the Lord. Yet God has given us power to struggle with and resist the evil, if we cannot in this world wholly conquer it. He has told us, that "His ways are not our ways," and, therefore, however incomprehensible to finite man, "in HIM shall the SEED of ISRAEL be justified, and shall glory." He has taught us in infinite compassion, what we must DO, and how FEEL, to be acceptable in His sight; not in the law alone, for if we study only that in our captivity, we shall be appalled by the ordinances we cannot now perform, but in His prophets and the Psalms, which, as rules of conduct and of feeling, will give us all we need.

As a statute of the Israelitish state, the law we have been considering is no longer obeyed; it cannot be, for we are not now in our own land; but it is the spirit of the ordinance which so nearly concerns us, more especially as women.

To recognise to its full extent the distinction between the ways of God and the ways of man, so beautifully displayed in this our law, let us think one moment on the policy actuating leaders and lawgivers of more modern times, men professing to be guided by the spirit of love and peace. Where, in feudal times, do we find provision thus made for the newly-wedded? A stigma, never to be blotted out, would have clung round the name and reputation of that man who would not turn from his home and young wife, even on his marriage day, at the first rude call to lawless, and often most unnecessary war. Where do we find lawgivers, princes, and nobles, ever taking into consideration the comfort and peace, we will not even say happiness, of their female followers? Where were laws ever issued for her, to guard with fostering tenderness her gentle virtues, her clinging affections, her domestic charms? Where, save in the law of God? To attract attention, to win respect, to obtain protection, she was compelled to be more *great* than *good*, to leave her natural sphere, and manifest fortitude, bravery, and devotedness, qualities indeed excellent in themselves, but, as proved in the middle ages, only valued for their near relation to the qualities of the warrior, and departure from woman's ordinary habits and home. And by what thousands of suffering women, of all ages, must these characteristics have been unattainable, and in consequence how many thousands left to all the misery of deserted homes, crushed affections, and the countless nameless tortures borne by woman in a lonely unprotected path? And much later than the feudal times, a period but very little removed into the past,—shall we say the horrible conscription which devastated France, and every conquered territory owning Buonaparte as master, manifested that care of woman, that tender sympathy in her every feeling, which we are told is only found with the believers in the gospel? We must judge of the divinity of laws by the spirit which, from their observance, emanates over those to whom they are binding. The Jewish law is, on many points, during our captivity, impossible to be observed. Yet we see the spirit of its ancient ordinances still guiding our homesteads, impelling the gentlest and most confiding spirit towards woman in every relation of life. The Hebrew may scarcely be conscious what actuates his tenderness towards his wife and children, but it comes from the spirit of that law, given to his fathers, in which woman was marked as the especial care and protection of the Lord. The law, in form, like the human frame, may die for a time, but the spirit of the ordinances, like the soul of the body, is immortal, and will revive again the shell from which awhile it may have flown.

The law of Vows is considered by some derogatory to the dignity of woman, by rendering her liable to the will of her husband, and subject to his approval, even in her devoting herself to her God. We will endeavor to prove that the supposition is mistaken. Equally acceptable and responsible as man in the sight of God, still, as we have said before, "her desires were to bow to her husband." She neglected her conjugal duty if she pursued any course, even under the pretence of religious motives, contrary to his will. A singular vow demanded a voluntary relinquishment of domestic duties and enjoyments, to devote herself in some way to His service; it is generally supposed in some employments of the Tabernacle, or in the service of His poor, or in the "binding oath to afflict the soul," giving herself up for a certain time to individual fast and prayer. Now few women in Israel, except orphaned single women, and childless widows, could be so independently situated as to make and follow up these vows without interfering with some nearer domestic duty. Woman's sphere in the law of God, without doubt, is HOME; her noblest attraction, devotedness to those with whom she is there thrown in daily intercourse. Some women there are, who find not only duty, but pleasure there—not only love, but safety. Others again, restless and discontented, fancy they should be happier, and better, and more useful, anywhere but where they are, and gladly seize the first pretence to turn aside.

Spiritual devotedness is too often a worldly snare, and the pride of holiness the most dangerous temptation which can possibly assail us. We have often heard (amongst the Gentiles indeed, not amongst ourselves, for we have unhappily too few enthusiasts of any kind) of what is termed a saint (we abhor the falsity of the term, but we are using now the language of the world). One avowedly devoted to the cause of religion; passing hours in her closet, surrounded by religious books, all, we may observe, *commentaries*, but not the *Word of Life* itself; or, with religious friends, wearing a peculiar dress, and most peculiar manners; visiting the poor, more often with tracts than food; censuring every innocent amusement as profane, and temptations of Satan; bearing words of humility on the lips, but of pride in heart; outwardly condemning and abhorring her own sins, but inwardly thanking God that she is so much holier than others; robing religion in such dark and terrible colors, that the young spirit shrinks from it, and plunges in the world with renewed zest, to escape from the faintest semblance of its acceptance.

If there be such, mistaken they certainly are; but their judgment rests with Him whom they seek after their own thoughts to serve, not with their brother man, who, without some more true and sacred guide, might equally be led astray. We have merely alluded to this class of religious enthusiasts, more clearly to manifest the evil which the law of vows effectually excluded, but which, without such law, might, from the holiness pervading God's people, have been more than likely to ensue.

Man did not need such restraint upon his "singular vows;" because, in the first place, he was more independent than woman; in the next, *reason*, not *feeling*, being his guide, he was not likely to fall into the temptation of ill-regulated enthusiasm, even in his holiest and dearest duty. Woman's guide in general is feeling: she is a creature of impulse, ever likely, unless strongly yet tenderly restrained, to turn aside from the safer and less excitable path of daily duty, wherever the affections or the enthusiasm of the moment may lead. More especially is she likely to fall into this temptation when first awakened to the claims, and beauty, and comfort of religion. The simple duties of home then seem little worth, compared to the service of heaven. Herself, her parents and brothers, husband and children, appear of slender consequence compared to the state of her affections and faith towards God. The perfect compatibility of her duties towards God and towards man is unperceived. She cannot realize that the unfatiguing, unexciting duties of domestic usefulness, infused with thoughts of God and of His word, is the path most acceptable to Him; and severing, instead of uniting, she neglects what she deems the lesser, to pursue the greater duty.

Many avenues were open to the wives of Israel to tempt the taking "singular vows." The birth of children, the recovery from illness, escape from danger, receipt of some unexpected blessing, dread of impending sorrow, or misfortune extraordinarily averted, and sin repented of, all these might, in the close links which, when the law was given, bound Israel to the Lord, and in the warm passionate emotions of Eastern women, have impelled either the vow of service, to make manifest their thanksgiving, or the vow of affliction by fasting and prayer, to propitiate the Lord and turn away His wrath. And this vow might be taken in a moment of strong feeling, without sufficient thought as to the possibility of its performance, without interfering with the comforts of her husband and children, or her duties to her household. Was it not, then, just and wise, that the impetuous feeling of woman should be guided and tenderly restrained by the calmer, stronger reason and foresight of man?

But that this dependence on her husband in no way subjected her to his *caprice*, is proved by the law which we will extract at length. "If a woman shall vow a vow unto the Lord, and bind herself by a bond . . . . . And if she had at all a husband when she vowed or uttered aught out of her lips wherewith she bound her soul; and her husband heard it, and held his peace at her in the day that he heard it, then her vows shall stand, and her bonds wherewith she bound her soul shall stand. But if her husband disallowed her on the day that he heard, then he shall make her vows which she vowed, and that which she uttered with her lips, wherewith she bound her soul, of none effect, and the Lord shall forgive her . . . . . Every vow, and every binding oath to afflict the soul, her husband may establish it, or her husband may make it void. *But if her husband hold his peace at her from day to day, then he establisheth all her vows, or all her bonds which are upon her. He confirmeth them, because he held his peace at her in the day that he heard them. And if he shall any ways make them void, after that he hath heard them,* THEN HE SHALL BEAR HER INIQUITY." (Numbers xxx. 3, 6, 7, 8, 13, 14, 15.)

We here find most particular care taken to shield woman from that indecision and caprice from which she is so often the innocent sufferer.

The honor, respect, and deference which should characterize a wife's conduct and feelings towards her husband, are first enforced. For the unperformed vow, or the breaking the vows of the lips, the Lord will forgive her, because they have been disallowed by her husband. But they must be disallowed *when taken.* If from indecision, or weakness, or unkindness, in the determination to thwart the wishes of his wife, he neither forbids nor confirms, but remains silent, that silence, in the sight of God and to his wife, is CONFIRMATION. He has no power capriciously to prevent the fulfilment of her bond or vow by declaring that silence is not consent, and he does not choose that her vow shall be performed. He cannot do this. His very caprice is effectually prevented, for, if he acts thus, the woman's breach of vows will indeed be forgiven to her, but HE SHALL BEAR ITS INIQUITY,—a law whose beautiful justice marks its divine origin more forcibly than almost any other guiding the conduct of husband and wife.

No human legislator could have enacted it, for what lawgiver of earth could have gone so deeply into the very heart of man, and guarded the domestic relations of life from such petty yet constant misery as caprice?

One most consoling truth we learn by this law: it is in itself a direct and positive refutation of the charge brought against us, that Jewish women have no access to God—no right whatever to interfere with the requirements and ordinances of religion. Were woman the creature of a day, passing hence to be no more, with neither hope of reward nor liability to wrath, beyond this world, why should she have the power of making vows at all; and so solemnly, that did man interfere with their due performance, he should bear her iniquity, and woman—aye, the despised and degraded woman—should be forgiven?

The candid and unprejudiced reader of the word of life, be his faith what it may, must perceive how mistaken is such a charge; and let not, then, our young sisters be tempted to quit their native fold for another, where they are told greater privileges await them, both as women and as immortal beings. Let them not be terrified by the charge that, as Jewish women, they are soulless slaves. But let them come to the word of God, and prove that *there* is their shield, *there* is their defence. That there their God Himself has revealed a love and care for His weaker children, too deeply, too nearly, too blessedly for them to need aught else; that there is their hope, as there is their consolation.

Yet more to protect his feebler creation from the fierce passions and unjust accusations of Eastern natures, the Most High, in his infinite mercy, instituted the law of jealousy, an awful and most terrible law, yet one which every *innocent* woman must have hailed with thankfulness, and which every *guilty* woman must have died ere she could have faced. The various sins prohibited by the voice of God Himself, in His Ten Commandments, are all in His sight of equal magnitude, and, therefore, without any reservation whatever, were all punishable with death. And well had it been for the purity, virtue, and happiness of man, had this blessed law continued in force as it was given, and thence had emanated over the whole world. It has been called a law of fire and blood, given but to destroy and be destroyed. But the charge is false. The Eternal knew the natures of those to whom it was given—that severity was needed for the time; and had that severity been used, and the law literally and purely OBEYED, even as it was intended, each generation would have been purer and more spiritual than the former, till that holiness was at length universally attained, which would indeed have brought "the days of heaven on the earth;" and Israel would not now have been persecuted and tortured in some lands, and an exile and a wanderer, houseless and priestless, in them all!

Adultery, even as idolatry, sabbath-breaking, murder, &c., was punishable by death. In Israel, the ruthless spoiler of man's dearest shrine—his home, sacrificed not only his honor (which, however high sounding, to such characters must be but a name), not only his standing and his wealth, but his LIFE. Aye, and not the tempter only, but the wife, the mother, who could fling misery upon a tortured husband, and undying shame upon her helpless babes. Yet amid a people irascible and fierce, too liable to jealousy to examine calmly and justly, as we know is the case at this very day with every Eastern nation, a law was imperatively needed to protect the helpless and innocent, alike from false charges and a husband's unjust hate. No man could take justice into his own hands. He dared not injure the reputation, or take the life of his wife, without having her guilt proved by God Himself. A false accusation had no power to fling shame upon her, or render her station doubtful, as it would now. The Most High Himself interfered in her defence, and proved, in the face of the whole people, her innocence and honor; as, were she guilty, He took into His own hands her punishment, and the manifestation of her guilt.

The law of jealousy is not in general regarded by the women of Israel as it ought to be. False refinement shrinks from it as a thing perfectly unnecessary and antiquated now. Nay, perhaps as a law so horrible, so indelicate, that they wonder that it is not expunged from the Bible. By us it is welcomed as another most consoling and unanswerable proof of the Eternal's tender mercy towards us. The full extent of its use and justice can only be realized by contrasting it with the statutes of the southern and eastern nations, with whose quick passions and excitability, Israel, when the law was given, had more in common than with the cooler and more dispassioned north.

With the followers of Mahomet does not a mere thought, a mere suspicion, unaided by the very shadow of proof, commit the helpless woman to a watery grave, with none to interfere in her behalf, or mourn her when at rest? None to clear her name, or bring the false and cruel husband to justice and to shame? And amidst those bearing the Christian name, do not the Italian and Spaniard make as murderous use of the stiletto or the drugged cup, as the Moslem of the sack? That such misery is seldom heard of in Protestant countries, comes not from actual law, but from that greater civilization and refinement, which must spring from public and private communion with the Bible. This is the safeguard of Protestant women, and this they owe to the spirit of that law given to us by God Himself. Some among the Gentiles there are, honest and spiritual enough to acknowledge this; and from our very heart we honor such honest lovers of truth. But others, and unhappily the greater number, there are who fling shame and dishonor upon the women of the very people for whose safety those blessed laws were framed, the spirit of which is now guiding the Protestants themselves.

By contrasting the law vouchsafed to us with those guiding

the Gentiles of all denominations, we learn to know the true value of the blessed faith which we possess, and are armed against all insidious efforts to turn us from it. But this can never be whilst the women of Israel regard the laws of Moses only in a national and local, not in an individual view, believing that, because they are no longer in actual use, they only relate to them in their several positions in Jerusalem, and do not in the least concern them now.

They do concern us, most nearly and most consolingly. He whose infinite mercy gave them has not cast us from His love, though, for a time, compelled for our sins to bear witness to the nations of His justice and His wrath. Yet for us, as a people, and each of us individually, He bears the same infinite long-suffering love which he bore to our ancestors in Egypt. We learn this from every prophet, who never spoke of sin without holding forth forgiveness, who never prophesied dispersion and banishment without comforting with the promise of restoration; and we know the extent of our Father's Love towards us, by every statute of His law.

The interference of the Most High in cases similar to those calling for the law of jealousy, the wives of Israel may no longer need: but are there none in minor circumstances wrongfully accused? None needing a Father who knoweth every secret thought and inward struggle, to whom to look when man may wilfully wrong, or blindly misappreciate? None who struggle on in the petty, but how sadly wearing, trials of daily life, to do what seems the best, to act the kindest, to banish every throb of self, and sacrifice all of individual comfort and enjoyment to further the comfort and the wishes of another, yet finds her every effort turned against herself, and armed with acutest woe? In such cases, and who shall say there are none such, where can woman turn, but to her God? Where find consolation, save in the belief that her innocence, her efforts, rest with Him, and He will one day make them known? Where shall her heart, bleeding and torn from its earthly rest, find peace, save in His love? Oh! what woman bearing the name of Israel, can hesitate one moment to pour forth her every grief to him, and feel she is individually his care, and He will plead her cause?

The express commands relating to the marriages of the priests is another beautiful proof of woman's perfect equality in Israel, and compatibility to be holy unto the Lord, by sharing the holiness of his elected servants; a proof, also, that in His service the Eternal demanded no sacrifice of human affections. They were, indeed, to be sanctified to Him, to be infused with His spirit, and so to become a blessing and a joy to His servants; but never to be annihilated, and so give temptation for the most awful abuses and crimes, as in the monastic seclusions of the Roman church. The sanctity, the purity, which was to attend the wife of the priest, was a further incentive to the purity and holiness of the women in Israel. Superiority of actual ranks there was none, but superiority in virtue there was, and to gain that superiority was in the power of all women under the guidance of the law. The priests were the very highest and noblest in the sight of the people, being the elect of the Lord, and the ministers of His will. How pure, then, and holy, must have been the ambition to become worthy of selection as the priests' wives; and how beautifully is the superior holiness and sanctity of the women of Israel brought forward by the simple fact that the priests of the Lord might only choose a wife from "their own people!"

It is evident, then, from every law we have regarded, that, instead of being degraded and enslaved, the wives in Israel were peculiarly and especially objects of the Eternal's love. For their safety, their honor, those laws were issued, now recognised by the greater part of the civilized world; and all those who deny this shake the very foundations of the whole system of morality, under whatever creed it may be found. The Gentile is in very truth "debtor to the Jew" for far more than he acknowledges; for every law unconsciously guiding and sanctifying his domestic relations, refining his own conduct, elevating his own mind, for every law blessing his home with a faithful wife, respected mother, and duteous child. That, therefore, any woman can fling odium on the Jewish law, can only excite our pity towards her. The innocence, honor and purity, and domestic, social, and religious duties of wives, being more clearly and unanswerably developed in the sacred canon of the Mosaic law than in any other, from the very simple fact that every other is founded upon them.

CHAPTER IV.

LAWS RELATING TO THE WIDOWS AND DAUGHTERS OF ISRAEL.

Before regarding the laws instituted for the widows of Israel, let us pause one moment on the full tide of anguish and unprotected isolation comprised to woman in that one word "widow," that we may comprehend our Father's love to the full extent. What woman's heart, awake to kind and generous feelings, can look upon a widow without sympathy—without the yearning prayer that consolation may be granted her, and her fatherless babes find friends to guide them through a stormy world? We know no description so thrillingly powerful of this, the heart's desolation, as the lines we subjoin.

"Lone sharer of a widowed lot,
Where is the language, though a Seraph hymned
The poetry of heaven, to picture thee,
Wrecked as thou art, *whose life has now become*
Affliction's martyrdom? for such is love
Doomed to remain on desolation's rock,
And look for ever where the past lies dead.
What is the world to thy benighted soul?
A dungeon! Save that where thy children's tones
Can ring with gladness its sepulchral gloom.
Placid and cold, and spiritually pale
Art thou. The lustre of thy youth is dimmed,
The verdure of thy spirit o'er. In vain
The beaming eloquence of day attracts
Thy heart's communion with creation's joy.
Like twilight imaged on a bank of snow
The smile that waneth o'er thy marble cheek."

Robert Montgomery.

Such, indeed, is the earthly sadness of the widow. *One* with him who has departed, how may she tread the earth's dark vales alone? Where look for love to supply the place of that now gone? Where find a father for those babes, clinging to her for that support, that love, which in her first bereavement she feels utterly unable to bestow? Where but in Him, who in His law so especially provides for her and for her fatherless children; and, by his prophets, reinforces the statutes already given, and brings forward their *neglect* as one of the manifold sins which called down His displeasure?

We find in his gracious word not alone the command, but the severe penalty attached to its disobedience, first in Exodus xxii. 22, 23, 24: "Ye shall not afflict any widow or fatherless child. If thou afflict them in any wise, and they cry at all unto ME, I will surely hear their cry, and my wrath shall wax hot, and I will kill you with the sword; and your wives shall be widows, your children fatherless."

Can any language more emphatically and forcibly denote the tender mercy of the Eternal? His love made their sorrows His own. As a positive sin against Himself, He threatened to afflict all those who dared afflict them by the infliction of similar suffering. He knew that, left to man's mercy, the widow and the fatherless would often meet with oppression, fraud, and injustice; be defrauded of their natural rights, and afflicted by hard creditors. Not only as a widow, called upon to bear "affliction's martyrdom," but as a mother, to behold her children a prey to suffering and want. In Israel this could not be. The widow and the fatherless were God's own, for He knew that not alone the wife, but the mother must be cared for.

"Leave thy fatherless children to ME," He said by His prophet Jeremiah, at a time when misery, desolation, and destruction were falling on Judea and her sons for their awful iniquity. "Leave them to ME, and I will keep them alive. And let thy widows trust in ME." Even then, when disobedience and idolatry had so cursed the land, that His wrath could no longer be withheld, He reiterated the gracious promise given in His law. Sunk into the lowest ebb of iniquity, how could the widow and orphan be protected if left to the care of man? Where might they look, at such a season, but to their God, who for them alone had mercy and long suffering still?

The ruin and worldly misfortunes and trials, so often now the portion of the widow, could not exist in Israel. The nation at large was commanded to provide for them, and in every feast of offerings or of festivals, and in the ingathering of their corn, and oil, and fruits, to include the widow and the fatherless; laws not once, but several times repeated. "When thou cuttest down thy harvest in thy field, and hast forgotten the sheaf in the field, thou shalt not go again to fetch it, but it shall be for the stranger, and the FATHERLESS, and the WIDOW, that the Lord thy God may bless thee in all the works of thy hands. When thou beatest thy olive tree thou shalt not go over the boughs again, it shall be for the stranger, the FATHERLESS, and the WIDOW. When thou gatherest the grapes at thy vineyard, thou shalt not glean it again, it shall be for the stranger, the FATHERLESS, and the WIDOW."

Nor was this all. The tithes of wine, corn, and oil, the firstlings of herds and flocks, all of which were devoted to the service of the Lord, that all worldliness and niggardliness should be banished from Israel, and "they should learn to fear the Lord their God always." The feast of Weeks and of the Tabernacles, when the families of Israel rejoiced before the Lord in the place which He chose, the WIDOW and the FATHERLESS were included. There was to be no affliction, no dependence, no sorrow in Israel (though the poor were not to cease out of the land) at these times. *All* were to rejoice before the Lord. And yet more in addition: "At the end of three years thou shalt bring forth all the tithe of thine increase the same year, and lay it up within the gates. And the Levite, because he hath no part nor inheritance with thee, and the stranger, and the FATHERLESS, and the WIDOW, which are within thy gates, shall come, and shall eat and be satisfied, that the Lord thy God may bless thee in all the work of thine hand which thou doest." And so important was obedience to this statute, that its profession was necessary in the confession of him who came to offer the basket of first-fruits, as a sign of his having come unto the land of his inheritance. "Then shalt thou say," proceeded the instruction of the priest, "before the Lord thy God, I have brought away the hallowed things out of mine house, and also have given them to the Levite and the stranger, and the FATHERLESS and the WIDOW, according to all thy commandments which thou hast commanded. I have not transgressed thy commandments, neither have I forgotten them" (Deut. xxvi. 12, 13).

Again, in Deut. xxiv. 17, it is not enough that we have already heard, "thou shalt not afflict them," under the awful penalty of similar affliction from the hand of God, but prohibition as to the manner of that affliction is expressly pointed out.

"Thou shalt not pervert the judgment of the stranger, nor of the FATHERLESS, nor take a WIDOW's raiment to pledge." Why? Because they had no earthly friend to redeem the latter, or plead for the former. Weak and unguarded, they were exposed to all these evils, had not the Eternal, in His tender compassion, taken them under His own especial care; and, instead of compelling them to depend on the insecure tenure of man's compassion, or even justice, instituting laws for their benefit, the disobedience of which was *sin* unto Himself.

Had these laws been obeyed, it was impossible for the widow and the fatherless, however destitute they might have been left, to suffer mere worldly ills. The agony of the widowed wife could not be increased by the thought of how she was to provide for her fatherless little ones. The Lord was their guardian, and He gave her and her children the gentle care and affection of their brethren in Israel; bidding her cry unto Him in sorrow or affliction, for He would assuredly hear her cry, and punish those who called it forth.

What nation, then, what code, however just, however perfect, ever framed such laws as these? "What nation," in truth, "has God so near to them as Israel in all we call upon Him for?" Were no other laws relative to woman instituted, these alone would be sufficient to mark that their very weakness rendered them objects, even more than man, of compassion and love; for where has God provided for man as for woman in the desolation of her widowhood?

That modern Judaism cannot obey these laws now, as when they were given, interferes not with the fact of their institution itself. This very charge, reiterated, enforced as it is, elevates woman, and excites towards her, not alone the humanity and tenderness, but the *respect* of man. How could he feel otherwise towards those whom God Himself has promised to protect? What stronger incentive could he have to be forbearing and gentle towards her, and in no way to afflict her, than that if he failed in kindness, his wife should be widowed, his children fatherless? Where shall we find a law to disannul this, proceeding, as it does, from the mouth of God?

To the women of Israel, at the present day, how inexpressibly consoling are these laws! In form they can no longer be obeyed; but, as in the case of the statutes relating to wives, it is the spirit pervading them which we must take to our hearts, till they swell in grateful thankfulness to Him who from His throne in heaven condescends to make widows His especial care. And He does so *now* as then. God is immutable—a Spirit of Truth, knowing not the shadow of a change; and, therefore, do we know and feel that the same love from which issued those beautiful laws, actuates His dealings with his people now. It is vain, utterly vain, to say we are cast off, and, therefore, cannot claim it. The Bible teems with passages relating to our banishment alone, and to the Eternal's deep love borne towards us while in captivity, and, consequently, towards us now. We could multiply passages on passages, from the Pentateuch, Psalms, and Prophets, to prove this. But the very words already quoted from Jeremiah would be almost sufficient. When they were pronounced, the sins of Jerusalem were far more heinous than those of Israel in her captivity. Yet even then God took the fatherless and the widow under His fostering care; separating them for the innocence of the one, and the unprotected weakness of the other, from the mass of iniquity which desecrated Judea.

As concerns His compassion towards us now, we shall find them so distinctly, so clearly enforced in Leviticus xxiv., particularly from verse 40 to the end, and in the whole of Deuteronomy xxx., that to doubt and keep back, from a supposition of our inability to approach our God, and claim His love in our captivity, becomes actual guilt, and is likely not only to throw a wider and wider barrier between Him and ourselves, but to expose us more dangerously than any other temptation to the sophisms of the Nazarene, who, in mistaken kindness, would terrify us from our sole rock of refuge and strength, by insisting that, cast out from the Lord's favor as we are, nothing can save us from eternal perdition but the acceptance of their faith. The more solid sense and unimpassioned reason of man may, and do, effectually guard him from such danger; but woman's quicker feeling and more easily blinded judgment need all the defence and rest in a divine love which the study of her own faith, and its manifold manifestations of the Eternal as a God of truth and love, alone can give. No argument is more likely to weigh with a strong-feeling, unguarded woman, knowing little or nothing but the mere formula of her own religion, than the idea, if pressed at a right moment, that the law of Moses is a law of fire and blood, given only to destroy, and that the religion of Jesus is one of love; that Jewish women can have no comfort in adversity, but that as Christians they will find all they need; that in the one Faith they must feel themselves degraded, as in the other exalted and secure.

Now, without affecting actual *creed* at all, temptations like these, unless fully and faithfully convinced that we, as women of Israel, have privileges still higher, must on some dispositions fall with sufficient weight as so to confuse and entangle, that even belief is adopted ere we are at all aware of what we are about. We allude not to those whom reason only guides—who, cold, unimaginative, passionless themselves, laugh at feeling, because they know it not—who find philosophy always sufficient for their need. But the larger portion of women, creatures of mere feeling and impulse, we would beseech to come to the Word of God, and derive thence, in the days of youth and happiness, that peace, love, and consolation, which if unknown till "the evil days come, and the years when thou shalt say, I have no pleasure in them," may be sought, from very blindness and wilfulness, in a stranger fold. The arguments we have quoted would fall to the ground by the simple answer, that as women of Israel, we *have* ALL we need; that God revealed His deep love to us ages before He became known to our Gentile sisters; that while we possess His blessed Word, we can never feel too unworthy to claim the tenderness he so proffers. He Himself has given us privileges in every relation and position in life which no other nation has, except as derived from us, and that, instead of fire and blood, the whole Jewish law to woman teems with LOVE.

These feelings, inculcated in childhood, felt and experienced in riper years, will be sufficient for woman, and enable her to realize all the blessed consolation which every law relating to her so spiritually bestows. Not to widows only, but to all who are in affliction, the Divine spirit infusing every law *must* bring comfort, by evincing how closely, how consolingly, she is drawn to God.

Can the widow and the fatherless in Israel recall this truth, yet not bless God that the record of His law is still our own, granted that in times of dispersion and banishment we might not despair, even though the form of the law must be, till our restoration, at an end? Oh, let the afflicted take comfort!

She has but to believe and obey, and the deep compassion of her God will perfect both, and render them acceptable. Let her but think on the magnitude of that love which has provided for her both as widow and mother. That by *name* she is singled out as especially the object of Divine solicitude, and, therefore, that the Eternal knew and knows the heaviness of her trial, the extent of her deep sorrow, the pressure of her cares. Let her recall every law given for the widow and the fatherless, and remember that He who gave them knows not the shadow of a change, and, therefore, feels for her now as tenderly as He did for her ancestors of old. What is time to Him? We look back with our finite gaze, and think there is such a wide distinction between past and present, that the laws given for the one can in no way concern the other. Customs, manners, all of *earth may* change, but not the nature of the immortal soul, nor of the human heart. From the beginning of the world, until the end, these *were*, *are*, and *will be* the same. And so is HE from whom they spring, and who guides and cares for them now as when HE first grafted them into man. What, then, is time to Him? Can frail finite humanity believe that *time* has changed His tenderness towards His afflicted children? Oh! who would throw such scorn, such disrespect on that word which repeats and enforces in every manner of expression, "I, even I, am He, that changeth not; therefore ye sons of Israel are not consumed?" Let the widows of Israel take to their hearts every law which manifests His love towards them as widows. They are as much theirs *now* as at the moment they were given. Let them not believe, for a single moment, that the superior holiness of their ancestors gave them greater favor in the sight of their God. He saith, "Not for your own sakes will I do this, O Israel, for ye are a perverse and rebellious generation, but for the sake of the covenant I swore unto your fathers, Abraham, Isaac, and Jacob." And again, in strong confirmation, "For mine own sake, even for mine own sake, will I do it; for how should my name be polluted: and I will not give my glory to another." (Isaiah xlviii.) With such words how may we hesitate? Come unto Him, ye widows of Israel, for ye are HIS. Clasp to your hearts His love. Think not ye can weary it, for "God is not man, that He should lie, nor the son of man that he should repent." Let no thought of unworthiness keep us back, for not in our own righteousness, but in His, must we trust. And oh believe in Him, trust in Him; and, as the widows of old, in our very affliction we shall be comforted, and to the Gentiles show forth His glory.

Our next section, the Daughters of Israel, while it principally relates to the duties of our younger sisters as inferred from the laws concerning them, also brings much important matter to light, regarding the equality of women.

In every command and ordinance relative to obedience to parents, to the eating of holy things (Levit. xi. 14; Deut. xii. and xvi.), to appearing and rejoicing at the various festivals (Deut. xvi.), daughters, equally with the sons, are so emphatically specified, that it is impossible to believe that the religious as well as the moral duties of the law are not equally incumbent on *woman* as well as man. It is useless to transcribe the verses which point this out, as they will be found, in their own simple force of expression, in the chapters of the Lord's own Word quoted above. Were the maidens of Israel to keep aloof from all religious observances, to be bound to household duties and frivolous employments, become authorized to leave all the concerns of an immortal soul and of eternity to the care of fathers, husbands, or brothers, we should find no mention of such a class of beings. Nay, had the Eternal even intended that their fitness or unfitness for His service should depend on the judgment of man, we should still find only the sons mentioned. But to remove this entirely, the attendance of the maidens of Israel at every rejoicing, etc., becomes an *absolute command* from God, and its disobedience, neglect, or change, was sin against Himself. Such laws as those of Mezuzzot or Tephilim were given in an indeterminate manner, requiring the aid of the priest to decide who should wear the latter, and how use the former; but the obedience of the daughters of Israel, with their brothers, unto every ordinance, is so clearly and simply put, that the mind must indeed be perverted who would seek to deprive them of such blessed privileges, and insist that religion is too deep a thing for woman.

God bade woman as well as man love Him with heart, and soul, and might; knowing that to all who did so, the comprehension of His will, His attributes, was comparatively easy, and obedience to His every statute a labor of rejoicing and love. To learn and to feel this in youth, woman, equally with man, must be *taught* to know and love the Lord, not left to the mere practice of forms; must be taught, that to appear at His festivals, to keep His ordinances, to obey His commandments, are privileges of joy, granted to them in the fulness of God's love, and mark the distinction between His rule and that of every other. They would be led to compare their station and their privileges as maidens of Israel, with those of the women of Greece and Rome, and every contemporary nation, and, in more modern times, with the women of many a Gentile land. Civilization, and a study and practice of the moral laws of the Bible, are doing their work, and pervading the customs and feelings of the Nazarene world; but their guiding law breathes not the Eternal's especial care for woman, in her every relation of life, more forcibly than ours does.

That the daughters of Israel must have had the power to obtain influence over their fathers, even to persuade them to evil, is proved by their being specially named in the law already quoted, regarding the punishment of all those, be they brother, son, DAUGHTER, wife, or friend, who enticed to idolatry.

Again, we are told in Deut. vii. 2, 4, alluding to the care needed to preserve the Israelites a holy people, and prevent all communion with the idolatrous nations around: "Thou shalt make no covenant with them, nor show mercy to them; neither shalt thou make marriages with them; thy DAUGHTER thou shalt not give unto his son, nor his daughter shalt thou take unto thy son. For they will turn away thy son from following ME, that they may serve other Gods, etc. For thou art an holy people unto the Lord thy God. The Lord thy God hath chosen thee to be a special people unto Himself, above all the people that are upon the face of the earth."

"Son," in the sentence "for they will turn away thy son," etc., evidently signifies both son and daughter, as both are specifically named in the preceding verse, and the Hebrew word בֵּן, though always translated *son*, is equivalent to the English noun *child*, for which there is no distinct Hebrew term. "Children of Israel," is written in Hebrew exactly as if it were translated, "sons of Israel" (בְּנֵי יִשְׂרָאֵל), but it evidently and unanswerably includes both sexes, by the words already quoted: "Gather the people together, men, women, and children," and other verses of similar import. As Israel had been already warned against giving his daughter in marriage to a son of Canaan, she is, of course, included in the danger thence ensuing, although only "son" is mentioned; the plural meaning of that "son" being evident from the pronoun following it being *they* instead of *he*. "For they will turn aside thy child from following ME, that THEY may serve other gods."

Now if nothing depended on women in Israel to uphold and make manifest the glory of their God, in obedience to His law and in serving Him, what necessity was there for this law? If her soul was of less moment than that of man, why should it have been so carefully guarded from pollution? This law of itself would be sufficient to prove to the daughters of Israel their solemn responsibility, not only individually, but *nationally;* and we shall find still more.

In Numbers xxvii., we read that the daughters of Zelophehad came "before Moses, and all the princes of the congregation," and, boldly stating the death of their father without sons, inquired, "why should the name of our father be done away from among his family because he had no sons? Give us, therefore," they continued, "a possession among the brethren of our fathers. And Moses brought their cause before the Lord. And the Lord spake unto Moses, saying, The daughters of Zelophehad speak right. Thou shalt surely give them a possession of an inheritance among their father's brethren, and thou shalt cause the inheritance of their father to pass unto them. And thou shalt speak unto the children of Israel, saying If a man die, and have no son, then shall ye cause his inheritance to pass unto his daughter."

Now this simple narration very clearly proves that the civil, as well as religious privileges were protected and insured. Here are five unmarried women, most probably young, and acting on no guidance but their own sense of right and justice, as inculcated by the whole law of Moses, unhesitatingly addressing their great Lawgiver, in presence of all the heads of Israel, and fearlessly stating their case. Their position must have been one of perfect freedom, or they could not so have sought Moses, and not only been heard, but, because he did not feel himself adequate to pronounce a decision on a case never before occurring, their cause was brought by him before the Lord, and God Himself deigned to reply. They had spoken right, the Eternal said;

the inheritance should be as they said, not only to them, but ever after, as a law in Israel.

We see here, not only the daughters of Israel protected and established in their birthrights, but the practical illustration of the Eternal's gracious promise repeated in Deut. x. 17, 18, "For the Lord your God is a God of gods and Lord of lords, a mighty and a terrible, who regardeth not persons, nor taketh reward, but does execute the judgment of the FATHERLESS and the widow." The daughters of Zelophehad were *fatherless;* perchance (for such is human nature), surrounded by those who disputed their right, deeming that woman could have no civil privileges; compelled to do violence to their feminine nature, and make an appeal; whereupon God, not man, took their judgment in His own hands and gave them right. The supposition of their having to encounter human opposition, is further confirmed by the event of the thirty-sixth chapter of Numbers. The chief fathers of the tribe of Manasseh, to which Zelophehad belonged, came before Moses and the heads of Israel, stating the inconvenience of female inheritance, as being likely to be lost by marriage with some other tribe; and in the jubilee, when every man returned to the inheritance of his fathers, the portion inherited by daughters would be amalgamated with the inheritance of the tribe whereunto they were received. This difficulty, to mere human reasoning, would have seemed so to interfere with the statute already given, that man would have been at a loss how to overcome it. But that which God has once said, He altereth not; and He bade Moses inform the children of Israel, that "the tribe of the sons of Joseph had said well. This is the thing which the Lord doth command concerning the daughters of Zelophehad, saying, LET THEM MARRY TO WHOM THEY THINK BEST; only to the tribe of the family of their father shall they marry. And every daughter that possesseth an inheritance in any tribe of the children of Israel, shall be wife unto one of the families of the tribe of her father, that the children of Israel may enjoy every man the inheritance of his fathers."

Even in this law, so important for the peace and harmony of the tribes of Israel, the Eternal disdained not to care also for the temporal happiness of His weaker children, by expressly stating, that their choice was to be *whom they think best;* bounded, indeed, by the tribe of their father, amongst whom as they principally associated it was most natural their choice should fall. No arbitrary law interfered with domestic happiness. Neither consanguinity, fortune, nor any of the modern reasons, impelling unions of convenience, of ambition, or of any kind but of the heart, interfered with woman's own choice of happiness. Heiress in her own right, with none daring to interfere with the judgment of God Himself, she might select whom she thought best to share the possessions accorded to her. No human judgment, no thought of man, would have so cared for woman. The law, indeed, might have been given, but those impressive words, "Let them marry whom they think best," speak but of the omniscient care and infinite love of God.

The law of vows we have already enlarged upon in our second section, the wives of Israel; yet, as its ordinance concerns the daughters of Israel also, we must briefly recur to it. The nature of those vows, and in what manner they are liable to abuse, we have already seen. A daughter might, perhaps, more easily than a wife, devote herself by a singular vow to the service of the Lord, but more easily also be led into its abuse. A young woman (for it is to such the laws refer—see Numbers xxx. 16), while in her father's house, performs her duty to her God, and proves her zeal in His service to greatest perfection, while evincing her obedience to the fifth commandment, and devoting herself as much as possible to the comfort and happiness of her parents, and to all the unobtrusive claims of home. This, as we have said before, is often neglected during the early enthusiasm of first religious impressions, and the wish to do something great and striking, to evince the fervor of her professions, occupies the mind to the exclusion of all else. This, in Israel, is effectually guarded against, by rendering the daughter dependent in some measure on the will of her father, and by so doing increasing the veneration, love, and submission, which, did she obey the fifth commandment, she could not fail to bear him, at the same time guarded, like the wife in Israel, from all capriciousness or indecision, and the petty trials thence proceeding.

That she had the power, even when in her youth in her father's house, of devoting herself by a vow unto the Lord, clearly evinces that even young women had access to the Eternal, and their prayers and service were graciously accepted by Him, without any interference of man.

This is the spirit of the law concerning us most nearly now, and which every young daughter in Israel should lovingly remember, that young, lowly, weak as she is, and dependent as she may be, she has yet the glorious privilege of devoting herself to the service of her God. No longer, indeed, by a singular vow, calling upon her to depart from home duties, and affections, for outward service, nor by a binding oath to afflict the soul by departure from her usual food and innocent amusements, but simply by associating the love of God and hope of His approval with all her thoughts, and the meek and unpretending effort to make manifest spirituality and holiness in every action, every trial, every blessing of her life. This will be less difficult to accomplish if she do but study, heartfully and prayerfully, His precious word, and read there, borne out by the whole beautiful world of nature, the blessed record of God's unfailing love; if she will but persevere in trust and prayer, and not despair if many many times she turns seemingly unanswered from the Fount of living waters, and her earthly nature tempt her to put her whole trust in "cisterns, broken cisterns that will hold no water." This was Israel's sin, which, more powerfully than any other, at length hurled on her the Eternal's long-averted wrath; and, knowing this, we shall sin threefold now if we strain not every nerve to resist all such specious coloring of earth, and cleave under every difficulty, spite of disappointment, of despondency, of doubt, unwaveringly to the Lord.

But let not the young daughter of Israel, rejoicing in her fond enthusiasm that she is so specially designated in His law, believe that to do His work is easy and all joy, as at first it seems. There must come a time, if she truly seek and pray to love Him, that He will try that love; not, it may be, with the afflictions publicly acknowledged as such, but with the coldness, deadness, utter stagnation of the spirit, as if all of religion, or even interest in religious things, had entirely departed. This is the most fearful period in the religious experience of the young. They doubt every feeling of piety which had been theirs before. They mentally ask, why should they be different to their more worldly companions, who are ever happy, ever gay? Why should they voluntarily resign such pleasures for a service that, instead of bringing comfort, does but make them miserable? Were they not over presumptuous to have supposed for a moment that God could care for such as they, and would it not be wiser and better to join the multitude, who, living but for earth and time, never cast a thought on heaven and eternity for to whom can they express feelings so impossible to be believed or understood?

Oh! let not such periods of trial turn the daughter of Israel from that better path which an earlier age has chosen. Come indeed they *must*, for God thus tries the extent of His children's love. The truly, sincerely, spiritually religious of every creed, of every class, have experienced all that they may feel. It is the dread "phantom of the threshold," which must be resisted by its only all-subduing foe—that faith which can ascend on the wings of prayer, and trust in God to give comfort, hope, and joy. It is no proof of superior holiness, of more rapid advancement in the one straight path, where these emotions are unknown. It is rather an unanswerable evidence that the spirit yet sleeps, unawakened to its weakness, its dependence. It does not yet know the workings of the Lord within; or that its fancied strength may be broken as a reed. Oh! let not the young daughter of Israel, when bowed and sorrowing beneath the strange despondency of heart and thought, envy these. God hath not departed from her. He doth but try the strength of her faith and love. If comfort, if spiritual joy always attended on religious service, where would be that necessity for faithfulness and constancy? Where the *trial* of love, if ever coupled with reward? Where its strength, its durability, if the first moment the object of its aspirings *appear* to forsake, to darken His countenance towards them, it takes wing to some more rewarding god? Would we love a mortal thus? And shall we do less for God, whose love we know to be so unending, so infinite, so exhaustless, and who never in reality withdraws it, though to try us He permits the human infirmities of frame to produce the darkness under which we pine?

Would we, in truth, follow the example of our ancestors, and devote ourselves to our God, we must endure this meekly and trustingly, as we would any more tangible evil, or more visible affliction. And even when this is removed, through His loving mercy, and again our souls spring up rejoicing, though more chastened, let us still "remember the days of darkness, for they shall be many." Religion in no way saves us from afflictions, but it supports us under them. It gives us what nothing else can give, the unvarying comfort of a Father's love, and an unfailing hope in heaven.

As in former ages a young woman could not devote herself by a singular vow without the approval of her father, although with her *spiritual feelings* he had no power to interfere, so now let every daughter of Israel abstain from every public or presumptuous evidence of religious profession which can interfere with the prejudices of her parents. The spirit of that beautiful religion which *was* granted to us, and which *will* again be ours, was "to turn the heart of the fathers to their children, and the hearts of the children to their fathers;" not to sow dissension and disunion. Whatever a young woman may feel, however grieve at what she may think is wanting in the theoretical or practical religion of her parents, it is her duty to *pray* and *wait*. God will answer in His own time, but it is no part of her duty either to condemn or cease to love. No parent will interfere with a child's religion, if, instead of being obtruded upon him, it does but guide alike conduct and feeling, impel obedience and cheerfulness, and strengthen to endure. The *motive* of these superior characteristics an irreligious and unbelieving parent may not, indeed, for long years perceive; but, almost unconsciously, he will learn to respect the prejudices of such a child; and if, indeed, it may please God to permit such earthly recompense, she may be the blessed means of leading him to the same God, the same immortal goal.

But this can never be if she obtrude religion, or in the slightest degree evince a supposition of her own superior holiness. It is indeed one of the hardest trials in life, to see any one of those whom we most love perseveringly reject all we feel the dearest, most important. But if we bring it before God, He will give us strength to continue constant in prayer for them, and lessen the evil we deplore. The case of a parent refusing to let his child serve God, and make religion her first object, is utterly unknown in Israel; but should it be, in this instance only a child is imperatively called upon to disobey. The commands of an earthly parent must be disregarded, if they interfere with and compel disobedience to the commands of God. Leviticus xix. 29 authorizes our upholding this. Although the case itself, in which there is a daughter guarded from an unnatural father, be different in details, yet it is equally protective in the present instance; and a child may be fully assured, if the command of her father compel disobedience to her God in any one of His commandments (for all are of equal sanctity to the one alluded to in the verse quoted), her painful duty must be to disobey.

But a state of things so fearful can never be in Israel, if a daughter's religion be practised as we have hinted above.

There may be indifference, there may be the apparent absence of all spiritual religion; but no man who wishes to be thought an Israelite, ever neglects the peculiar forms of his faith, and his daughter, therefore, has no cause for dividing herself from him, however more earnest, more spiritual, may be her individual views. She may have to bear with the neglect or disregard of some ordinances which her heart tells her are sacred, but if she have the will she has the power to keep her own way undefiled; and if she be truly and sincerely a daughter of Israel, every parental disregard of holy things will bring her to her God yet more earnestly in prayer.

One other point we would urge ere we quit the subject. Let not Israel's young daughters fancy, that to devote heart, mind, and soul to God, demands the relinquishment of those innocent pleasures and enjoyments for which God himself has framed our hearts. There are many among the Gentiles who believe religion wholly incompatible with recreation and amusement; that all social pleasures must be resigned; only certain books perused and even some accomplishments forbidden, as likely to lead to sin. The religion of God is, on the contrary, so consistent with man's capabilities and yearnings, that we never can believe these things incumbent upon us. The first grand object of our lives, in truth, it must be; and that gained—which, if we inculcate the immortal spirit of religion as well as its more perishable form unto our children, it will be—we need not fear that enjoyment either of social intercourse or of intellectual resources will turn us from it. God has framed us to give and to receive pleasure. He has stored our hearts with sweet emotions, our minds with inexhaustible resources. We best make manifest our deep and grateful sense of His loving-kindness by its enjoyment. "God loveth a cheerful giver," we have somewhere read. And in no religion is this sentiment so truly, practically illustrated as in ours, coming, as it does, from God Himself. A knowledge of ourselves, which, if we are accustomed in youth to examine our hearts by the standard of God's word, we shall undoubtedly obtain, will warn us of those weaknesses and failings most likely to lead us into temptation; and we shall guard against these, and either conquer them through His infused grace, or shun them till the strength we implore is granted. There is no need to become different in seeming from our fellows, and tacitly condemn and chide every innocent amusement and resource by our refusal to join in them. The idea that no amusement is innocent, that nothing we do, think, or feel is free from sin, is not—blessed be God!—the creed of Israel. He hath appointed our religious and moral duties; He hath laid down our earthly path; He hath taught us how to look to Him, and how by faith we shall be justified, and through His infinite mercy be received with Him. He hath stored our souls and minds with exhaustless capabilities of happiness, even upon earth. He hath gathered around us in His beautiful world a thousand objects to call forth love, gratitude, and joy; and He who is truth and justice would not have done these things, were we so incapable of righteousness, as from our birth to be blackened with such sin as only blood can wash away.

Let me not be misunderstood, or accused of contradicting my own theory, so to speak, for my theory is the theory of the Bible. Liable to every weakness—more inclined to the evil than the good—we are; but such is inherent from the time that our heavenly origin was changed and marred by the dominion of the passions, infirmities, and weakness of earth. And it was for such beings the law was given, to aid them to subdue natural corruption, to give them opportunities to exercise righteousness, virtue, and faith; to awaken the immortal part of our nature; to arouse all those better, higher, and purer feelings, which, however *dormant*, cannot *die*, for they have been breathed into us by the spirit of the Lord; and for which, if we neglect and let them ever sleep, because we fancy we either possess them not, or are too closely bound to arouse them, we shall be called to a fearful account. Not one single point of the Eternal's precious word—the Bible which we acknowledge—authorizes a belief in the Gentile creed.

The particular mention of the superior sanctity of the priests' daughters, evinces that the holiness of the fathers was shared by the daughters. They were to partake of the holy meats, not only in their youth; but if widows, or divorced, without children, had the power of returning to their father's house. A further proof of the holiness incumbent on her as the daughter of the Eternal's appointed servant, and one who had power by her conduct either to exalt or "profane her father," we find, in Levit. xxi. 9, a different and more awful death appointed for her, if she became sinful, than the usual mode of Hebrew executions. These laws, of course, cannot concern us now (though would that they could, our priests being, as they ought to be, the first in rank and consequence of our nation), but the spirit of them, as of every other relative to the women of Israel, tends to mark their equality, their elevation, and their immortal responsibility, so forcibly as to prevent all possible rejoinder. Were the prayers of man sufficient for the welfare of woman—had she no individual soul to render account of—there would be less necessity to notice the wives and the daughters of the priests than any other. The superior sanctity of their husbands and fathers would surely be more than sufficient for them. We trust, however, we have said enough to convince our young sisters that, as Daughters of Israel, they have higher and nobler privileges than the daughters of any other race; that their God Himself has deigned to give laws and ordinances for their especial guidance and protection, which cannot be gainsaid without verging on impiety. And that, therefore, much, very much, depends on them, one and all, to uphold His glory through their own religious and moral dignity, and give evidence, alike to their own hearts, and to those nations, by word, thought, and deed, that they need nothing more than their own beautiful religion to guide them through earth and time, and fit them for eternity and heaven. They *can* do this, and will they fail?

CHAPTER V.

MAID SERVANTS IN ISRAEL, AND SUNDRY OTHER LAWS.

Our fifth section alludes to a class which (we say it with grief) no longer exists amongst us, and, therefore, can only be looked upon as a still further proof of the Eternal's loving care for His female children. It cannot guide us till once more we have maid-servants of our own faith amongst us. How often, how constantly, this subject has engrossed the thoughts and wishes of the writer, that by any possible means, the daughters of our poorer and dependent brethren could be received as domestics in our families, and so enable us to adhere to the laws framed for them, can be known but to the Searcher of all hearts; for when spoken to man, the idea is received but as high-flown folly, impossible to be realized. If so considered by the mass, there is no help for it, and so it must remain till it please God to put His spirit once more within us, and enlighten the darkness which, in some instances, has gathered around us, rich and poor.

That it is only the rich and influential who can bring about reform in our poorer classes we quite acknowledge. Their religious education must be carried on on a different basis. The spirit and meaning of every form must be inculcated, or they can never rise from the ignorance and superstition in which, through long ages of fearful persecution, they are plunged. The mind and heart alike must be enlarged; their own dignity, their own responsibility inculcated; the distinction between essential and local laws; the superior, the unchangeable sanctity of the law of God, combined with reverence and love for the fence which good, and wise, and holy men have raised around it. Were these things inculcated, there would be many eager to accept the offers of service in Jewish families, and find their obedience to their God quite compatible with their duty to their employers. Of course we allude not to those establishments in which but one or two servants only are kept. We simply mean those classes where there are upper and lower domestics—where one day in the week the former may not be called upon either for servile work, or to break through any of the forms which hallow the Sabbath day. There are such things, we have heard, as head nurses, who, even though Gentiles, have nothing to do with the servile work of their nursery kingdoms. Ladies' maids, who have nothing to do but needlework, dress hair, and attend to their mistress and young ladies. Housekeepers, even housemaids, where there are upper and lower. All these situations might, were they properly educated for it, be filled by the maid-servants in Israel, without interfering one tittle with their adherence and obedience to their Faith.

There must, indeed, be a WILL on both sides, the employers and the employed, but were that WILL found, the WAY would be easy.

Every law instituted in Israel for the safety, happiness, and welfare of the man-servant, mentioned by name the maid-servant also. In obedience to the fourth commandment, in the protection of the tenth, in every festival and fast, every ordinance binding on Jewish families as well as individuals, we find the maid-servant expressly named; thus proving that, though her actual rank was subordinate, though her duties were distinct, she was as carefully and tenderly provided for as the daughters of a family themselves. Even in the eating of holy things, which some might suppose a privilege only granted to the heirs of households, she was associated. No man could rejoice before the Lord by himself; sons, daughters, widows, fatherless, men-servants, and MAID-SERVANTS, all were included, and so distinctly enumerated, that not one could be omitted without a decided breach of law. The twenty-first chapter of Exodus and fifteenth chapter of Deuteronomy treat powerfully on the protection and kindness demanded towards male and *female* domestics. The simple words, "they shall not go out as men-servants do," reveal the loving care for their protection, that they should not be exposed to all the rougher labor of the field and out-door service incumbent on the males. To sell her to a strange nation, which would be the natural desire of the injurer and the deceiver, to conceal his sin, no man had power; for, if he did so, she could not regain her freedom at the end of seven years, and be restored to her family, as was the law in Israel. If he betrothed her to his son, she was to become even as a daughter; and if, as was the custom of the East, another wife were taken, her food, her raiment, her duty of marriage, he had no power to diminish. If he failed in either, she was free and spotless, alike in the sight of God and man. These beautiful laws appear, not only pretty convincing of the equality of female servants with their male brethren in the same class, but rather a startling manifestation of the falsity of the charge, that *wives* in Israel are degraded and abased. If even a female slave, when raised to become the wife of her master's son, was to be regarded as a daughter, to retain her every privilege as first-selected wife, however the capricious heart of her husband might select another of his own rank, we rather imagine that every grade of Hebrew wives was equally protected by the Lord, and that no man whatever had power to degrade them.

All injury committed on a female servant exposed her master to punishment of equal severity as the injury of a male. He dared do her no hurt, for if he did, whether through predetermination or momentary passion, she was his slave no longer. She had power to appeal from him to the representatives of her God, His priests, and she knew justice would be done her, for to do it was the ordinance of God. And, even without injury, the term of servitude was over in the seventh year. The extremity of destitution might have compelled a parent to sell, or rather to devote, his child to servitude; or reasons less imperative might urge his doing so, knowing that his children, even though they worked, would be better provided for, and perhaps more easily enabled to keep every ordinance of the Lord, in the family of their master, than struggling on for a scanty subsistence, nominally free. The poor were not to cease out of the land, that the people might obey the words of their God, in which He bade them, "Open thine hand *wide* unto thy poor brother, to thy poor and to thy needy in thy land;" and then, as a practical illustration of how the hand is to be opened *wide*, we are told that when our brother a Hebrew man, or a Hebrew *woman*, has been sold, and served in a family six years, we were not only to let him, or her, go free, which, did we act according to the finite judgment of man, there would be many to think sufficient; but they were to be furnished liberally out of the flock and the floor (i. e. barn, meaning corn), and out of the wine-press; of all wherewith the Lord had blessed us we were to give unto them. And not satisfied with having already mentioned the Hebrew woman, as included with the Hebrew man, in these laws, the law again enforces the equal rights of both, by repeating, "and also unto thy maid-servant thou shalt do likewise;" adding, with that exquisite spirit of love infused through every law, "It shall not seem hard unto thee, when thou sendest him away free from thee, for he has been worth a double hired servant, in serving thee six years, and the Lord thy God shall bless thee in all thou doest." Now, had there been no other mention of woman, these beautiful laws would have been sufficient to prove her equality with man in the sight of the Eternal. The *illustration* of these laws was given *before* the *precept*, in the Most High's dealings with Hagar, as we have already seen; as a bond-slave, and one not even of His chosen. He had compassion and love for her; and that His people should endeavor as strongly as lay in their power to follow in His own paths, He laid down statutes, the obedience to which would make every maid-servant as much the object of her master's care, tenderness, and liberality, as Hagar had been to Him.

The command relative to the maid-servants' attendance at the feast of holy things, on every Sabbath festival, etc., is rather convincing of religion being as incumbent on her as on man; nay, that her master himself was liable to punishment if he neglected to associate her, as well as every other of his household, in his religious exercises.

Some over-refined natures are horrified at the idea of being sold to service—of the very term *slave* (the Hebrew word עֶבֶד, by the way, signifies *servant* or *domestic* also); and, taking up the position that the law of Moses countenanced similar traffic as the slave trade in all its modern horrors, make it the grand objection to regarding the religion as the revelation of God. Yet no one who really studies the Word of God, can entertain an idea so erroneous for a moment. Perpetual slavery—that awful sacrifice of all home affections, all human emotions, that horrible system which permitted man to regard his brother man as a beast of the field, to be bought and sold, live and die at his will—was utterly unknown in Israel. The term "selling" a son or daughter, simply signified the receiving *beforehand* the price of six years' labor, in which six years the slave (so called) was equal to his master in everything but actual labor. He was to share in every feast, every rejoicing, sit at his master's table, listen to the law, accept every covenant of God, be clothed, fed, and cared for, and at the term of his release be so liberally treated individually, as to enable him, if he pleased, to quit service, and enter into independent business for himself, or remain, from *pure affection or voluntary relinquishment* of freedom, for ever with his master. This was the actual state of slavery in Israel, productive of a three-fold good. It saved many a parent from beholding the utter destitution of his children; gave him the means of working for himself by the price received for their six years' labor, assured him of their temporal and spiritual welfare and of their being cared for, on their release, far better than he could for them, much as he loved them; prevented all those horrible incentives to crime and misery produced by the abject destitution of many a Gentile land; united master and servant in the sweet and holy ties of brotherhood, alike of religion, tribe, and land; subject to one law, worshipping one God, caring for the helpless and the weak, and making every household where the laws of God were obeyed one of heavenly harmony and love. In Israel there was no surplus of hands for work; none of those fearful temptations to sin in being thrown out of employ, in the inability to meet the heavy taxes and other drains upon the poor. The law in its every item spoke of God, and revealed Him as a God of love. He alone could have framed statutes entering into every man's household, guiding his conduct from his parents to his very servants; shielding, compassionating, loving every individual in Israel, from the high priest to the lowest slave.

Having now regarded all the laws instituted expressly for woman, in her several positions of mother, wife, widow, daughter, maid-servant, we have but to throw together all the remaining statutes relating to her generally. In every offering, be it of trespass, of thanksgiving, or of purification, we find in Leviticus, Numbers, and Deuteronomy, woman was so emphatically included as to be the subject of laws set apart for herself. The ordinances were binding on both man and woman, and care expressly taken to mark the guiding line of obedience for both. There was nothing left for inference, but all which was necessary was distinctly laid down. In the very particular law for lepers, *woman* was named as well as *man*. Nothing was left to human judgment; every item concerning its treatment, its care, and its purification, precisely written down. In the laws for the Nazarite (Numbers vi.), woman is specified so clearly, that it is utterly impossible to retain a doubt of her service being equally acceptable, or that she had not the same power as man, to separate herself by a vow unto the Lord. That which was to guide man in this devotion, must equally have been given to guide her, or we should not see it so expressly stated, "when man or WOMAN shall separate themselves to vow the vow of a Nazarite," etc. A woman who could wish to devote herself, appears to us to have been an independent single woman, and, therefore, not one of the daughters and wives specified in the latter law regarding vows, which, judging from the beautiful precision of the laws of God, would, had it alluded to the Nazarites, have been so expressed. The singular vow mentioned in Leviticus xxvii., including, as every other ordinance, woman as well as man, may or may not relate to the same kind of vows as mentioned in Numbers xxx. But whether it be or not, the law for the respective valuation of male and female service, proves that woman could make a singular vow, and either fulfil or redeem it with equal freedom and acceptance as man. That her service was valued at a less rate, is no proof of her inequality, but simply that the service she could render the Temple was, from the weakness of her frame, and the retiring nature of her sex, of less use and importance than man's. Compare the work and capability of a man from the age of twenty to sixty, to those of a woman during the same period. There would be full the worth of "twenty shekels" difference. After the age of sixty, or in early childhood, the difference of valuation was much less, because the capabilities of both drew nearer each other. We see, then, the real meaning of these differing estimations. The law of God, while it elevates and spiritualizes woman to an equal share of immortality and responsibility before Him, in no way permits or encourages her coming unduly forward or exalting herself above man. Her weaker frame, her less mighty mind, her more easily excited emotions, all mark the necessity of a more retiring and dependent station. She may contend for equal earthly rights, she may deem our assertion of her inferior capabilities of frame and mind an unfounded aspersion cast upon her, she may say she is equally independent, equally strong, in reason and power, yet to *prove* this, we fear she will not find quite so easy. Certainly not by the word of God, her only sure test of reason and feeling. And how much more just and graceful is her voluntary adherence to her own allotted path, and her determination to adorn that path with all the winning qualities, the devotedness, the affections, peculiar to her own sex, than the vain struggle to be in all things as man; a struggle in which she can but make manifest her weakness, and finally be so vanquished, that even her natural claims are denied her, or conceded as a favor, not as a right.

The equality which we contend for (and which we uphold is so clearly demonstrated, in not only our holy law itself, but in the mention of every female of the Bible), is not, in our capability, our station, humanly considered, but simply as immortal children of the Most High; having equal access to His gracious ear, equal power to win his condescending reply, equal responsibility in the performance of our every duty, in the just exercise of our several faculties; which faculties, so peculiarly adapted by our merciful Father to our wants, happiness, and duties, are of equal valuation in His sight as those of man. This is woman's equality, proved by the very law which, by some misguided spirits, may be twisted into her abasement. What would be the need of marking her human valuation, if she had not the power of devoting herself by a singular vow unto the Lord, in any period of her life, from a month old to above sixty? Or, if she have no access to God, save through man, what could be the use of her vow? Were she to be degraded morally and mentally, where would be even her inclination for this spiritual service? Surely there need not have been any reference to her in this law, if the women of Israel were to be considered slaves and heathens.

By this twenty-seventh chapter of Leviticus, we see too that *female* infants might be devoted by their parents to the Lord, another beautiful and unanswerable manifestation of their perfect equality with their brothers from their very birth, and must entirely do away with the idea that has been so idly brought forward, that the festival attending the naming of male children in Israel, compared with the quiet reception of the female, at once proves in what an inferior light the latter is regarded. The festivity which hails the entrance of the new-born son of Israel into the holy covenant of his fathers, is an immemorial national usage, descending to us from "the time that Abraham made a great feast, the day that Isaac was weaned," and has nothing whatever to do with the claims of one sex over the other. To my own heart, the different reception of male and female children is an exquisite illustration and type of their respective paths. The world and man must be the theatre and the fellow-actor of the *boy;* he must go forth armed with a religious heart and unbending spirit to meet the temptations of pleasure, ambition, and a host of other passions and emotions, which must assail his more public path. But, to the *girl*, home is her theatre, her God her only stay. Why should festivity and idle revelry hail the birth of one, in whose own heart must be her purest pleasures, distinct from every pleasure (so called) of the world; whose path must be one of quiet and unostentatious retirement and usefulness? Her name is given in the house of God, and by one of His elected servants. Taken to the most holy place, which, in our captive and desolate state, His house presents, by that ceremony to be received into the congregation of His people, does the female babe need more? Cannot the Hebrew mother thus realize the devoting her child to the faith and service of her God, more powerfully, more solemnly, than in even the festive circle which gathers round to hail the naming of her boy? We think, were these several rites more seriously considered, the idle charge we have quoted above, merely to disprove it, would find little resting in the heart of our fellows.

The express prohibition relating to woman's adopting, on any pretence whatever, the garments of the male, is another beautiful ordinance marking her natural sphere, and proving that any departure from it was not acceptable to the Lord. It was not only the act itself which is so forcibly brought forward, that Deut. xxii. 5 tells us, "All that do so are *abomination* unto the Lord thy God," but the thoughts and feelings included in such an act, the temptation to depart from the retirement, the modesty, the purity of that home station which woman should so quietly fulfil. Were she not an equally responsible moral and religious agent as man, why need this law have been given?

Again, we find that *women* who have wrought wickedness, *women* who have a familiar spirit (that is, sought to deceive by pretended spells and enchantments), *women* who have enticed to idolatry—all these, as well as similar sinners amidst the males, were to be stoned to death on the evidence of two witnesses. Now the very power to work such wickedness, supposes a perfect freedom of thought and will, wholly distinct from the power of man. Were woman so entirely the slave of man that her very prayers must be guided by his, and could only be acceptable through him, there could be no justice in condemning her as a free agent; her sins must be the sins of her father or husband, not her own, if her merit were only acceptable through his. She could not possibly be bound to obey the law, or punished for its disobedience, if it were only given to, and incumbent on, man. If she were to be made a slave and heathen, how does it happen that, wherever there can be a doubt as to both sexes being included, either in religious observances, or prohibiting of customs which were abominatior unto the Lord,

WOMAN is expressly mentioned in conjunction with man? The very wrath threatened in case of her trangression proves her equality quite as powerfully as the rewards promised to obedience, and the laws instituted for her adherence.

Three times a year it was a *positive enjoinment* for every *male* to appear before the Lord in the place appointed for His temple. That woman was not included by name, was, instead of being a proof of her lesser importance and responsibility, a beautiful manifestation of that divine tenderness and justice, which, in their perfection and prescience, God only could display. A nameless variety of causes might intervene to prevent woman's leaving her home in the distant provinces of Judea to accompany her father and husband to Jerusalem. Many a man might be enabled to obey the law himself, who would have been prevented doing so, had he been under a *positive command* to bring with him wife and children.

Locomotion is man's native element, and he can more often indulge in it without interfering with home duties than woman. It was right and just, that he who so frequently travelled for pleasure should do so three times a year in obedience to the will of God. But many causes, in her own physical inability or maternal anxiety in the illness of some member of her family, might occur to prevent woman, and therefore the law was not made *binding* upon her, as it was on man.

That this distinct mention of "all thy males" in no way degraded her, however, is clearly proved by the simple fact of her being required, when it was possible, and in all her positions in life, to rejoice before the Lord in his appointed festivals, to listen to the reading of His law at the Feast of Tabernacles, to attend to the offerings instituted expressly for her, to abstain from all wickedness and idolatry, and to come unto the Lord in every event, thought, act, desire, public or private, of her life. "Ye stand this day all of you before the Lord your God," Moses exclaims, in the twenty-ninth chapter of Deuteronomy; "your captains of your tribes, your elders, and your officers, with all the men of Israel, your little ones, your WIVES, and the stranger that is in thy camp, from the hewer of wood to the drawer of water, that thou shouldst enter into covenant with the Lord thy God, and into His oath, that He may establish thee to-day for a people unto Himself, and that He may be unto thee a God, as He hath said unto thee, and as he hath sworn unto thy fathers, to Abraham, to Isaac, and to Jacob. Neither with you only do I make this covenant and this oath, but with him that standeth here with us this day before the Lord our God, and *also* with *him who* is *not here with* us this day, lest there should be among you any *man*, *woman*, family, or tribe, whose heart turneth away this day to go and serve the gods of these nations."

In these few verses, and yet more powerfully in the whole chapter, to which we entreat our readers to turn, we have all which, as women of Israel, we need to seal the scriptural truth and basis of the position which we have adopted and set forth. Every class, grade, and condition of women, as of men, must have been present when Moses spoke these emphatic words—all included in the terms, "little ones and WIVES." And they heard, that Moses addressed not only *them*, but their *descendants*, lest any man, WOMAN, family, or tribe, should, by their idolatry, or other transgression, hurl down on the whole nation the awful curses which he proceeds to enumerate. Would he, need he, have been thus particular, were the women of Israel destined to be but slaves to man, nonentities before God? Alas! whatever the falsely accusing Gentile, or mistaken Hebrew, may assert, we have but fearful evidence in the monarch of Israel of the influence of woman, manifesting too terribly the prophet's prescience in including her, as leading herself and man to sin, and so hastening the great and terrible wrath of the Lord.

We have now drawn to the conclusion of our Second Period, the women of Israel's most momentous era: the delivery and establishment of that law, which, in the very midst of revolutions, changes, new creeds, and their awful persecutions,—in the very midst of denial, abuse, and heavy darkness,—yet remains the hope, the guide, the protection, the defence, the elevation of woman, whatever her station, whatever her country, aye, and whatever her creed may be;—more especially the blessed inheritance of the females of that people on whom our God Himself bestowed it, and one, therefore, which should be their glory, their privilege, their delight, to render so exalted, by their individual and national conduct, in the sight of a Gentile world, that none dare fling odium on the female Jewish name, or seek to heathenize and degrade them.

We have sought to bring together every law relative to woman; but the subject is so momentous, the field so wide, we can scarce hope we have accomplished it as fully as we could wish. We can only hope and pray, that a perusal of these pages may lead our sisters in Israel to seek their *foundation* yet more earnestly than the *frail superstructure*, and find for themselves, in their Bibles, all that we may have omitted, or failed to treat as largely as we might. The more our beautiful law is studied, the more must we feel, that, as women, we are especially objects of the Eternal's loving protection and care; that we are privileged in every feeling as well as every act to come to Him, alike in thanksgiving and prayer; that we have no need whatever, in obtaining our eternal welfare, for the aid and interference of man. The more we study, the more we must feel that we have, as women of Israel, a station to uphold alike before God and man; that as the first, the only people to whom God Himself deigned to provide a law, we should be the very first in holiness, purity, spirituality, and divine love, amid the nations. We may be captives, we may be awhile under the Eternal's wrath, but that truth in no way lessens our responsibility, or diminishes the necessity for our firmly upholding our heavenly heritage and guiding law. We may be captives, but, and oh! let the blessed truth be remembered and clasped to our hearts, we are NOT CAST OFF. Our chastisement is not the sign of divine wrath alone, but of that DEEP LOVE which punisheth to save, to amend, to bring back to the blessed paths which we have deserted, NOT to annihilate, as in the case of so many other nations. Our very existence through so many centuries of darkness would alone prove this, even had we not the whole word of God to assert that so it would be. Every prophet abounds in the divine entreaty, so fraught with forbearing love, "O Israel, return unto the Lord thy God; why hast thou fallen by thine iniquity?" And shall we, as women, reject these gracious proffers? Oh, let us indeed ever come unto the Lord our God, and make manifest to the Gentiles, to ourselves, how deeply, how earnestly we feel, that alike our protection, innocence, honor, purity, elevation, all that can make life dear and holy, all that is provided to lighten our temporal toil, with eternal hope to strengthen our weakness, to guide our daily path, and bless our daily work, is of the Lord, not man. That every pure throb of love, every sweet tie of life, every aspiring prayer and grateful thanksgiving, comes from and is hallowed by Him, who, in His deep love, entered into the heart and home of woman, and so fenced them round with just and beautiful laws, that it was impossible to perform a single duty, social or domestic, parental, filial, conjugal, or fraternal, without being holy unto the Lord! Can we think on this important and most blessed truth without lifting up our yearning hearts in the fervent prayer for that guidance, that blessing, which will enable us to remember our solemn responsibility, our heavenly heritage; and, in the midst of captivity, and its varied ordeals of adversity, stagnation, and prosperity, that we may still join heart to heart and hand to hand in the persevering effort to make manifest to our God, that we would indeed be once more His own, and to the nations, that, cast off for a "little moment" as we are, WE ARE STILL, and SHALL EVER BE, the CHOSEN PEOPLE of the LORD?

THIRD PERIOD.

CHAPTER I.

MIRIAM.

Having now considered the law of God under all its various bearings relative to woman, it only remains to prove, from the female characters of Scripture, in what manner that law was obeyed; and whether it be possible to discover any trace of statutes, which, in direct contradistinction to the changeless law of the Eternal, tend to degrade, instead of to elevate, the female character; or whether we cannot bring forward some sufficiently convincing arguments in favor of our deeply studied theory, that the law of the Eternal is explained, by its practical illustration, through the whole history of the Bible.

To the oralist, or non-oralist, this consideration ought to be of equal weight. Keeping aloof entirely from the discussion which has of late too painfully agitated the whole Jewish nation, we would yet present to both parties the simple fact, that the supposed degradation of the women of Israel can have no existence whatever in the Oral Law, or we must find some trace of this abasement in this and the succeeding periods of our history. If both were given at the same time, the women of Israel whom we are about to bring forward, must have lived under the jurisdiction of both; and as their lives, feelings, and actions, are all in exact accordance with the spirit and the form of the written law, it is clearly evident, that the modern accusation against us can have *no* foundation whatever in the Oral Law, or we must have discovered it in the female characters of Scripture. Nor will the groundless assertion of our individual inferiority and social abasement find confirmation in the writings of our ancient fathers, whose beautiful parables and tales all tend to illustrate alike the spirit of our law, and the axiom of our wise man, "Who can find a virtuous woman, for her price is far above rubies?"

We will proceed, then, without further introduction, to our history, convinced that were the word of the Eternal more deeply studied, the love and peace it breathes must infuse themselves unconsciously in every human heart, and strife and discord melt away before the inspired transcript of the love and mercy of our God.

The character of Miriam is one of the most perfect delineations of woman in her mixed nature of good and evil which the Bible gives. Her first introduction we have already noticed—a young girl, watching, at the command of her mother, the fate of the ark which held her baby brother, and boldly addressing the princess of Egypt in the child's behalf.

Her next mention is her sharing the holy triumph of that brother, and responding, with apparently her whole heart, to the song of praise bursting forth from the assembled Israelites on the shores of the Red Sea. "And Miriam the prophetess, the sister of Aaron, took a timbrel in her hand, and all the women went out after her, with timbrels, and with dances. And Miriam answered them, Sing, sing ye to the Lord, for he hath triumphed gloriously, the horse and his rider hath he thrown into the sea."

The Hebrew word, הַנְּבִיאָה, here used, and translated prophetess, means also, a *poetess*, and the wife of a prophet, and is applied sometimes to a singer of hymns. In this latter meaning, and perhaps, also, as a poetess, it must be applied to Miriam, as she was neither the wife of a prophet, nor, as in the case of Deborah, and afterwards Huldah, endowed by the Eternal with the power of prophecy itself. She appears to have been one of those gifted beings, from whom the words of sacred song flow spontaneously. The miracles performed in their very sight were sufficient to excite enthusiasm in a woman's heart, and awaken the burst of thanksgiving; and Miriam might have fancied herself at that moment as zealous and earnest in the cause of God as she appeared to be. But for true piety, something more is wanted than the mere enthusiasm of the moment, or the high-sounding religion of flowing verse. By Miriam not being permitted to enter the promised land, it is evident that she "had not followed the

Lord fully," but had probably joined in the rebellions and murmurings which characterized almost the whole body of the Israelites during their wanderings in the wilderness. The very next mention of her after her song of praise, is her presumptuous attack upon Moses, and daring insult to the power of the Lord, contained in the twelfth chapter of Numbers. Some chronologists believe this incident occurred only one year after the passage of the Red Sea, a period not sufficiently long for circumstances to have changed the character of Miriam so completely, had not jealousy and presumption been secretly inmates of her heart before; unknown, perhaps, even to herself, for how few of us know our "secret sins," until they are roused into action by some unlooked-for temptation in an unguarded moment, and we are startled at ourselves.

The feelings of Miriam, recorded in this chapter, are so perfectly accordant with woman's nature, that surely no woman of Israel will turn from it, believing the length of time which has elapsed removes all the warning which it should inculcate. One of the most prominent of female failings is secret jealousy, quite distinct, however, from the fearful passion so called. We allude simply to that species of secret and unconfessed jealousy, which is the real origin of *detraction*, so often, unhappily, practised by woman upon woman. We are not now writing of any class, or creed, or people in particular, but of women in general. There never yet was gossip, without some species of detraction spoken or implied; and never yet has detraction been probed candidly and fairly (disregarding the pain of so doing) to its root, without being traced to either jealousy or envy of some quality, or possession, of the more favored being so unkindly judged.

Women, and single women more especially, are more liable to petty failings than men, simply because they have less to engross their minds, and less of consequence to employ their hands. Unless taught from earliest years to find and take pleasure in resources *within*, they must look *without*, and busy themselves with the characters, and conduct, and concerns of their neighbors. Now acknowledged merit to such characters gives very little food for cosy chat; it wants *esprit*, and so they are never content, till something doubtful or suspicious is discovered, or supposed to be, and then the lovers of gossip may be found in full conclave, marvelling, and wondering, and turning, and twisting, and blaming, and pitying, till the very object of such animadversion might find it difficult to trace of whom they speak, and know infinitely less of her own concerns, intentions, and feelings, than her reporters.

As Miriam acted, so would most women, unenlightened by that pure spirit of religious love, which alone can conquer the natural inclination towards detraction, and subdue secret jealousy, by making us aware of its existence. "And Miriam and Aaron spake against Moses, *because of the Ethiopian woman whom he had married.*" The very thing to arouse jealousy and disturbance in an unenlightened woman's mind.

Miriam had never been thrown in contact with her sister-in-law till within the last few months: Moses having sent his wife for safety, with his two sons, to her father Jethro, during the troubles in Egypt and their subsequent redemption. From the silence with regard to Zipporah, we are led to infer that she was a woman of meek and retiring habits, but of course, as the wife of their great leader Moses, held in higher repute by the people than his sister. And this, trifling as it seems, is now, as it always has been, a trial to some of our sex. Few single women there are who can look upon the elevation of a brother's wife without some secret feelings of pain, which will be subdued and changed into warmest affection, or gain ascendency and violence, finding vent in petty malice or half-concealed detraction, according as religion, and candor, and self-knowledge are, or are not, predominant in the sister's character. Perhaps it is hard, in some cases, to see one younger and fairer, and only known but a few years or months, as the case may be, usurp entire possession of a beloved brother's heart; wherein we, who have been his hand-in-hand companions from earliest infancy, must now be content with but a very secondary place; but such is one of the many trials peculiarly woman's,—permitted, that from her very loneliness below, she may look above for that fulness of love and tenderness for which she yearns. And thrice happy is that woman who, conscious of this, can yet be content with, and value as before, the love her brother has still to spare for her; who will so subdue natural feeling as to find in very truth a friend and sister in a brother's wife, and subjects of deepest interest in her children.

Miriam, as we may infer from her punishment, was not one of these. That an Ethiopian should be raised above herself, who was a daughter of Israel, was, to one of her evidently proud spirit, unendurable. Unable, however, to discover aught in Zipporah herself for a publicly-avowed scorn, she sought to lessen the holiness and greatness of her brother, by daring to declare that the Lord had spoken through her and Aaron also. That this jealousy arose because of the "Ethiopian woman whom he had married," Holy Writ itself informs us; and from Miriam's name being mentioned before that of Aaron, and yet more, from the wrath of the Lord being manifested towards her alone, it is evident that hers was the greater sin. Her individual assumption of prophetic power, she knew, would avail her nothing, but, uniting Aaron in the declaration, she sought to make it appear that God had breathed His spirit into every member of Amram's family. She had too much policy to endeavor to deprive Moses of all his granted and allowed privileges. Her only wish was, to decrease the value and spirituality of those privileges to him individually, and elevate herself and Aaron on his descent; emboldened so to do by the excessive meekness and forbearance of Moses, which she knew would shield her from all *human* reproof. She might, perhaps, have so dwelt upon her own imaginary importance, as really to believe what she asserted, and so feel more and more galled at the little account in which she was held.

It is quite possible for woman so to feel and so to act, and for all to proceed from the petty feelings of jealousy and malice, first excited by the higher grade and more considered position of a brother's wife. "Hath the Lord indeed spoken only by Moses? hath he not spoken also by us?" were the words they said; brief, and perchance of little weight considered by themselves, but in a people ever ready to revolt and murmur, more than likely to kindle sedition and disturbance. "And the Lord heard it, and the Lord spake suddenly unto Moses, and unto Aaron, and unto Miriam, Come out ye three unto the tabernacle of the congregation: and they three came out, and the Lord came down in the pillar of the cloud, and stood in the door of the tabernacle, and called Aaron and Miriam; and they both came forth."

Where now could have been the presumptuous self-importance of Miriam, called thus by Him at whose word might be annihilation? With what fearful terror must she have heard that summons, and listened to the reproving words of the Eternal?—exalting Moses above even His inspired prophets; for to them He declared He would make Himself known in a vision, and speak unto them in a dream, "but my servant Moses is not so, who is faithful in all mine house. With him will I speak mouth to mouth, even apparently, and not in dark speeches; and the similitude of the Lord shall he behold: wherefore then were ye not afraid to speak against my servant Moses? And the anger of the Lord was kindled against them; and He departed. And the cloud departed from off the tabernacle; and, behold, Miriam was leprous, as snow: and Aaron looked upon Miriam, and, behold, she was leprous."

It is from this awful chastisement, inflicted by the Lord Himself, that we must judge of the heinousness of her sin; that presumption and arrogancy are no small crimes in His sight, and that God Himself was insulted in the insult offered to His chosen servant. "My servant Moses," He ever designates him; implying the severest reproof in those simple words. Even were they endowed with prophetic power, He tells them they would be less than Moses; for to Moses alone would He deign to speak mouth to mouth. Had Miriam's sin been but the impulse of the moment, the reproof would have been sufficient, as we see in other cases in Scripture; but, effectually to root out the sinful presumption which probably had lain dormant for months, the Eternal, in His perfect justice, inflicted such chastisement as would cause her to be shunned and loathed by the very people whom she had sought to impress with her individual importance. Human reproof, indeed, she had not; for Moses, "meek above all the men which were on the face of the earth," had not even answered the detracting words, conscious that his power was not his own, and that He who gave it, would, if needed, appear in his defence. Had Miriam's heart been perfect towards God, neither her sin nor her punishment would have taken place. Pride and presumption *cannot* exist with true piety; and we are therefore justified in supposing, that the awful infliction was not only a chastisement for present sin, but to awaken her to all the neglectfulness and presumption dividing her from the Lord in years long past. She was now not only to feel His stupendous power, but the true forgiving meekness and piety of the brother she had scorned and spoken against, only "because of his Ethiopian wife."

Stunned and appalled with the suddenness of the infliction,

and dumb perhaps from awakening shame, Miriam herself stood silent before Moses: and Aaron therefore appealed for her.

"Alas, my Lord, I beseech thee, lay not the sin upon us, wherein we have done foolishly, and wherein we have sinned Let her not be as one dead, of whom the flesh is half consumed as in the moment of his birth." And Moses, without pause, without one word of reproof, or just indignation at being thus appealed to by the very persons who had sought to injure him, lifted up his voice in earnest prayer unto the Lord, saying, "Heal her now, O God, I beseech thee." And God heard the prayer, and in His infinite goodness so answered it, as to temper justice with mercy, promising to withdraw His hand after seven days, during which time, in obedience to the already instituted laws for lepers, she was to be shut out from the camp. "And the people journeyed not till she was healed."

As there is no further mention of Miriam, except her death, in Numbers xx., we may infer that her chastisement had its effect, and that her haughty and seditious spirit was sufficiently subdued. We learn, from her brief history, much to guide us as women in general, and much to support our position as women of Israel. In the former, we see in what light presumption is regarded by the Lord—that would we retain His favor, we must be content with our own position, and in no way interfere, or seek to depreciate those whom, even in our own families, it may have pleased Him to set above us; that even from so small a beginning as jealousy of a brother's wife, simply because she was the daughter of a stranger, sin gained such powerful ascendency, as to demand the most awful punishment for its subjection. We learn, that according to the nature of our transgression, so will be its chastisement. Miriam sought to raise herself not only above her brother's wife, but to an equality with that brother himself; and, by the infliction of a loathsome disease, she sank at once below the lowest of her people. No one dared approach her; she was cut off even from employment, from every former object of interest, banished from the camp; and she would have thus remained till her death, had not Moses interfered to beseech and obtain forgiveness.

The direct interposition of the Lord in punishing sin, and rewarding virtue, is no longer visible; but few who study His word, their own hearts, and the face of the world, both past and present, will not acknowledge that He is still the same, retributing and rewarding as when His ways were made manifest to all. By the example of Scripture characters, He reveals to us now that which is still acceptable or unacceptable to Him. Presumption, jealousy, the scorn of individual blessings, in the coveting others, may no longer be punished by leprosy, but "the Lord's arm is not shortened," and He may afflict us in a variety of ways, and through the very feelings which we so sinfully encourage. Let us beware, then, of detraction, of jealousy, of presumption; for our Father in Heaven abhors these things. Let us look only for the blessings granted us individually, in our inward and outward lot, and comparing them with the sorrowing and afflicted, bless God for what He has given us; not insult Him, by looking with an eye of envy only on those to whom His wisdom has given more. There is not a thought, not a feeling, unknown to Him; and oh! let us so guard our hearts, that we may be aware of the first whispering of sin, and banish it, even if it be in seeming but a thought.

As women of Israel, the history of Miriam is fraught with particular interest, from its so undeniably proving that woman must be quite as responsible a being as man before the Lord, or He certainly would not have deigned to appear Himself as her judge. Were woman unable of herself to eschew sin, Miriam's punishment would have been undoubtedly unjust. Nay, were she not responsible for *feelings*, as well as acts, God would not thus have stretched forth His avenging hand. Her feelings had only been formed into words, *not* yet into *actions;* still the Lord punished. And would He have done so, did he not wish to make manifest, in the sight of the whole people, that both sexes were alike before Him? Were woman in a degraded position, Miriam, in the first place, would not have had sufficient power for her seditious words to be of any consequence; and, in the next, it would have been incumbent on man to chastise—there needed no interference of the Lord. We see, therefore, the very sinfulness of Jewish women, as recorded in the Bible, is undeniable evidence of their equality, alike in their power to subdue sin, and in its responsibility before God.

That the Eternal graciously pardoned at the word of Moses, is no proof that Miriam *needed* the supplication of man to bring her cause before the Lord, but simply that forgiveness and intercession from the *injured* for the *injurer*, are peculiarly acceptable to Him, and will ever bring reply. Miriam had equal power to pray and be heard, as Rebekah, Hannah, and other female characters of Scripture; but her punishment was no doubt to be increased by the painful feelings which, if she were not quite hardened, must have been excited by the appeal of Moses in her favor, and in receiving the remission of her sentence through him. It at once proclaimed his power with the Lord, which she had sought to depreciate, and his still continued affection for herself. That the whole camp of Israel should halt in its march seven days for her alone,—that she should suffer less than were she shut out from her fellows in the act of travelling, argues pretty strongly, that her being a woman in no degree lessened her importance, or rendered the men of Israel less careful for her comfort. They could not have done more, had the chastised been Aaron in her stead.

CHAPTER II.

FEMALE WORKERS OF THE TABERNACLE.—CALEB'S DAUGHTER.

In a history of the women of Israel, we must not forget those who are mentioned as aiding the holy work of the tabernacle. Proclamation was made throughout the camp, that every man and woman who had a *willing heart* should bring an offering unto the Lord, either of gold, silver, or brass, blue, purple, and scarlet, and fine linen, and goats' hair, and oil, and spices, and sweet incense, and onyx stones, and stones of all kinds; and that every one who was *wise-hearted* among them should come and make all that the Lord had commanded, which Moses proceeds to enumerate (see Exod. xxxv. and xxxvi.). The congregation then departed to their several tents, but speedily came every one *whose heart stirred him up*, and every one whom his *spirit made willing*. "And they came, both men and WOMEN, as many who were willing-hearted, and brought bracelets, and earrings, and rings, and tablets of gold," &c. "And all *the women* who were *wise-hearted* did spin with their hands, and brought that which they had spun, both of blue, and of purple, and of scarlet, and of fine linen. And all the women *whose heart stirred them up in wisdom*, spun goats' hair. The children of Israel brought a willing offering unto the Lord, every man and *woman*, whose heart made them willing." In such quantities were these free offerings, that another proclamation was soon made; for "they spake unto Moses, saying, The people bring *much more than enough* for the service of the work, which the Lord commanded to make. And Moses gave commandment, and they caused it to be proclaimed throughout the camp, saying, Let neither man nor *woman* make any more work for the offering of the sanctuary. And the people were restrained from bringing."

We have quoted all these verses, at the risk of being thought tedious, on account of the very important truths they contain. In the first place, we see that, notwithstanding the innumerable rebellions, seditions, and murmurings of the Israelites, there was still a vast multitude, whose hearts so stirred them up for the service of the Lord, as to bring more valuable offerings than could be used. In the text, by the constant allusion to the *willing hearted*, and to those whose spirits made them willing, we read, that only those gifts were acceptable which were offered from the *heart*. No mere formal profession could here avail. The *spirit* within was to be the prompter, not the outward appearance. In the third, the frequent mention of the wise-hearted, or those whose hearts stirred them up in wisdom, we learn, from the context, specified more especially those whom God Himself had gifted for the work; and that all those arts of engraving, of embroidery, of weaving, of cunning work, of spinning, nay, every kind of male and female work, came originally as much from His inspiration, as every other higher branch usually denominated "natural gifts," "talents," or "genius." Spinning, weaving, engraving, and embroidery, are now so common, that we have quite forgotten from whose inspiration they originally came; and were we told that these very resources of the mind and fingers should be amongst the innumerable daily blessings for which we should thank God, we might be accused of enthusiasm and religious romance; yet who can read this chapter of Exodus, without feeling the truth of our position, and bidding the heart glow with thanksgiving for the innocent and happy resources of daily life?

In the fourth place, by both proclamations being addressed to

WOMAN as well as man, we have another unanswerable proof of their equality, not only in the power and freedom to bring offerings, but in their being equally gifted by the Eternal for the work. We peruse with admiration the self-devotion of the women of Carthage, when bringing together all their gold and silver ornaments to form arms for the defence of their city, even cutting off their hair to make strings for bows and other weapons; and our admiration is just: but how much more strongly should it be excited towards the women of Israel of old, who, from pure love of God, and zeal in His holy service, brought all their ornaments, bracelets, earrings, tablets, rings, jewels of gold and silver, every article of value which they could collect, and set themselves, heart and hand, to spin, weave, embroider, and use all their talents in His service by whom they had been bestowed. The women of Carthage were roused by a sense of rapidly approaching danger, by the excitement of war, by that pure love of home and land which God has implanted in every breast. The women of Israel were under no excitement; nay, they were wandering in a wilderness fraught with much to exhaust and weary mere *human nature*, however the immortal spirit might be sustained by the presence and revelation of the Lord. Their goal was in *perspective*. The voice of murmuring, of disbelief, was constantly sounding around them. "Wherefore is it, that thou hast brought us up out of Egypt, to kill us and our children?" were words, not once nor twice, but countless times repeated, with every new trial of their faith. And what is so infectious in a "mixed multitude" as unbelief—ay, even in the very face of miracles performed in their behalf? Yet, at the first call, there were still very many wise and willing-hearted to come forward. The women of Carthage were actuated by the mere feelings of humanity, by *palpable* danger, by the clearly traced issue of their efforts. The women of Israel worked through FAITH. Hoping for no earthly reward, seeking no worldly glory, sacrificing ornaments most prized (for dress, as we shall presently see, was considered rather too much than too little by our ancestors), knowing that once given they could not be recalled, keeping neither time nor talent back, but using both perseveringly and indiscriminately, and all simply and solely out of pure love to God.

There is something both beautiful and consoling in this portion of our history. It informs us, that in the very midst of constant rebellions and constant fallings away, there were, and will always be found, many to love and serve their God. That He will never leave Himself without witnesses upon earth; and that, therefore, however we may mourn the lack of energy and spirituality in Israel—however we may grieve and deplore the cases of infidelity or indifference, or even direct departures from His most Holy Law—still God is with us to retain many an unsuspected one in fidelity and zeal. Despondency, even in His cause, is more than wrong; it is sinful, for it doubts Him who is so strong to save; whose word is passed, that "Israel shall *never* cease to be a nation before Him;" and who, even from the deepest darkness, can and will bring forth light. It causes feelings towards our fellows, both of injustice and pain; and in ourselves deadens every effort after holiness and righteousness, by the supposition, that the struggles of one individual must be all in vain. Despondency treads so closely upon indifference, that every effort should be put in force to prevent its ascendency. We cannot have faith either in God or man if we despond, and thus we are gradually led into sin, alike against our Father in Heaven, our brother man, and ourselves.

To us as women, the particular mention of our female ancestors, as bringing offerings and working for the tabernacle, is inexpressibly consoling. It assures us that, lowly as we are, retired as is our natural sphere, incapable as is our weaker frame for the exertions of man in the Lord's service, still we are acceptable—still He will graciously look down on our "willing hearts," and the humble work of our hand, and bless them with such love, as will give us peace even upon earth. It tells us, that from Him comes every employment and resource, alike of mind and hand; and that, in consequence, all should be used to His glory; not, indeed, for the service of the tabernacle, for we are not now so called upon to work, but in the happiness which His gifts should bestow upon ourselves and our fellow-creatures. Had we but these two chapters in our Holy Law, we should have sufficient to confirm our spiritual privileges;—that our Father asks but a willing spirit, a heart that is stirred within us to do His service, whatever it may be, to resign whatever He may call; but it MUST BE a willing heart: mere lip-service is mockery and sin. Let it not be said that the Jewish religion is a religion of mere form, incumbent only on the males, and therefore debarring woman from all religious exercises, all access to God. Bid those who throw such foul wrong on Israel, come hither to the pure unadulterated fount of the Living God, and then say, if the religion of the Nazarene were the *first*, and *only one*, to teach woman her holy privileges, and to preach that pure spiritual piety of the heart, that simple working through faith, which is revealed so blessedly in our Law, and confirmed by every inspired prophet of the Lord. And that religion of the heart is ours still.. We need no other to replace it.

The age of chivalry is generally supposed to be a powerful proof of the respect and consideration with which women were regarded amongst the Gentile nations during the middle ages. Their position was marked; their love, their hand, the greatest reward, the most powerful incentive for the young warriors to distinguish themselves. Marvellous deeds were done, and dangers dared, all for the smiles of woman; nay, evil passions were often subdued: generosity, magnanimity, kindness, and many other virtues, were called into play by woman's influence, without which those ages would have been dark indeed. Her individual position might have been too elevated; but still, that elevation was far more often used for good than evil. Chivalry *did* bring forth good with regard to woman's influence on man, and no one assuredly will deny, but that to have been held up as the rewarder of valor, the incentive of virtue, must have made her a subject of consideration, respect, and love, very different to slavery and degradation.

Now, the very first instance of chivalry which history records, is found in the Bible, and in the history of that very people to whose women similar privileges are denied. "And Caleb said, he that smiteth Kirjath-sepher [also called Debir], and taketh it, to him will I give Achsah my daughter to wife. And Othniel, the son of Kenaz, Caleb's younger brother, took it: and he gave him Achsah his daughter to wife. And it came to pass, as she came unto him, she moved him to ask of her father a field; and she lighted off her ass; and Caleb said unto her, What wouldst thou? and she said unto him, Give me a blessing; for thou hast given me a south land; give me also springs of water. And Caleb gave her also the upper springs and the nether springs." We find all these verses, first in Joshua xv. 16–19, and repeated without any variation in Judges i. 12–15

Caleb was a prince of the tribe of Judah (Numb. xiii. 6), so high in favor with the Lord, as to be joined with Joshua in being permitted to enter the promised land, and designated by the Eternal as "My servant Caleb, who hath followed me fully."

Caleb seems to have been, like Joshua, a prince and warrior of high repute, dauntless, and faithful before God and before man. His daughter (though not an only child, for we read in 1 Chron. iv. 15, that he had also three sons) shared the consideration proffered to her father. Caleb must have seen the high respect and admiration in which she was held, or he never would have dreamed of offering her as the reward of valor. That which is of no value, lightly won, and lightly held, and, when obtained, to sink merely into a household slave, was not at all likely to excite young men to the arduous task of smiting and taking a fortified city, defended as it was by the sons of Anak, whose immense stature and extraordinary prowess had formerly caused them to be considered as "giants," in whose sight the children of Israel were but as "grasshoppers." Nor can we regard this as merely a solitary instance: it is a proof of the *general condition* of Hebrew women at that period; and also that Othniel was not Achsah's only admirer.

"He that smiteth and taketh it, to him will I give Achsah my daughter to wife," is a general appeal, supposing her hand to be a sufficient incentive to all the young men of the tribe; and that His Law, regarding the inheritance of daughters, should not be transgressed, the Eternal blessed the valiant efforts of Othniel, Caleb's own nephew, with success; and the coveted maiden became his wife.

That it was solely Achsah herself who was sought and won, with no idea of her wealth, is clearly proved by the simple words "she moved him [her husband] to ask of her father, a field or piece of land;" the wish for possession came from her, not from Othniel, who was in all probability fully satisfied with the recompense he had gained; and when Caleb had granted this request, as we know by the words in which she afterwards addresses him, she approached him herself, and lighting off her ass, a token of the respect natural to Israel, Caleb asked her, "What wilt thou?" and she answered him, "Give me a blessing:" meaning, possibly, a further token of his love for her;

"for thou hast given me a south land [alluding to that already given at Othniel's request], give me also springs of water: and Caleb gave her the upper and the nether springs."

Without springs, land, in so hot a country as Judea, was of little value; and therefore is it that Achsah craves this boon in addition to that already granted. The affectionate confidence subsisting between the father and daughter is beautifully illustrated in this simple little incident. Though Achsah held her father in such respect as not to prefer her request while *sitting* on her ass before him, yet she feared not to make her wishes known, fully conscious that, were they in his power, he would grant them unhesitatingly; and his instant reply proves how much reason she had for her confidence.

We learn too from this, that woman must undoubtedly have had the power of possessing landed property in her own right, and in a degree exclusive of her husband;* else Caleb would have made over the portion intended for her to Othniel on his marriage, instead of waiting for Achsah to ask, and granting it to her alone.

The beautiful law of our God was then in full force among every rank and condition of man; and surely we can find no trace in the history of Achsah to confirm the false position of our being degraded. Does it not rather elevate us to a perfect equality with our brother man, and prove undeniably that the Israelites were the very first nation in the world to hold forth the love and hand of woman as the pure and holy incentive to deeds of manliness and valor?

* And exclusive also of her brothers; for if landed inheritance were to be man's only, she could have had no claim to any portion. The above was written originally, under the impression that Achsah was Caleb's only child: a further study of the genealogies in Chronicles proves that she was not.

CHAPTER III.

DEBORAH.

THE promised land was gained, deeds of extraordinary valor and military skill and prowess marked its conquest and subdivision; but God's express command was disobeyed; and, in consequence, the tribes, even after they had settled in their respective territories, were continually "doing evil in the sight of the Lord," and at war, as a chastisement, with their idolatrous neighbors. God had ordained the extermination of the former inhabitants of Palestine, because of their fearful state of idolatry, and various abominations. He had deferred bringing in the seed of Abraham to their appointed land, because "the iniquity of the Amorites was not yet full." He might in His wisdom have exterminated them by fire, water, or disease; but He appointed the swords of the Israelites as the instruments of His wrath, simply to try their faith and obedience, and bid them *earn* the rest, peace, spiritual and temporal glory, which he had held forth as the recompense of perfect obedience.

This fact is very frequently disregarded in a mere superficial reading of the history of Canaan. There are those even to doubt and cavil at the ways of their God, because He commanded His people to obtain possession of the promised land at the edge of the sword; forgetting that so doing was at once a punishment for those who had insulted Him by their awful iniquities (having full power to subdue sin, and keep in the straight path, as did the inhabitants of Mesopotamia even without direct revelation), and also to try the obedience of His people. Disease, fire, or flood, would have accomplished the first of these designs equally with the plan adopted; but not the second. Yet the former would at once have been recognised as the hand of God; no one questioning the agency of either the deluge, the destruction of Sodom, or the earthquake and the plague, punishing the rebellion of Korah. Why then should not the sword of slaughter be traced to the same Divine ordination, whence alone in fact it proceeded?

The Israelites, however, failed in their commanded obedience. Instead of exterminating, they entered into friendly leagues with the enemies and insulters of their God; and the Eternal, in His just anger, permitted them, in consequence, to remain as "thorns, and pricks in their sides, and their false gods as a snare unto them." And so it was: "They took their daughters to be their wives, and gave their daughters to their sons, and served their gods; and the children of Israel did evil in the sight of God, and forgat the Lord their God, and served Baalim and the groves." And this fearful state of things occurred repeatedly; rousing the anger of the Lord each time to sell them into the hands of their enemies, and yet whenever they cried unto Him in returning faith and repentance, His infinite mercy raised up deliverers in whom He put His spirit, and saved them.

Othniel, the nephew and son-in-law of Caleb, Ehud, and Shamgar, had each in his turn been thus selected by the Lord; and during their respective sways Israel was at rest and obedient. But between each, they had relapsed into idolatry and rebellion; and after the deaths of Ehud and Shamgar, who appear contemporaries, falling anew into evil, the Eternal sold them into the hands of Jabin, king of Hazor, who mightily oppressed them twenty years, and caused them again to cry unto the Lord.

But even in these periods of anarchy and rebellion, all were not idolatrous. There must still have been many "seven thousands who had not bowed the knee to Baal," else would not the Lord have thus repeatedly compassionated and relieved them. Amongst these faithful few, the law was of course followed, and the people judged according to the statutes given through Moses. Had there been the very least foundation for the supposition of the degrading and heathenizing the Hebrew female, we should not find the offices of prophet, judge, military instructor, poet, and sacred singer, all *combined* and all *perfected* in the person of a woman; a fact clearly and almost startlingly illustrative of what must have been their high and intellectual training, as well as natural aptitude for guiding and enforcing the statutes of their God, to which at that time woman could attain.

"And Deborah, a prophetess, the wife of Lapidoth, she judged Israel at that time. And she dwelt under the palm tree of Deborah, between Ramah and Bethel, in Mount Ephraim: and the children of Israel came unto her for judgment." This simple description evinces that the greatness of Deborah consisted not at all in outward state, in semblance of high rank, or in any particular respect or homage outwardly paid her; but simply in her vast superiority of mental and spiritual acquirements which were acknowledged by her countrymen, and consequently revered. The office of judge in Israel was not hereditary. It only devolved on those gifted to perform it: and, by the example before us, might be held by either sex: rather an *unsatisfactory* proof of the degradation of Jewish women. We are expressly told that Deborah was a prophetess, and "the wife of Lapidoth." Now, by the arrangement of this sentence, confirmed by the context, it is very evident that Deborah was a prophetess in her own person, wholly and entirely distinct from her husband, who was a mere cypher in public concerns. The Eternal had inspired her, a WOMAN and a WIFE in Israel, with His spirit expressly to do His will, and make manifest to her countrymen how little is He the respecter of persons; judging only by hearts perfect in His service, and spirits willing for the work: heeding neither the weakness nor apparent inability of one sex, compared with the greater natural powers of the other.

Yet so naturally are her public position and personal gifts described, that we cannot possibly believe her elevation to be an extraordinary occurrence, or that her position as a wife forbade her rising above mere conjugal and household duties. We never hear of a slave, or leper, or heathen, being intrusted with the prophetic spirit of the Eternal, simply because the social condition of such persons would and must prevent their obtaining either the respect, obedience, or even attention of the people. For the same reason, had woman really been on a par with these, as she is by some declared to be, she would never have been intrusted with gifts spiritual and mental, which Deborah so richly possessed. She never could have been a prophetess, for her words would only have been regarded as idle raving. She could never have been a judge, from the want of opportunities to train and perfect her intellect, and to obtain the necessary experience. Now it is clear that instead of this, her natural position must have been so high, that there needed not even adventitious state and splendor to make it acknowledged; and her intellect and judgment so cultivated, as not only to bring the people flocking to her for judgment, but to occasion Barak's refusal to set out on a warlike expedition unless she accompanied them.

We find the first recorded instance of her using her prophetic power in Judges iv. 6: "And she sent and called Barak the son of Abinoam out of Kedesh Naphtali, and said unto him, Hath not the Lord God of Israel commanded, saying, Go and draw toward Mount Tabor, and take with thee ten thousand men of the children of Naphtali and the children of Zebulun? And I will draw unto thee Sisera, the captain of Jabin's army, and his chariots and his multitudes; and I will deliver him into thine hand. And Barak said unto her, *If thou wilt go with me*, then I will go: but if thou wilt not go with me, then will I not go. And she said, I will surely go with thee: notwithstanding the journey shall not be for thine honor; for the Lord will sell Sisera into the hand of a woman."

We should be at a loss to understand the feeling in Barak, which impelled his reply, might we not infer it from Deborah's rejoinder. It would appear that, like many of his countrymen, while he obeyed, he was still wanting in the perfect faith which would have given him a glorious triumph in his own person. The presence of Deborah could in no way give him greater increase of safety and glory, than had he gone without her. She was but the instrument of the Lord, making His will known to her fellows. The words were not hers, but God's; and Barak should have acted on them without either reservation or doubt. Instead of which we find him making a *condition* to his obedience; and refusing to obey, if that condition were not complied with. What could the presence of a woman avail him? Her being a prophetess gave him no more assurance of conquest than the word of the Lord had already done; and *because he trusted more in the woman than in her God*, the journey would not be to his honor; a *woman's* hand should accomplish that complete downfall of Sisera, which would otherwise have accrued to his individual glory. It is evident that this is the real rendering of this rather obscure sentence, else we should not have it so expressly stated that the "journey would not be for his honor."

Deborah however arose, and went with Barak, first to collect the necessary troops from Zebulun and Naphtali, and then to Mount Tabor, where Sisera and his immense armament of nine hundred chariots of iron, besides infantry, marched to meet them. Still we find Barak but secondary, doing nothing without the word of the Lord through Deborah. And Deborah said, "Up! for this is the day in which the Lord hath delivered Sisera into thine hand: is not the Lord gone out before thee? So Barak went down from Mount Tabor, and ten thousand men after them;" and the Lord gave them such complete victory, that but Sisera escaped, to receive his death at the hand of a woman, according to the Eternal's word. Nor was it a single victory, for "the hand of the children of Israel prospered and prevailed against Jabin, king of Canaan."

We next find Deborah exercising that glorious talent of extempore poetry only found amongst the Hebrews; and by her, a woman and a wife in Israel, possessed to an almost equal degree with the Psalmist and prophets, who followed at a later period. Her song is considered one of the most beautiful specimens of Hebrew poetry, whether read in the original, or in the English version. We find her taking no glory whatever to herself, but calling upon the princes, and governors, and people of Israel, to join with her in "blessing the Lord for the avenging of Israel." In the fourth and fifth verses, she alludes, by a most beautiful figure, to the power of the Eternal. That before Him "the earth trembled, and the heavens dropped, and the clouds dropped water. And the mountains trembled, even Sinai, before the Lord God of Israel," thus manifesting that his power, not man's, had brought delivery to Israel. Then in the sixth and eighth verses she describes the condition of the people before she arose a mother in Israel; that they were compelled to travel in by-paths, because of the high roads all being occupied by their foes; and from the villages all the inhabitants had ceased, from their being continually exposed undefended to the enemy. Nor was there a shield or spear seen in the forty thousand of Israel. The simplicity and lowliness of the prophetess's natural position, is beautifully illustrated by the term she applies to herself—neither princess, nor governor, nor judge, nor prophetess, though both the last offices she fulfilled —"until that I, Deborah, arose, until I arose a MOTHER in Israel." She asked no greater honor or privilege for herself individually, than the being recognised as the mother of the people whom the Lord alone had endowed her with power to judge. "My heart is towards the governors of Israel," she continues, "that offered themselves willingly among the people. Bless ye the Lord," meaning those who, rising from the idolatry and sloth which had encompassed the people, offered themselves willingly for the service of the Lord. She bids them speak,—all classes of people,—from those princes who rode on white asses, and those who sat in judgment, and those who walked by the way, to even the drawers of water who had before been harassed by the noise of the archers coming forcibly to disturb their domestic employments; and all were to rehearse the righteous acts of the Lord, for to Him alone they owed their preservation. "The Lord made ME have dominion over the mighty," she says, in verse thirteen, thus retaining her own dignity and power in Israel, yet tracing it to the Eternal, not to herself. The poetry describing the downfall of their foes, calling forth the imagery of nature to give it force and life; the death of Sisera, and the waiting and watching of his mother at her lattice—"Why is his chariot so long in coming? why tarry the wheels of his chariots?" and the answer, alike from her ladies, and her own heart, "Have they not sped? have they not divided the prey; to every man a damsel or two; to Sisera a prey of divers colors, a prey of divers colors of needle-work, meet for the necks of them that take the spoil?" as if to fail with his mighty armament were impossible; and thus sung by the lips of the conquerors, infused with a species of satire, giving indescribable poignancy to the strain; and then the glorious conclusion, "So let all thine enemies perish, O Lord: but let them that love thee be as the sun when he goeth forth in his might;" form altogether one of the sublimest strains of spiritual fervor in the Bible; and mark forcibly, by her conduct, both as prophetess and judge, that in Deborah, even as in Gideon, David, and the prophets of later years, God disdained not to breathe His spirit, but made a WOMAN His instrument to judge, to prophesy, to teach, and to redeem.

"And the land had rest forty years," we are told at the conclusion of Deborah's song; words which, as no other judge is mentioned, would lead us to infer that Deborah continued "a mother in Israel" all that time, retaining the people in fidelity, and consequently in temporal and spiritual peace. Even if she did not live herself to govern all those years, it is evident that her influence and instructions were remembered and acted upon, for it was not till *after* these forty years that "Israel again did evil in the sight of the Lord," and so again required a redeemer, which was granted in the person of Gideon.

The silence preserved regarding the subsequent life and death of Deborah, is a simple confirmation of the meekness and humility with which we found her judging Israel under her own palm-tree, before being called to a more stirring scene. The land was at peace, the power of prophecy and foresight in military matters was no longer needed, and Deborah resumed her personally humble station, evidently without any ambitious wish, or attempt to elevate her rank or prospects. It was enough that she was useful to her countrymen; that she was a lowly instrument in the Eternal's hand to work them good. What, now, did she need to satisfy the *woman nature*, which she still so evidently retained? Her judgments, her works, are covered with the veil of silence, but we learn their effects by the simple phrase, that "the land had rest forty years"—the land, the whole land, not merely that which was under her direct superintendence. Virtue, holiness, and wisdom, though the gifts of but one lowly individual, are not confined to one place, when used, as were Deborah's, to the glory of God, and the good of her people. Silently, and perhaps unperceived, they spread over space and time; and oh! how glorious must be the destiny of that woman, who, without one moment quitting her natural sphere, can yet by precept, example, and labor produce such blessed effects as to give the land peace, and bring a whole people unto God!

In a *practical* view, perhaps, the character of Deborah cannot now be brought home to the conduct of her descendants, for woman can no longer occupy a position of such trust and wisdom in Israel; but, *theoretically*, we may take the history of Deborah to our hearts, both *nationally* and individually. With such an example in the Word of our God, it is unanswerably evident that neither the Written nor the Oral Law could have contained one syllable to the disparagement of woman.

Men were in no condition to have permitted the influence of woman, had they not been accustomed, by the constant and emphatic enjoinments of the law, to look on her with respect, consideration, and tenderness. Mentally and spiritually, Deborah was gifted in an extraordinary degree, leading us to infer that the women of Israel must have had the power to cultivate both mind and spirit, and to delight in their resources, for we have the whole Bible to prove that the Eternal never selected for the instruments of His will, any but those whose hearts were inclined towards Him, even before He called them—witness the history of Abraham, Joseph, Moses, David, and others. All and every talent comes from God, but will not work and influence by His sole gift alone. They are given to be improved, persevered in, perfected, by those to whom they are intrusted, and then used in the service of their Giver. It is evident, then, that Deborah had the *inclination* and the *power* to cultivate, perfect, and use the gifts of her God; and this would have been quite impossible, had her social condition been such as the enemies of *scriptural* and *spiritual* Judaism declare. With the history of Deborah in their hands, the young daughters of Israel need little other defence or argument, to convince their adversaries that they require no other creed, nor even a denial of the Oral Law, to teach them their proper position, alike to themselves and their fellows, and in their relative duties towards God and man.

Deborah being a wife, confirms this yet more strongly. There must not only have been perfect freedom of *position*, but of *action;* even more than is found in the history of any modern nation, for we do not find a single instance of a wife being elected to any public office requiring intellect and spirituality, secular and religious knowledge, so completely distinct from her husband. Yet the history of Deborah in no way infers that she was neglectful of her conjugal and domestic duties. There is an unpretending simplicity about her very greatness. The very fact of those she judged coming to her under her own palm-tree, supposes her quiet and retired mode of living. She never leaves her home, except at the earnest entreaty of Barak, which urges her to sacrifice domestic retirement for public good. To a really great mind, domestic and public duties are so perfectly compatible, that the first need never be sacrificed for the last. And that Lapidoth in no manner interfered with the public offices of his wife, called as she was to them by God Himself through His gifts, infers a noble confidence and respectful consideration towards her, evidently springing at once from the national equality and freedom tendered to Jewish women; and from a mind great enough to appreciate and value such talents even in a woman; a greatness not very often found in modern times.

To follow in the steps of our great ancestress is not possible, now that the prophetic spirit is removed from Israel, and the few public offices left us fall naturally to the guardianship of man; yet many and many a Jewish woman is intrusted with one or more talents direct from God; and if she can stretch forth a helping hand to the less enlightened of her people, let her not hold back, from the false and unscriptural belief that woman cannot aid the cause of God, or in any way attain to religious knowledge. His word is open to her, as to man. In Moses' command to read and explain the Law to all people, woman was included by name. And now the whole Bible, Law, Historical books, Psalms, and Prophets, are open to her daily commune, and shall it be said that she has neither the right nor the understanding to make use of such blessed privilege? Shame, shame on those who would thus cramp the power of the Lord, in denying to any one of His creatures the power of addressing and comprehending Him, through the inexhaustible treasure of His gracious word!

Every married woman is judge and guardian of her own household. She may have to encounter the prejudices of a husband, not yet thinking with her on all points; but if she have really a great mind, she will know how to *influence*, without in any way *interfering*. She will know how to serve the Lord in her household without neglecting her duty and affection towards her husband; and by domestic conduct influence society at large, secretly and unsuspectedly indeed, but more powerfully than she herself can in the least degree suppose.

To unmarried women, even as to wives, some talent is intrusted, which may be used to the glory of its Giver. Life is not lent us to be frittered away in an unmeaning little satisfactory run of amusements, or often in their mere fruitless search. There surely is some period in a single woman's existence, when the hopes, ambition, and even favorite amusements, of girlhood must come to an end. Because unmarried, is woman still to believe herself a girl, hoping for, and looking for, a change in her existence, which will in reality never come? Would it not be wiser and better, aye, and incalculably happier, if woman herself withdrew from the sphere of exciting hopes and pleasures which she had occupied in girlhood? If she sought perseveringly and prayerfully some new objects of interest, affection, and employment, which she might justly hope would become a stay and support in rapidly advancing years, and thus entirely prevent the ennui, and its attendants, love of gossip, frivolity, and often sourness and irritability, which are too generally believed to be the sole characteristics of single (and so of course supposed disappointed) women? Have we not all some precious talent lent us by our God, and for the use of which He will demand an account? Is there not the whole human family from which to select some few objects of interest, on whom to expend some of our leisure time, and draw our thoughts from all-engrossing self? Were there but one object on whom we have lavished kindness, and taught to look up to God and heaven, and to walk this earth virtuously and meekly—but one or two whom, had we the pecuniary means, we have clothed and fed—a sick or dying bed that we have soothed—a sorrowing one consoled—an erring one turned from the guilty path—the repentant, or the weak, strengthened and encouraged—we shall not have lived in vain; or, when we come to die, look shudderingly back on a useless life and wasted gifts; on existence lost in the vain struggle to arrest the flight of time, and still seek hope and pleasure in thoughts and scenes, whose sweetness has been too long extracted for aught to remain but bitterness and gall. Deborahs in truth we cannot be; but each and all have talents given, and a sphere assigned them, and, like her, all have it in their power, in the good performed towards man, to use the one, and consecrate the other to the service of their God.

CHAPTER IV.

WIFE OF MANOAH.

SEVERAL years passed since the death of Deborah. Gideon, Tolo, Jair, Jepthah, Ibzan, Elon, and Abdan, had successively judged Israel, often with interregnums of rebellion, apostasy, and anarchy. After the death of the last mentioned judge, "the children of Israel again did evil in the sight of the Lord, and He delivered them into the hands of the Philistines forty years." We now come to another incident in the history of the women of Israel demanding our attention. In the tribe of Dan was a certain man of the city of Zorah, named Manoah, whose wife had no children, always a source of grief in the families of Israel; *not*, as the Christians believe, from the idea of becoming the mother of the promised Messiah (who is scarcely mentioned till the time of the prophets, when the awfully threatened chastisement of the Eternal needed such consolatory promises), but because children were always considered proofs of the Lord's love, a privilege granted from Him as the recompense of faithful service; as we read in the words of David, "Lo, children are an heritage of the Lord: and the fruit of the womb IS HIS REWARD," Psalm cxxvii. And, again, "Thy wife shall be as a fruitful vine by the sides of thine house: and thy children like olive plants around thy table. Behold, *thus shall* the man *be blessed* that feareth the Lord. Thou shalt see thy children's children, and peace on Israel," Psalm cxxviii. To go down childless to the grave, and so prevent the name from being "built up" in Israel, was deemed a heavy affliction, inferring, for some secret sin or public transgression, the anger of the Lord.

Sacred Writ is silent as to the reason of the Eternal's selection falling on the family of Manoah for a deliverer in part from the Philistines, but we are justified in inferring from the context, that they were one of the few faithful followers of Israel, by whom the Law was in all points obeyed. Be that however as it may, this is certain, that it was to the WOMAN, not to the man, the Most High deigned to send His angelic messenger, with not only the blessed revelation that He would grant her a son; but deigning to instruct her as to the food and drink she was to refrain from taking herself, and to the devoting her babe as a Nazarite to the Lord, even from his infancy; thus making the direct commands of the Immutable agree in all points with the Law which His wisdom and mercy had already given.

Naturally astonished, for such revelations were not even then common in Israel, we find "the woman" following the impulse of her confiding nature, hastening on the instant to her husband, and informing him that a man of God had come unto her, and his countenance was very terrible (signifying, not actually terrible, but grand and imposing), like the countenance of an angel of the Lord; but "I asked him not whence he was, neither told he me his name." From this description of the heavenly messenger, it appears that the woman did not consider him in reality an angel, supposing him a man of God or prophet, bearing a message from the Most High, as was usual in Israel, yet still struck by the imposing beauty of his countenance, and feeling it possessed something beyond mortality.

Equally astonished, but *believing*, Manoah lost no time in idle speculation, but betook himself instantly to prayer; thus confirming our idea of his faithfulness and piety, and proving one grand and important national truth, that the Israelites needed no *mediator* whatever, be he man or angel, to bring up their prayers before God, and obtain His gracious reply. Here was Manoah, living on his own estates, in his own tribe, far removed from the priests of the Lord and the tabernacle, through the first of whom alone it is declared, by our opponents, that the prayers of Israel could be acceptably offered up. No priest near, of whom he could either ask or obtain counsel; no wise man or judge, of whom he might demand advice or explanation. Yet the law was then in force all over Israel, and if it had been illegal and derogatory to the dignity of the Lord to address Him in prayer from any place, or at any time, we should have found Manoah hastening without a moment's delay to the appointed spot, and offering sacrifices to obtain the mediation of the anointed priest, knowing that through him only he could obtain reply.

Instead of which, we find him, without even pause or hesitation, believing the words of his wife so implicitly, as to offer up a prayer of such simple construction that it clearly proves how little the Most High regards mere formula in prayer, when springing, as did Manoah's, from humility and faith. "Then Manoah entreated the Lord, and said, O my Lord, let the man of God which thou didst send come again to us, and teach us what we shall do unto the child that shall be born." Here is no doubt expressed as to the reality of the blessing proffered: "The child that shall be born," reveals how fully he believed in the promise; but, as was natural to humanity, he entreated a confirmation of the instructions vouchsafed, not knowing how far the imagination and the fears of his wife might have tinctured her relation.

"And God hearkened to the voice of Manoah." Did we

need any further incentive to "entreat the Lord" in all things, surely we have it here. Manoah had simply spoken the thoughts of his heart in words, which would be their natural vehicle of expression. He had prayed through the merits of neither dead nor living, man nor angel, but in lowly trusting faith, and God hearkened and answered. Again His messenger appeared unto the woman as she sat in the field, Manoah not being with her, and she ran to inform her husband, saying that the man had again appeared unto her, the same who had come previously; and Manoah, no doubt in secret adoring the Beneficent God who had thus deigned to answer his prayer, went with his wife, and demanded of the messenger, if he were indeed the man who had visited them before. And being answered in the affirmative, he besought a repetition of how to "order the child;" and the angel condescended a full reply, reiterating all his previous instructions. Still believing him a man, as himself, only gifted with the spirit of the Lord, Manoah, with the hospitality peculiar to the Hebrew, besought him to remain until "we shall have made ready a kid for thee." And the angel of the Lord said unto Manoah, "Though thou detain me, I will not eat of thy bread. And if thou wilt offer a burnt-offering thou must offer it unto the Lord; *for Manoah knew not that he was an angel of the Lord.* And Manoah said, What is thy name? that when thy sayings come to pass, we may do thee honor. And the angel of the Lord said unto him, Wherefore askest thou thus after my name, seeing it is secret? So Manoah took a kid with a meat-offering, and offered it upon a rock unto the Lord. And it came to pass, when the flame went up toward heaven from off the altar, the angel of the Lord ascended in the flame of the altar, and Manoah and his wife looked on it, and fell with their faces to the ground. And the angel of the Lord did no more appear unto Manoah and his wife: then Manoah knew he was an angel of the Lord. And Manoah said, We shall surely die, for we have seen God [i. e. a messenger direct from God.] But his wife said unto him, If the Lord were pleased to kill us, He would not have received a burnt-offering and a meat-offering at our hands, neither would He have showed us all these things, nor would as at this (second) time have told us such things as these." (Judges xii.)

We have quoted this chapter almost at length, because it contains so much which it is almost imperative for us to consider in a national point of view, before we can come to regard it in its bearings on our history as women. Any elucidation or defence of our national belief will not, we trust, be deemed out of place in a Jewish work, however little it may be pronounced to have to do with the main point of its subject. In an age when so much of controversy is going on, when even the intimate association, and often friendships, between Hebrew and Gentile may bring forward peculiar points of belief, to inquire their differences or varying modes of interpretation—it becomes imperatively necessary for the young Hebrew of either sex to be provided with such defence as will, at least, satisfy his own heart and conscience, and render him invulnerable to the peculiar expositions proffered to his attention, however little such defence may weigh with the hereditary prejudices of his opponents. There is a wide difference between an argument seeking the conversion of another, and that merely defending our own belief in the same sacred authority as gives a supposed foundation for the belief of an opponent. As long as the Christian confines his arguments and quotations to the New Testament, the Israelite feels perfectly secure, from his entire rejection of such authority as Divine. But when the words of the Old Testament are so explained as to bear almost startlingly upon the creed of our adversaries, then it is we need careful, though perfectly simple, training, to provide us both with reply and defence. To be kept in ignorance of the Nazarene readings of the Bible does no good whatever; for there are very few who can hope to pass through life, particularly now that social intercourse is so unrestrained, without some approach to the differences of belief, and their causes. Much better is it to know clearly the danger we are not unlikely to encounter, and how to avert it, than to come upon it wholly unprepared. Not in childhood indeed, for it would be folly to perplex the young mind with the tenets of *two* beliefs: then it is simply necessary to impress and explain the essentials of their own creed; but in maturer years, when the opening mind is not only capable of understanding, but feels itself restless and anxious for something more than the mere education of childhood: then let them compare their belief with that of others; let them know what and why their opponents so believe, through the enlarged and liberal views of a spiritually Jewish instructor; let the light of reason and revelation be their guide, and we shall find both male and female of the Hebrew youth so confirmed in their own blessed faith, as to live and die for it, yet eschewing all of illiberality, uncharitableness, and scorn, towards those of other and less enlightened creeds.

The chapter under consideration is one of those much regarded by the Nazarene, and always brought forward in controversial discussion. From Manoah's simple words, "We have seen God," they believe, that wherever the "angel of the Lord" is mentioned, it signifies the second person of the Godhead; and that as He took visible form to our ancestors of old, so we might equally believe in His taking the form of Jesus to save the world.

To a mere superficial thinker this argument might prove dangerous; and we are therefore anxious to explain this chapter according to the Israelite's belief. In the first place, we refuse to see in this messenger anything more than the Word of God declares, "an angel of the Lord," simply because the Eternal said unto Moses, in answer to his earnest entreaty, "Show me thy glory, THOU CANST NOT SEE MY FACE: FOR THERE SHALL NO MAN SEE ME, AND LIVE." And we therefore know, that no man has or ever can see His face, and live; for God is a God of truth, and knows not the very shadow of a change. That which He has once said is immutable, unwavering, changeless as Himself. That there may be, even in the books of Moses, one or two verses seeming to contradict this assertion, as in Exodus xxiv., verses 10 and 11, and in verse 11 of chapter xxxiii., is of no importance, being either a wrong translation, or the mere manner of writing, to bring down the solemn appearance of the glory of God to the comprehension of the mixed multitude, and impossible to be weighed a single moment with the words of the Most High Himself. Would He declare the solemn truth in one part of His Holy Word, confirming it by every prophet, and in another part command His people, as a condition of their salvation, to believe on His appearing on earth, and conversing face to face with man, first as an angel, and then in human form? The very words of Manoah confirm this belief, and prove it was entertained as strongly by the ancient as the modern Jews. The Nazarenes take only the last member of this sentence, forgetting the important fact, "*We shall surely die, if, indeed*, we have seen God," for such is the real meaning of his words, and that he did not die; and the simple truth of his wife's suggestion convinced him, no doubt, as it convinces us, that it was not God whom he had seen, but one of those angelic messengers whom it sometimes pleased the Lord to employ to deliver His missions unto man. The nature of such beings it needs not now to inquire; but the belief in the existence of angels is so twined with the belief in the Bible, that if we disbelieve the one, we must disbelieve the other. The very word מַלְאָךְ, derived from the Arabic לָאַךְ, *to send*, or *employ*, signifies merely a messenger, a legate, used indiscriminately for one employed by a king as ambassador, or by the Lord as an angel, prophet, or priest; and sometimes also applied to whatever is sent by the Eternal to execute His will, even as winds and plagues.

The grand and imposing aspect of the angelic countenance, as we have seen, struck Manoah's wife; but that neither she nor her husband supposed him anything more than a prophet or priest, is evident by their manner of addressing him, and their entreating him to tarry for refreshment. The angel's reply is strong confirmation of what we have already stated concerning his real office. To eat of their bread would be confirming their idea that he was but a man; to accept their burnt-offering would be arrogating to himself what was due only to his Heavenly Master. "If thou offer a burnt-offering thou must offer it unto the LORD;" not to him, who, though of an angelic nature, was still nothing but a messenger. Still ignorant that he was an angel, Manoah asks his name, to do him honor; and *because he knew how liable were even believing Israelites to turn aside from the worship of the immutable God to worship others, and jealous for the glory of his Master*, the angel refused to tell his name, declaring it was secret—that when his words came to pass, Manoah or his wife might not have even a *name* to turn aside their thoughts from the one sole God; still, to convince them he was not a mere mortal, but came direct from the Lord, he ascended, or disappeared, in the flame of the altar, as had been the sign of the divine acceptance of the offering, from the sacrifice of Abel downwards. And it was knowing this, and recognising the immediate agency of the Most High, in thus sending one of His own messengers, that so overwhelmed Manoah and his wife with religious awe, as to cause them to fall with their faces to the ground, not daring to look even upon the semblance of His glory.

A layman, and a lowly individual of his father's tribe, it was not unnatural that Manoah should even be more awe-struck, than rejoiced, at the revelation so graciously vouchsafed; and whilst the mistaken idea engrossed him, if, indeed, it ever did, that he had conversed with God, he could not do otherwise than fear instant death, for, like all his brethren, he knew the God of Israel was a God of truth; and, therefore, if he had seen him, he must cease to live. The ready answer of his wife removed these groundless fears; and while it told him, that if it had pleased the Lord to kill them, He would not have accepted offerings at their hands, or so revealed His will, it must equally have convinced him, as a believer in the revelation of the Lord through Moses, that it was *not God*, but his messenger whom He had seen.

Such is the simple rendering of this very simple chapter; while the second commandment, and the words already quoted, "No man can see me, and live," with the firm belief that God is TRUTH, are all sufficient wherewith satisfactorily to explain, both to our own hearts and to those of our children, every verse that may seem to read slightly contradictory, and supply us with an impenetrable shield, against which the reasonings of our opponents must fall blunted and harmless to the ground.

Regarding this narrative in its bearings on our history as Women of Israel, it is confirmation strong of our always attested declaration, that neither Written nor Oral Law interfered with the perfect equality of man and wife. The chapter before us displays a simple and natural picture of conjugal confidence and equality, and of the respective peculiarities of man and woman. It is impossible to read this chapter, without perceiving that Manoah's wife was a perfectly free agent, only bound by the links of love and confidence which the marriage law enjoins. As the mother of the child selected to deliver Israel in part from the Philistines, she was even of more importance in the sight of God than her husband, a fact inferred from the angel appearing both times to *her*, and only addressing Manoah when addressed by him. We find, too, Manoah including her alike in all he said and did. "Let *us* detain thee, until *we* have prepared a kid," &c. In the religious observance of the burnt-offering, and in the lowly prostration acknowledging the divine power, Manoah and his *wife* are separately named, proving her perfect equality in all religious observances, and her *right* to partake of them. That the angel never again appeared either to Manoah or his *wife*, is the proof to them that he was a messenger from the Lord. The words, "we shall surely die," included her in the penalty supposed to have been incurred, and mark the female as equally a responsible agent as the male. Still more clearly demonstrative that the Hebrew wife really occupied the free and equal position which the laws of God Himself assigned her, is the fact that it was her ready wit, and quickness of intellect, which reassured her husband. She had been awe-struck like himself, but yet, perfectly in accordance with woman's nature, was the first to comprehend the real intention of the revelation. Man's more solid nature and deeper thought, require time for mature judgment—woman's quicker fancy, and often more easily excited feeling, give her the advantage in the rapidity of comprehension, and, very often, in the correctness of judgment, which man's greater solidity strengthens and matures.

But that Manoah's wife could thus comprehend, and thus correctly judge, implies a domestic and social position which not only permitted, but exercised these peculiar faculties. In an enslaved and degraded position, their possession was practically and theoretically impossible.

We find, then, much even in this brief chapter to interest and instruct us, alike as Hebrew women, and as women taken generally. In the latter, we shall do well to reflect on the simple trusting confidence of Manoah's wife, seeming the more tender and deferential from the greater correctness of judgment manifested afterwards. And so it should always be. However woman may be naturally endowed with superior attainments, with, perhaps, even a greater share of strength and firmness, and a quicker aptitude for intellectual acquirements, still it is her bounden duty so to guide and use these gifts, that they shall never in any way jar upon the feelings of the one chosen as her husband; and check mutual confidence and love by that assumption of superiority, even granted it exist, of all things most irritating to man's nature. It is woman's province to *influence*, never to *dictate;* to conceal, rather than assume superiority. She may find many and many an opportunity to use it for the good of her husband and children, as was the case with the wife of Manoah; but never let her display it—never let her permit her husband to feel his inferiority—never let her withhold confidence, from the mistaken notion that as her judgment is as good, if not better than his, she cannot need his advice or interference—for if she does, she may rest assured that from that instant her influence is at an end for ever.

CHAPTER V.

NAOMI.

We now come to a portion of our history as women of Israel, which, from the loveliness of female character that it displays, has in neither history nor romance been equalled. In the Bible it is termed the book of Ruth; but as Ruth does not properly belong, by birth and ancestry, to the women of Israel, Naomi must be the subject of our consideration. With her history, however, Ruth is so entwined, that we cannot reflect on the one without also pausing on the touching beauty of the other.

The country of Moab, situated in the north-east part of Arabia Petræa, was separated from Judea by the desolate tract of the Dead Sea, and the river Arnon. It could not probably be said ever to have formed part of the land of Canaan; but was one of those nations which the Eternal expressly commanded His people to spare: see Deut. ii. 9.

The Dead Sea was also the boundary of the tribe of Judah; and it is rather a remarkable fact, that Judah and Simeon are the only tribes of Israel who appear to have driven out all the previous Canaanitish possessors. Judah was the first appointed by the Most High to go up against the land; and, accompanied by his brother Simeon, evinced not only more obedience but more valor and military skill. We do not read of them, as of Benjamin, Manasseh, Ephraim, Zebulun, Asher, Naphtali, and Dan, who, with scarcely any fighting, entered into peaceful covenants with the Canaanites, and permitted them to dwell with them even in their cities. Nor, in consequence, do we find recorded of the tribe of Judah those awful crimes and wilful idolatries practised by his brethren. In the early part of Jewish history, Judah was undoubtedly the most faithful tribe, else had he not been the chosen branch, from which, in God's own time, will spring our Restorer and Messiah.

Elimelech was a man of this valiant tribe, and, in consequence of a severe famine which devastated Judea (the punishment, in all probability, of national sin), he removed his family, consisting of a wife and two sons, to the country of Moab, not far distant from their native city, Bethlehem-Judah or Ephratah. Elimelech died in Moab, not very long after he sojourned there; and his two sons, Chilion and Mahlon, took them wives of the women of Moab, and dwelled there about ten years. Such unions were contrary to the given Law of God; and we may infer that, notwithstanding the virtue and attractions of those selected, the act itself as disobedience was displeasing in the sight of the Lord, from the early deaths, without leaving children, of Elimelech's two sons. This, however, is a mere suggestion which may or may not be, and does not infer Divine displeasure against either Orpah or Ruth; as those not under the Law were not bound by its instructions.

During the lifetime of her husband and sons, we hear nothing of Naomi; but it is by her conduct and sentiments in adversity, and the strong affection borne towards her by her daughters-in-law, that we may judge of her previous character.

A faithful wife, an affectionate mother—gentle, meek, trusting—manifesting a simple, guileless piety in every relation, every circumstance of life; such she must have been, or we should not find her in affliction the character which the Word of God displays.

It is not always in prosperity that we discover the true graces of a spiritual character. The quiet, unostentatious discharge of domestic duty—the fond, unwavering affections of domestic life—these strike us not; nay, we often pass them by, wondering at the simplicity and tame-spiritedness which can rest content in such unexciting scenes. But when adversity comes, and strength and piety is to an extraordinary degree displayed, then it is we learn that it *is* in unexciting scenes woman's character is best matured; and we may chance to envy those whom we had before almost despised.

The heart of the Hebrew widow yearned towards that lovely land, from which she had been so long a willing exile for her husband and children's sake—yearned towards it, for it was the land of her brethren, where the Lord had set up His only Tabernacle; where His law had assured her of His especial protection—for she was a *widow* in Israel; where her full heart could pour itself before Him in the congregation of her people—could worship Him in all points according to His law. In Moab she was alone of her race and faith. No wonder she yearned once more to rest in her native land; or that, lonely and aged as she was, she should yet set forth on the weary way. Another reason, also, might thus have urged her: she heard that "the Lord had visited His people with bread," and, therefore, she was no longer guiltless in continuing to sojourn in a heathen land.

Accompanied by her daughters, she departed from "the place where she was;" but, after going some little way together, she tenderly besought them to return, each to her mother's house, praying that the Lord might deal kindly with them, even as they had dealt with the dead and with her; and grant them each rest and peace, with a husband of their own people. Then she kissed them, and they lifted up their voices and wept, saying, "We will surely return with thee unto thine own people." They had lived with her ten years—a long period for the character and conduct to have been tried—and we see what Naomi's must have been, by the grief of her two daughters—unable to part with her, even to return to their own parents. To Naomi, such separation must also have been a heavy trial; but she was too unselfish to wish them to accompany her to a land of strangers. With renewed tenderness, then, she sought to turn them from their purpose, telling them she might no longer give them husbands; thus alluding to the law of her people, which commands the brother or nearest kinsman of the deceased to take unto himself the childless wife; and then only do we hear this meek and pious mother in Israel revert to her heavy affliction. "It grieveth me much, for your sakes, that the hand of the Lord is gone out against me." She recognised the hand of the Lord, and met her individual sorrows not only with uncomplaining resignation, but feeling yet more deeply for her daughters than for herself, and seeking to console them—leaving her own consolation to Him who had smitten and would heal. No wonder that her fond words increased their grief and bade them weep again: but the effect on the sisters was different. Orpah was one of the many, feeling painfully at the moment, passionately desirous to evince that she felt, but liable to be easily diverted from her purpose. Penetrating no deeper than the surface, she, perhaps, believed Naomi's words as neither desiring nor requiring her further company; and, therefore, repeatedly she kissed her mother-in-law and wept, but at length turned back to her own home. Much as she loved the aged Naomi, earnestly as she wished to serve her, she had not sufficient firmness and steadiness of character to *act of herself*, and set at naught the persuasions of affection. Gentle and yielding, it was easier for her to *grieve* than to *act;* and is not this the nature of many women? They fear to abide by their own judgment when two alternatives are presented to them. They hesitate and linger, fearing to commit themselves by decision, and so are guided by a breath. Accustomed to express all their own impulses and feelings without regarding others, such natures cannot possibly understand those firmer and less selfish ones, who would do violence to their own wishes, to secure what may seem the greater share of happiness for another. That Orpah was one of these, solves her conduct far more justly and agreeably than to suppose her, as many do, merely *professing* a love and regret which she could not really feel—else, she too would have followed Naomi. Orpah was woman in her *weakness;* Ruth, woman in her *strength;* and both are as beautifully true to woman's nature now as then.

Ruth's own unselfish character gave her the clue to her mother-in-law's words. She could understand that Naomi might persuade them to return home, and yet cling to them as her last ties on earth. To Ruth action was better than passive grief, deeds than the tenderest words; and, therefore, when Naomi besought her to follow her sister-in-law, and return to her own people, Ruth's sole answer was couched in words exquisitely illustrative of the deep tenderness, the firm devotion, the beautiful deference of her individual character:—"Entreat me not to leave thee, or to return from following thee. Whither thou goest, I will go; and where thou lodgest, I will lodge. Thy people shall be my people, and thy God my God. Where thou diest, I will die, and there will I be buried. The Lord do so to me, and more also, if aught but death part me and thee!"

Not the most carefully studied oration could breathe more

undying, changeless, self-submitting devotion, than these few and simple words. Naomi was evidently poor. The riches of the Hebrews did not consist then of such wealth as would provide for their families after their death; land and its produce constituted their possessions; and these, where there were no males to cultivate, could not prevent the female survivors from being poor as well as bereaved. Naomi's return to her own land would, of course, according to the law of God, secure her provision; but in the constant rebellion and disobedience of the people, it was precarious and uncertain—she might not even be recognised by her countrymen, so long a time had elapsed since she had left Ephratah. By her earnest entreaties for her daughters to return, it is evident that sufficiency and comfort marked their own homes. Yet Ruth unhesitatingly resigned them all to share her mother-in-law's fate, whatever it might be. Bidding farewell to the friends, scenes, and associations of her youth, not for a time, but for a life, some cause for this pure devoted love there must have been. Ruth's simple words not only reveal the beauty of her own character, but that of the aged Naomi. Affection is ever the impulse to devotion and unselfishness. The human heart ever needs something to which so to cling as to be drawn out from self, and Ruth was not a character to devote her affections and energies to an unworthy object. We know what the character of Naomi must have been in those ten or twelve years of which we hear nothing, by the simple devotedness of Ruth in her adversity.

And what a comfort to that lone heart must have been the soothing words and "steadfast mindedness" of the Moabitish damsel. Must not she whom we shall find, under every circumstance of joy or grief, looking to the Lord alone, and tracing all things from His Almighty hand, have felt this comfort came from him—and that even then she had not trusted in vain. In the midst of affliction He sent consolation; in her deepest loneliness, raised up an earthly friend. Here, as we have already seen in the love of Isaac for Rebekah, we find the tender compassion of the Eternal for His creatures manifested in giving human comfort; He not only pours spiritual balm into the bleeding heart, but provides some being on whom its quivering affections may again find rest, and whose faithful love shall fill the aching void. To the bereaved wife and mother, left in her old age alone, a withered tree from which every leaf and flower has gone, with no hope of ever bearing more, Ruth's affection must have been indeed a precious balm. Without her, Naomi had been *alone*, and oh, at all times, how fearful is the suffering included in that word! Yet more in the adversity of bereavement and old age!

We do not hear how long the travellers journeyed, but Holy Writ simply, yet forcibly, brings before us the wonder and sympathy excited by the Bethlehemites on Naomi's return, "and it came to pass, when they were come to Bethlehem, that all the city was moved about them, and they said, 'Is this Naomi?'" Can we not fancy the whole city flocking to look upon the travellers, to discover if indeed the rumor of Naomi's return could be correct—and anxious, if it were, to give her kindly welcome? Struck by her look of years and sorrow, remembering her only as the fair and pleasant-looking wife of Elimelech, then in her freshest prime, marvelling one to another, can this indeed be Naomi? It is a complete picture of that primitive union of family and tribe, peculiar to early Judaism. Men were not then so engrossed with self, as to feel no sympathy, no interest, out of their own confined circle. They could spare both time and feeling to "be moved" at the return of a country-woman, who had been absent so long; and to grieve with her at those heavy afflictions which caused her to reply to their eager greetings, "Call me not Naomi, call me Mara, for the Almighty hath dealt very bitterly with me; I went out full, and the Lord hath brought me home again empty. Why then call ye me Naomi, seeing that the Lord hath testified against me, and the Almighty hath afflicted me?"

Again we find Naomi in meek submission referring all the events of her life to her God, yet uttering no complaint; she alludes to her heavy afflictions indeed,—alludes to them *as afflictions*, as God himself ordained—not as some enthusiasts would seek to persuade us, that all bereavements are to be considered joys, and so received with thanksgiving and praise, that pain is not to be pain, if sent by the hand of the Lord. This is not the spirit of the Jewish religion, as taught and practised in the Bible. Our Father demands not such violence done to the heart which He hath so mercifully and so wisely stored with such vast capabilities of pleasure and of pain. He demands not that sorrow is to be looked on as joy, and joy to be despised as leading us far from Him. When He tries us in affliction, where would be its spiritual improvement in faith and submission, if we are to welcome it as joy? Where would be the trial of pain, if it be not pain? No! God loves us too well to forbid the healing and saving influence of that holy grief, which, without detaching us from the sweet and lovely links of earth that He Himself vouchsafed, will yet lead us to Him, convinced that He afflicts for our eternal good; that He acts, even in bereavement, through His changeless love, and that He who smote, in His own time will heal. No sorrow has yet been soothed by the vain philosophy which would seek to lessen either its pang or its extent. The sufferer must weep and mourn awhile; but if it be in the spirit of Naomi there will still be comfort found.

Naomi makes no complaint; but how deeply she feels the contrast between her return to, and her departure from, Bethlehem, we read in her shrinking from the name of her youth, which, signifying pleasantness, sweetness, and grace, too painfully recalled the days when those terms were applicable, not only to the charms of her personal character, but the pleasantness and sweetness of her daily life. Bitterness and sadness were more applicable to her present lot, than the sweetness and joyance which had characterized it heretofore; and therefore she bids them call her Mara—but it is not complaint; it is but the natural shrinking of humanity from the memory of the past, contrasted with the suffering of the present.

It was at the beginning of the barley harvest Naomi and her daughter-in-law arrived at Bethlehem. There, it appears from the context, the former sought a retired and very humble dwelling. Notwithstanding that she had a wealthy kinsman, of the family of Elimelech, who, had she applied to him, was bound by the law to give her all the relief she needed, the gentle, unassuming nature of the widow preferred retirement and lowliness, to *claiming* the attention of her wealthy kinsman. The contrast between their respective positions was too great; and how beautifully does this shrinking from making herself known to Boaz, or even from revealing his existence to Ruth, betray her gentle dignity!—and that self-esteem, ever proceeding from true piety. The character of Naomi is consistent in all its parts, forcibly marking one who, from youth to age, was found true to herself and to her God.

The holy narration tells us, that "it was *Ruth's hap* to light on a part of the field belonging to Boaz." Had she known his near connexion, her refinement and delicacy of feeling would have led her to any other field in preference. The whole scene which follows is a most beautiful illustration of the domestic manners and customs of the early Jews, and all in exact accordance with the given law. The kind and conciliatory manner of Boaz, "the mighty man of wealth," to his dependents; his salutation, and their reply; evince how completely the thought and recollection of the God of Israel was entwined with the daily work of his people. The intimate acquaintance which Boaz must have had with all his household, male and female, from his instant discovery of the youthful stranger, and the reply of the reapers, all breathe a refinement and civilization of feeling and action, found at this period only amidst the people of the Lord.

Boaz confirmed the kindness of his dependents, by addressing Ruth in words of such gentle courtesy, peculiarly adapted to reassure and soothe her. He not only tells her to glean in his field alone—there was no need for her to go further—but to abide by his maidens, thus removing unconsciously all painful feelings on her being a Moabitish stranger, which would keep her aloof. He told her, too, to follow close after the reapers, that she should receive neither harshness nor insult, and when she was athirst, to drink freely from that which the young men had drawn.

With the respect ever proffered to real goodness, and astonished at such unexpected kindness, Ruth replied in words, the meekness and humility of which increased Boaz's prepossession in her favor, and confirmed all which rumor had already proclaimed concerning her. "Why have I found grace in thy eyes," she said, "that thou shouldst take this knowledge of me, seeing I am a stranger?" And how must her heart have throbbed with natural pleasure at Boaz's rejoinder, "It hath been fully showed me all that thou hast done unto thy mother-in-law, since the death of thine husband: how thou hast left father and mother, and the land of thy nativity, and art come unto a people which thou knewest not heretofore. The Lord recompense thy work, and a full reward be given thee of the Lord God of Israel, under whose wings thou art come to trust." Deserved approbation *is* sweet, however some stern Stoics may say that virtue is its own reward, and if conscience approves we need no more. Ruth must at once have felt that it was not the mere kindness springing from a good heart, which dictated Boaz's conduct to her, but that she was known and appreciated, stranger as she was. A coarser and more worldly nature than that of Boaz, even while it equally benefited, would have *exalted itself*, not the being it served; would have manifested kindness only because it would obtain personal praise, and care little for the feeling of the person served. Boaz, on the contrary, removed the idea of obligation to himself by elevating Ruth, and making her believe that to her own virtue, not to his kindness, she owed the attention she received. "Let me still find favor in thy sight, my lord," was her grateful reply; "for thou hast comforted me, and hast spoken friendly to thy handmaid, though I be not like one of thine own handmaidens." We never find Ruth forgetting her origin, nor in any way assuming the privileges which her acceptance of and belief in Naomi's God might naturally have assigned her; a lowliness which secured her, unasked, the privileges which, from a contrary conduct, would, no doubt, have been refused.

Not content with desiring her freely to share the meal provided for his reapers, Boaz himself reached her the "parched corn,"—seeing that she ate till she was sufficed; and when she rose up again to glean, he gave orders to let her glean amid the sheaves, and reproach her not, and also "to let fall some handfuls on purpose for her." His generosity, and her own perseverance, enabled her to take home an ephah of barley. And Naomi, eager to bring her child refreshment, not knowing how she might have fared during the day, "brought forth and gave to her the food which she had reserved for her;" affectionately asking from her, at the same time, where and what she had gleaned, and fervently blessing him who had thus taken knowledge of her. Ruth's reply elicited a burst of thanksgiving from Naomi. "Blessed be the Lord, who hath not left off his kindness to the living and the dead." She felt it was no chance, but her God, who had guided Ruth to the field of their kinsman, and infused his heart with kindness towards her. Convinced now that their restoration to their rights would be brought about by the direct agency of her God, she no longer scrupled to impart to Ruth the near relationship of Boaz; and when Ruth repeated his injunctions, to keep fast by his young men until they had ended all his harvest, Naomi, still tracing divine agency, gladly replied, "It is good, my daughter, that thou go out with his maidens, that they meet thee not in any other field." And Ruth, in unquestioning obedience, "kept fast by the maidens of Boaz, to glean unto the end of the barley and wheat harvest, and dwelt with her mother-in-law." Not all that was in all probability reported of her devotion and beauty, could tempt her to turn aside from her lowly path of usefulness and good. Novelty and change could have had no glare for her, or she might have restlessly longed to join the gleaners of other fields. She was too grateful for the friendly kindness of Boaz, too devoted to her mother-in-law, to wish to go beyond the field of the former, or the humble house of the latter. "Where thou lodgest I will lodge." she had said, and her words were but the index of her actions.

But the time had now come when her earthly lot was to undergo a material change. Naomi, who had, in all probability, passed the intervening days in thought and prayer, determined on seeking the rest and prosperity of her devoted daughter, according to the dictates of the law. She therefore gave Ruth the necessary directions—directions which to us may appear strange, and even revolting, but which seem, in the time of Naomi, to have been authorized by custom, and therefore containing nothing whatever indelicate or forward. To Ruth, as a Moabitess, the whole proceedings might have felt unusual, and perhaps even painful; but we have neither remark nor hesitation. She asks not wherefore, but simply says, "All that thou sayest unto me I will do." She had *proved* the affection and wisdom of her mother-in-law much too long to doubt them now, however her own feelings and judgment might shrink from the course of action proposed. Naomi's influence had ever been that of *love*, not of authority, and therefore was she ever sure of unquestioning obedience.

Human means Naomi refused not to adopt, but still she left the entire *end* of these means to the justice and mercy of her God. She knew that in His hand was the heart of Boaz, and therefore she merely told Ruth how to obtain his attention, leaving it to him "to tell thee what thou shalt do;" convinced that the Lord, in whom she trusted, would order the end aright.

All took place as she had anticipated.

Waking in terror at midnight—a terror not a little increased by finding some one lying at his feet—Boaz demanded, "Who art thou?" and received such a reply as at once calmed his affright, and roused him to a renewal of all the nobleness and generosity of his character. Some of our Hebrew translators of this book suppose Ruth's words, "Spread, therefore, thy skirt over thine handmaid, for thou art a near kinsman," to signify, "Give me thy protection as a husband;" and, as such, was in exact accordance with the law; we rather incline towards the opinion.

The reply of Boaz reassured the trembling suppliant; for steadily she had adhered to the straight path of duty, "following neither young men, neither rich nor poor," so that the whole city "knew that she was a virtuous woman." He proceeded to inform her that he was indeed their near kinsman, but there was one still nearer, whose duty it was to perform the husband's part; but that if he refused, even he, Boaz, pledged himself to do so, as the Lord liveth, bidding her lie down till morning; but ere the day broke so that one could recognise another, Ruth rose to depart, encouraged so to do by him with whom she had so fearlessly trusted herself, and whose care for her reputation was tender and thoughtful as a brother's. Nor did he send her away empty. Fearful lest she and her mother-in-law might be in want ere the business could be settled, he filled her veil with six measures of barley, with which she returned to her home; and Naomi bid her sit calmly down until they knew how the matter would fall.

There is no need to transcribe the events detailed in the fourth chapter, from the 1st to the 12th verse. A reference to the word of God itself is all that is needed on the part of our readers, to impress them forcibly with the beautiful picture of the manners and customs of our ancestors which it presents. The gate of the city was always the place of public judgment, that all the people might be aware of what was going on, and give their suffrages, and witness for or against. Thither Boaz repaired the very next morning after his interview with Ruth, and sat him down, waiting the appearance of the person he had named as the nearer of kin than himself. He hailed him on his approach, and the man willingly turned aside from his intended path, and sat down by the gate. Boaz next assembled ten elders, and stated his business. The field which Naomi wished disposed of, the kinsman seemed willing to redeem: but the remainder of his duty, to raise up the name of the dead to his inheritance, he refused, on the plea that to do so would interfere with his own inheritance; requiring Boaz, in consequence, to redeem the right for himself, as he, the nearest kinsman, could not; loosening at the same time his shoe, or glove, as some commentators believe, and giving it to his neighbor, as confirmation of his words. Boaz then addressed the elders and the people, bidding them be witness that he had purchased of the hand of Naomi all that was Elimelech, Chilion, and Mahlon's, and Ruth, the wife of Mahlon, to be his wife, that he might raise up the name of the dead, and so let it not be cut off from his brethren, or the gate of his place. And the elders of the people bore witness joyfully, coupled with earnest aspirations that the Lord might make the woman he had chosen, like Rachel and like Leah, who had built up the house of Israel; and that he himself might "do worthily in Ephratah, and be famous in Bethlehem."

And so he was: for as the great-grandfather of David, the name of Boaz must indeed be still famous in Judah, and dear to Israel. The uncomplaining submission and lowly trust of Naomi, and the filial obedience and devotion of Ruth, were both alike rewarded; for the latter not only became the wife of the generous and noble-minded Boaz, but, in due course of time, God granted her a son; and Naomi, who had believed herself but a withered branch, to which neither joy nor fruitfulness might ever return, "took the child, and laid it on her bosom, and became nurse to it." We may read in the lively greetings of the women of Bethlehem, the joy which this event occasioned, and their affectionate sympathy in Naomi's previous affliction. "Blessed be the Lord," they said, "who hath not left thee this day without a kinsman, that his name may be famous in Israel. And he shall be unto thee a restorer of life, and a nourisher of thine old age, for thy daughter-in-law, who loveth thee, and who is *better to thee than seven sons*, hath borne him."

How beautifully do these words express the women of Israel's appreciation and love of the gentle Moabitess! The babe would be a restorer of Naomi's life, and a cherisher of her old age, *for he was Ruth's son.* She who had been to Naomi better than seven sons (in the Hebrew the number is unlimited), would not fail to rear up her child in such virtue and holiness as would make his name indeed precious in Israel, and a blessing to his grandmother. Nor can we doubt that the affection and devotedness marking their mutual intercourse in adversity, was lessened in prosperity. The love which had been so mutually proved was not likely to decrease, but would rather deepen with every passing year.

With the genealogy of Boaz, down to David, this most interesting book concludes; and before we proceed to notice the beautiful lessons of domestic life which it inculcates, we would endeavor to prove how mistaken is the objection, sometimes brought forward, that Ruth, a Moabitess, should have been the ancestress of David, the elected servant of the Lord. When Ruth resigned alike home, parents, and the gods of her youth, she voluntarily engrafted herself upon the children of God; and we know that such engrafting was permitted, not only from the Law, but from its after-explanation by the prophets. In the Law we repeatedly find the command to save the *virgins alive*, even of those nations whom they were commanded to exterminate, that they might be brought to the worship of the One true God, and multiply Israel. In the Prophets we read, that those of the stranger, whether male or female, who voluntarily accepted the covenants of the Lord, and kept His sabbaths and appointed feasts and ordinances, even had they been only eunuchs before, were (see Isaiah, chap. lxvi. 3–8), instead of being despised, to receive a place and a name in His house, better even than sons and daughters, an everlasting name which shall not be cut off, to be brought to the holy mountain, and made joyful in His house of prayer; and their burnt-offerings and sacrifices, the essential privilege of the Holy People, accepted on God's altar. In the Law, too, we find repeated injunctions,—"love ye the stranger, for ye were strangers in the land of Egypt;" and by the whole history of Ruth we see how precisely this law was obeyed. She was one of those coming under the denomination of "the stranger," and who yet, from her acceptance of the Lord's sabbaths, covenants, &c., all of which is implied in her own words, "thy God shall be my God," deserved and received the privileges enumerated above.

She was yet more than a daughter in His sight, because her acceptance of, and obedience to the Law, were entirely *voluntary;* not merely received from education and as heritage. That God is no respecter of persons, we read throughout the whole of His changeless word. Faithfulness and virtue, the *heart*,—but neither birth nor appearance—are valued by Him. And when, therefore, Ruth turns from all the associations and scenes of her youth, to adopt and accept the religion of Naomi, and faithfully serve her God, she is in act no longer a Moabitess (and is only called so to designate her as a stranger amidst Israel), but as worthy, if not even more so, to be the ancestress of David, than the lineal descendants of Abraham, who were Israelites, because God had selected them so to be; *not* for their own sakes, or their own worth, but simply for the love He bore, and the promise He made unto His favored servants. Ruth became an Israelite from *voluntary adoption*. Her filial devotion and reverence was the most exquisite illustration of *how* she not only accepted, but obeyed the Law; and, from the character of David, still more than even his selection, we may easily infer how faithfully she not only obeyed the Law herself, but transmitted it to her descendants. That the Eternal should have selected a king whose great-grandmother was of Moabitish descent, cannot, then, we think, with any justice be brought forward as matter either of wonder or objection. If it were unlawful for any stranger to be engrafted upon Israel we should not find so many laws regarding "the stranger" in the Mosaic code itself, nor their *practical commentary* in Isaiah, as quoted above. Her virtue and goodness gave her favor in the sight alike of God and man, and rendered her worthy of being the ancestress of that holy line whence the Messiah himself will spring—while her voluntary acceptance of the God, and of course the faith, of Naomi, removed from her own Moabitish birth all reproach, and gave her yet a dearer name in the eyes of God and of His people than even that of daughter.

To us, as women of Israel, the whole book of Ruth teems with unspeakable consolation and support. It is a picture so vivid of the manners, customs, aye, and even feelings of Israel at that period, that even Gentile writers are struck by it, and refer to it with high eulogiums on its touching beauty and impressive truth. Shall we then value it less, and refuse to draw from it the strong confirmation which it contains of our contested point—the refined and elevated position of the women of Israel themselves, and the tender yet respectful consideration with which they were regarded by their brethren? Will any one point of Naomi's character permit us to suppose, that during her husband's lifetime she was merely a slave, with neither religious, moral, nor intellectual training? Had she been such in Elimelech's lifetime, such she must have remained. Instead of which, from her determination to return to her own land, and worship her God once more amongst her own people, we perceive that she was a woman of strong mind and unfailing energy; while from the affection of both her sons' wives, and the devotion of one, we must equally infer that she possessed, and in her domestic duties must have displayed, such winning and amiable qualities, as to call such affection forth; these characteristics, and all which follow—the refined and retiring dignity, the correct judgment, and also the patient faith in her God—all were quite incompatible with a degraded position either individually or socially. It is very clear, then, that not in any received Law of Israel could the position of the women of Israel have been that which our enemies so ignorantly report. If *two* Laws were in action at this period, one must have been an exact repetition of the other, or in a book like that of Ruth, so strikingly illustrative of the national character and customs, some difference must have been discernible.

If, then, the charge on modern Judaism be really founded on apparent truth, it must be a state of things brought about by the awful horrors of persecution, and their natural effect in narrowing and brutalizing the human mind. In all that relates to Ruth too, we see the real light in which the Hebrew woman was regarded, very clearly. We should not find her filial devotion and individual goodness so appreciated by all the Bethlehemites, female as well as male, were not virtue and goodness in woman subjects of admiration, of cherishing, and respect. It was not only in obedience to the Law, which commanded love and kindness to be shown towards the stranger, that Boaz so encouraged and cherished her when first gleaning in his field. He expressly states the wherefore, *because of* her devotion to her mother-in-law, and her having given up her father's gods to accept Him under whose wings she had come to trust. "A full reward shall be given thee from the Lord," he says; thus marking her as accepted and cherished by God as well as man. The most reverential yet fatherly care marks the whole of his conduct towards her; and here we see very strongly marked the obedience to the law instituted for the benefit of the stranger; he not only "showed kindness," but literally left for her the "gleanings of his field."

The third chapter of the sacred story most emphatically proves the superiority of morality and civilization in Israel, over the known world. In what other nation could Ruth have so trusted herself, as she did to the honor and justice of Boaz? How fully must Naomi have been assured of the safety of her child, or how could she have counselled such a mode of proceeding? and how completely she was justified in her confidence, we read in Boaz's anxiety to save Ruth from all insulting remarks, by letting it "not be known that a woman had been to the floor."

Again, in Boaz's instant pursuance of Ruth's suit, we very clearly perceive that women must have been considered of some account; and also another important point in a national view, Boaz's exact obedience to the formula of the Law, in calling the nearest kinsman to give his attention to the subject, and decide, notwithstanding his own evident anxiety to obtain Ruth as his wife, unquestionably proves, that as the Law was so strictly kept in *one point*, so it would be in *all;* and consequently there could have been, neither practically nor theoretically, any one single statute to the disparagement of woman.

The very joy of the whole people in Boaz's decision to make Ruth his wife; their hearty congratulations, and earnest wishes for his welfare, and hers, that she might be as Leah and Rachel; the delight of the women, and their joyous sympathy with Naomi at the unexpected issue to all her misfortunes; all prove the beautiful unity and love marking the people of the Lord. All seemed to vie with each other in making their respective tribes as one affectionate family, bound by the same ties, hoping the same hope, trusting the same God, weeping with those that wept, and rejoicing with those that joyed.

Such a state of things could never have existed if the women of Israel had not been, morally, spiritually, and intellectually, on a perfect equality with man.

Regarding the book of Ruth in its final bearings—that is, as it concerns women in general—we are particularly struck with the exquisite lesson of maternal and filial affection which it teaches. The beauty of Ruth's words and actions sometimes occupies attention alone, to the exclusion of the tenderness characterizing Naomi, which, to our feelings, is equally touching and impressive. Ruth's determination to quit her own land, her parents, and their gods, was indeed one of beautiful self-devotion; but it was evidently LOVE, not duty, which impelled it, and that love must have been called forth by the tenderness she had originally received. Seldom is the love of the young excited to such an extent towards an elder, unless by affection and appreciation from that elder, invited so to love; and not only *invited* but *retained* by unwavering kindness and regard. That such feelings had always actuated Naomi towards her daughter-in-law, we infer, from the caressing tenderness with which, in all that passes between them, she invariably addressed her. We never can read either coldness or indifference, much less the harsh mistrust, breathing often more in *tone* than actual words, which sometimes characterizes the manner of an elder towards a younger. All she says, either in persuasion to return, or in advice or inquiry, is with the same caressing love. In her bringing forth on Ruth's return the remains of the day's meal, which she had been compelled to take while Ruth was absent, how touchingly we read the love lingering with her absent child, the thought of saving for her the evening meal, and bringing it with eager haste the moment Ruth appeared, not knowing how she might have fared during the hot and weary day.

Oh! while we would have our young sisters imitate, as they cannot fail to love, the conduct of Ruth, will not their elders do well to ponder on, and imitate, the tenderness of Naomi? Youth will not, *cannot* love, a pure unselfish love, unless invited so to do; no, not even in the sanctuary of home, not even parents, unless love, not only *felt* but *displayed* in confidence and caressing kindness, marks the parental conduct. Duty done on either side is not enough, for it is not according to the spirit of the Lord, and of His word. There love predominates, and so should it predominate in the homes of His children. We do not deny that it does, but we would have it displayed as well as felt, by every member of that hallowed temple, HOME. Brothers and sisters, parents and children, twined together in that sacred silvery link, unbroken even by death; for they know it is immortal. Love not only felt, but breathing in every tone, and actuating every deed; confidence and trust—mutually given, mutually felt. How thrice blessed would such things make home! The parental heart would not then bleed in secret, at what seems like neglect and unkindness, if not an utter want of love. Nor would the young spirit shrink within itself, chilled and sad—yearning for affection *spoken* as well as felt; and utterly unconscious how truly and how deeply they may still be loved. How different is that home where no gentle word is heard—no caress asked for, or voluntarily bestowed—no interchange of mutual thought; but each member walks alone, seeking no sympathy save from the stranger, caring not to shed one flower on the parental hearth, and believing they have no place in the parental heart *save as a child*, words of which, until they are parents themselves, they know not, guess not, the unutterable meaning. How different is such a home to that where love is *visible!* Where parents and, as its natural consequence, children vie with each other, as to who can *prove* it most; and by the words and manners of daily life, throw such a beautiful halo even over its cares and sorrows, as inexpressibly heightens its sweetest joys.

There are some to doubt the love that dwells in caressing words and a loving manner. Yet why should it be doubted, till its absence has been proved? Why should the gentle power be despised, which will make daily life happier, and so inexpressibly soothe the sickness and sorrow which ask but love alone. No! It is the icy surface we must doubt, for never yet were there warm and unselfish loving hearts, who could think it necessary to suppress such fond emotions in the sweet sanctuary of *home.* It is the cold at heart who never give *domestic* affections vent, and can therefore never hope so to attract the young, as to rouse them to evince the love they could have felt, or proffer more than the cold, dull routine of daily duty. *We must love to be loved*—we must evince that love, would we so unite young hearts to our own, as, if needed, to sacrifice all of self for us, or to devote life, energy, hope, all to our service. Would we have our daughters Ruths, we must be Naomis; we have no right, no pretence, to demand more than we *evince*, as well as give. Reserve, coldness, command, may win us duty, but duty in the domestic circle is a poor substitute for love. Even kindness *in act* is often undervalued, nay, absolutely unknown, if it be not hallowed by the kindness of manner and of word. In the *world*, words and manner may be deceiving, but not in the temple of home; for the love which would there dictate kindness of manner must equally incite kind deeds. The latter may exist without the former, and if only one may have existence, we may grant the superiority of good deeds, though there are some griefs, some trials, which kindly *words* may soothe, where *action* has no power. Oh! let us unite the two as Ruth and Naomi—and however dark and troubled our earthly course, a light will shine within our homes, which no sorrow, nor care, nor even death, will have power to darken or remove. God is Love—the spirit of His word is Love; and would we indeed walk according to His dictates, Love, proved alike in *word* and *deed*, must be the Guardian Angel of our homes!

CHAPTER VI.

HANNAH.

In the history of the Jews by Josephus, the story of Hannah is mentioned as taking place before that of Ruth. We prefer following the arrangement of the Bible, although it is not improbable that Ruth and Hannah lived much at the same time; for we find the son of Hannah, when a very old man, visiting the grandson of Ruth, then in his prime, to choose from his household his youngest born as the anointed of the Lord. The period of the existence of these two beautiful female characters is in itself of little importance; but it is interesting to trace the intimate connexion of their descendants, thrown together as they were so closely in after life.

There was a certain man, living in the city of Rama Sophim of Mount Ephraim, an Ephrathite by descent, named Elkanah, who had two wives, Hannah and Peninnah. It is a remarkable fact, that this is the very first mention of a man having two wives since the days of Jacob. Joseph, Moses, Aaron and his sons, Caleb, Othniel, Lapidoth, Manoah, Elimelech, Chilion, and Mahlon, all had but one wife; a striking confirmation of our former assertion, that though polygamy was permitted, from its being an immemorial usage, *it was not*, in the early days of Israel, considered a necessary part of their domestic policy; and that almost every great and good man selected by the Eternal to work His will, before the monarchy, had but the one wife for whom the laws were given; and so evinced, in their own persons, the incipient dawnings of that more refined and elevated state of being and society, which in the natural progression of humanity would undoubtedly ensue.

The abuse of the permission to have more than one wife without transgressing the Law, which grew to such an awful height during the continuance of the monarchy, is no evidence of the degrading nature of the Law, but is the literal fulfilment of the threatened wrath of the Eternal, when the people insisted upon having an earthly king to rule over them, like other nations. That he would not only take unto himself their store and their fields, and their olive-yards and vineyards, but even their sons and their daughters to minister to his service and his pleasures; and, of course, the licentious conduct of the sovereign would be followed by equal license in his subjects.

But before the monarchy, though the people were ever in rebellion and disobedience, still no such domestic abuses had existence. Even when there were two wives, as in the case we are about to consider, we find the beautiful laws, instituted for domestic equity and peace, entering and guiding a man's household, as the Eternal had intended in their bestowal. Yet even these, while they prevented all justice on the part of the husband, could not entirely do away with the evils of a divided household, which Sacred Writ never fails to record for our warning.

"And Elkanah, with his wives and household, went up out of his city yearly to worship and sacrifice unto the Lord in Shiloh," then the residence of God's holy ark, and of his priests,—a *practical* confirmation of the law so to do, which we have already noticed. At these times, "he gave to Peninnah his wife, and to all her sons and daughters, portions, but unto Hannah he gave a double portion; for he loved Hannah: though the Lord had not granted her any children,"—loved her for herself, even above Peninnah, though she had given him a goodly progeny, and Hannah had but her own gentle virtues, which were sufficient for her husband.

But in Israel the denial of children was considered too sad a reproach, too painfully a proof of individual unworthiness in the sight of God, for the meek spirit of Hannah to endure it without bitter grief; a grief painfully aggravated by the provocations of her more favored rival, whose unkind reproaches increased with every year that diminished Hannah's hope. Still, Holy Writ tells us of no complaint on the part of Hannah against Peninnah. As the more beloved by her husband, had she told him of the continual provocations she received, she might have been sure of such interference as would have effectually shielded her from them in future, though at the expense of alienating Peninnah from her husband, and causing domestic strife. But such a course of acting was not according to Hannah's character. It was easier far to suffer than to complain; sweeter far to endure herself than seek revenge upon another.

Each visit to Shiloh excited anew the reproaches of Peninnah; and as this took place some years before Elkanah noticed the deep grief of his favorite wife, we may in a degree suppose the extent of Hannah's gentle forbearance. Hers was no trial of a day, or even a month, but of years; and can we imagine anything more trying to the heart and temper, than to live with one whose tongue was ever bitter with reproach? because it is not likely that it was *only* during their visits to Shiloh that "Peninnah provoked her sore, to make her fret," and provoked her for no fault; for nothing which Hannah herself could remedy, but simply for being less favored by the Lord. And yet, how many are there like her! How many love to reproach instead of soothe, as if sorrow and disappointment were the *fault* of the sufferers, not the loving sentence of the Lord! How many there are who thus make a daily life bitter to their fellows, instead of, as they might do, rendering grief less sad, and inexpressibly heightening joy.

Their visits to Shiloh must have been fraught with deep suffering to Hannah. It was not only the signal of Peninnah's aggravated unkindness; but the very sight of all her fellow-countrymen flocking to the temple of the Lord,* with their goodly show of sons and daughters, must have made her pious

* Though that house of God which we are accustomed to regard as the Temple was not built till the reign of Solomon, the residence of the Ark of God was always called the Temple. See 1 Sam. i. 9.

heart shrink deeper and deeper within itself in its own unspoken woe: and it is shown in her spirit's sad but unmurmuring inquiry, "Why had the Lord whom she loved and sought to serve, so reproached and forsaken her?" That this was really the case, and her grief was never spoken, never found vent in reproachful words, we know by Elkanah's gently reproving address. "Hannah, why weepest thou?" he said, "why eatest thou not? and why is thy heart grieved? Am not I better to thee than ten sons?" Here there is no reference to anything but Hannah's visible sorrow, and to Elkanah's natural supposition as to the cause of her grief; and in perfect accordance with the meek enduring beauty of her true womanly character, she makes no complaining answer. It would have been easy for her to exculpate herself for too repining sorrow by invectives against her happier rival; but she who had borne so much and so long, was far too spiritual for such petty revenge. Answer to man, save such as affection would dictate, the struggle to smile and be happy for a loved one's sake, she made none; but sought relief, where alone it might be found, at the footstool of her God—woman's best and surest refuge. For how may man, even when most loving, most beloved, so know the secret nature of a woman's heart, as to bring the balm it seeks, and give the strength it needs? Elkanah's words reveal the extent and truth of his love; and had it not been for the daily provocations of Peninnah, he might indeed have been to Hannah "better than ten sons:" but she had griefs and trials of which he knew nothing,—peculiarly her own, as what woman has not?—and these, in childlike faith and voiceless prayer, she brought unto her God.

The condition of married women amongst the Jews, in the time of the Judges, must have been perfectly free and unrestrained. We find her rising up after they had eaten and drunk in Shiloh, and without even imparting her intentions to her husband, much less asking his consent, going perfectly unattended and unrebuked to the temple of the Lord. There, in bitterness of soul weeping, she prayed unto the Lord of Hosts; and, in perfect accordance with the Mosaic Law, which expressly provided for such emergencies, she vowed a vow, that if the Eternal would in His infinite mercy remember His handmaid, and grant her a male child, she would devote him unto the Lord all the days of his life, and not a razor should come near his head.

But she prayed not aloud, nor in any stated formula of prayer; she prayed merely as the heart dictated: "she spoke in her heart," as we have it in the touching language of Scripture,—only her lips moved, but her voice was not heard; and Eli, the high priest, who sat beside one of the posts of the temple, marked her mouth, and hearing no word, combined with the agitated figure before him, believed she was drunken, and, reproaching her, bade her put her wine from her.

It must have been an aggravation of her sorrow to find herself so misunderstood by one, who, as high priest, she might with some justice believe would have required no explanation on her part, but, in the name of the Eternal, have proffered her relief at once. Still we find nothing in her touchingly beautiful reply to evince a failing in the firm faith which brought her there. "No, my lord," she answered, "I am a woman of a sorrowful spirit; I have drunk neither wine nor strong drink, but have poured out my soul before the Lord. Count not thine handmaid for a daughter of Belial; for out of the abundance of my grief and complaint have I spoken hitherto. Then Eli answered and said, Go in peace, and the God of Israel grant thee thy petition that thou hast asked of Him:" and, without doubt, without question, Hannah simply answered, "Let thine handmaid find grace in thy sight,"—meaning, to remember her in his prayers,—and then "she went her way, and did eat, and her countenance was no more sad."

The exquisite lesson and consolation which these verses contain (1 Sam. i. 9–19) we will defer to our concluding observations, now merely narrating the history itself. At the conclusion of the festival, Elkanah and his family returned to Ramah, where the Eternal in His mercy remembered His faithful servant, and taking from her her reproach, in due course of time granted her the son for which she had so earnestly prayed; and in joyful acknowledgment that it was in answer to her prayer he had been given, she called him Samuel, or "asked of the Lord."

The time again came round for Elkanah and his family to make their yearly offerings in Shiloh; and by the allusion to a vow of Elkanah's (see verse 21) we may infer that Hannah had of course imparted to him her vow, and received not only his unqualified sanction, but that he was anxious, in his next visit to the temple of the Eternal, himself to confirm it. We find, too, as we ought previously to have noticed, the day after Hannah had been to the temple, that *they* (probably herself and her husband) rose up in the morning early, and "worshipped before the Lord;" a worship, possibly, of thanksgiving and rejoicing on the part of both; on Elkanah's that his beloved wife was no longer sad, on Hannah's that her prayer was heard; for that it *was* heard, it is evident she never entertained a doubt, long before she could have had proof that it really was so. That this early worship had to do with the vow is, however, of course a mere suggestion: the Word of God is open to all; we would not compel the adoption of any suggestion, to which both reason and feeling cannot give reply.

Hannah, however, when the time of the yearly sacrifice arrived, refused to go up, saying to her husband, "I will not go up, till the child is weaned; and then I will bring him, that he may appear before the Lord, and there abide for ever:" a resolution freely approved of by Elkanah. "Do what seemeth thee good," he replied, "tarry until thou hast weaned him." This incident is a striking confirmation of all which we brought forward in the Second Period of our history, regarding the appearance and the non-appearance of the female part of a Jewish household in the Temple at the times appointed.

The history of Elkanah and his family illustrates this law exactly. That women as well as men were to appear in the house of the Lord, and join in his worship, is proved by both Hannah and Peninnah, with the latter's children, attending their husband to Shiloh; and that the law to go up thrice a year was only *binding* upon males from the many causes which might prevent females, particularly mothers, from so doing, we perceive by Hannah's tarrying till her child was weaned, and having her husband's free permission so to do.

The time at length came, when in obedience to her voluntary vow, Hannah must part from her boy, and deliver him up to the service of the God whose mercy had bestowed him to her prayer. Her only one, precious beyond all price! yet we find no hesitation, no thought of delay, no idea of forgetting that which she had vowed, though the nature of her vow, nay, that she had vowed at all, was unknown to all, even to the high priest, who had promised that her prayer should be granted without knowing what it was. Without listening to the maternal anxieties that must have engrossed her, we find her, directly the child was weaned, taking him with her to Shiloh, and three bullocks, and one ephah of flour, and a bottle of wine,—offerings from the store, and the field, and the vineyard,—all in exact accordance with the written Law, and they came unto the house of the Lord, and they slew a bullock there, and brought the child to Eli. "And she said, O my lord, as thy soul liveth, my lord, I am the woman that stood by thee here praying unto the Lord. For this child I prayed, and the Lord hath given me my petition which I asked of Him, and therefore also have I lent him to the Lord: as long as he liveth he shall be lent to the Lord. And he worshipped the Lord there,"—rather an obscure phrase, but probably signifying that Eli worshipped the Lord, in acknowledgment of His divine goodness, in thus permitting his words to come to pass, and giving the woman that which she desired.

The prayer, or rather hymn, of thanksgiving in which Hannah poured forth her gratitude to her God in a strain of the sublimest poetry and vivid conception of the power and goodness of Him whom she addressed, is a forcible illustration of the *intellectual* as well as the spiritual piety which characterized the women of Israel, and which in its very existence denies the possibility of degradation applying to women, either individually, socially, or domestically. Their intellect must have been of a very superior grade; while the facility of throwing the aspirations of the spirit into the sublimest poetry, evinces constant practice in so doing, and proves how completely prayer and thanksgiving impregnated their vital breath. It is useless quoting this beautiful song of praise, when the blessed word which contains it is open to all classes and ages of readers; but we would beseech our young friends not to be satisfied with this uninspired notice, but to turn to the word themselves, and mark the soul-felt clinging piety throughout. It is as exact a transcript of the swelling gratitude of a truly pious heart, as her prayer before had breathed its bitterness of grief. Some there are who gladly come to their God in sorrow, but quite forget that the seasons of joy should be devoted to Him as well. Hannah was evidently not of these; but one of the most perfectly spiritually pious characters of the Bible. There was no self-exaltation in her song of praise; no supposition that for any individual worth her reproach had been removed; or even that any peculiarly meritorious fervor in her prayer had wrought reply. No; all was of the LORD. All came from His exceeding mercy—His omnipotent power. It was he who had made bare His holy arm, and to the barren given children. He who gave strength to those that stumbled, while the arms of mighty men were broken—He who maketh poor, and maketh rich—He who bringeth low, and lifteth up—He who killeth, and maketh alive —for "by strength no man shall prevail."

Nor was it only because she was permitted thus to rejoice, and behold the power she exalted, that Hannah so magnified the Lord, and believed in His wisdom and love to do all that He willed. She must have known and felt all her hymn expressed in her time of grief, else we should not have seen her in lowly supplication, prostrate in the court of the Lord's house —beseeching His relief. She must have *believed*, else she could not thus have prayed.

Lonely and sad must have been the feelings of this true Hebrew mother when she returned to her house at Ramah, leaving her beautiful boy with the high priest, and knowing that but three times in the year might she behold him; and then not to receive from him the service and caresses of a son, but only to look on him as one devoted to his God and to His service! How must her heart have yearned for the engaging prattle, the caressing playfulness, the lovely looks of clinging love, which had so blessed her since his birth! What a blank in her existence must have been his absence! and what but spiritual trust and devoted love to her God, could have brought her consolation? The feelings alike of her human and spiritual nature are so exquisitely portrayed by that beautiful delineator of woman's spiritual character, Mrs. Hemans, that we can but refer our readers to her pages, convinced that it will aid them to enter into the full beauty of Hannah's character, and the extent of her trial in parting from her boy.*

Licentiousness and sin had crept into the very bosom of the Temple, through the conduct of the high priest's sons. Yet, in the midst of impurity, under the too indulgent control of an aged man whose laxity of parental discipline exposed him to

* See Mrs. Hemans's Poems, vol. iv. p 169.

the anger of the Lord, still was the child Samuel kept pure and undefiled even as he left his mother's roof, and, while yet a child, ministered before the Lord. His so doing explains and confirms the law of the Nazarite, and singular vow, to which we alluded in our Second Period, as implying devotion to the Lord's service, which even children might perform (see Lev xxvii. 6) by some personal service. It is thus we so repeatedly find the Hagiography, or historical parts of the Bible, containing the *practical illustration* of the *theoretical* statutes, exactly as Moses gave them, and so rendering the Holy Scriptures in very truth the verified transcript of the Eternal will. Moses' instructions to the elders regarding the practical obedience to the law, must have been in exact accordance with that which, being written, was, and is still, open to our perusal; or we should have found some traces of its difference in the manners and customs of our ancestors. All, therefore, in Modern Judaism, which is accused of contradicting the spirit of the eternal holy word, cannot have had its origin in either of the laws, oral or written, transmitted by Moses. We are anxious always to notice, as forcibly as may be, those portions of the Bible containing the *practical* confirmation of the written laws of Moses, because we have heard (though we can scarcely believe it) that the written word of the Eternal is pronounced by some as imperfect and incomplete. The promulgators of such a fearful doctrine are not perhaps aware that by so doing, and so depriving our females and youth of both sexes of their only stay, and strength, and consolation, they are opening a wider avenue and offering a greater temptation to embrace Christianity, than was ever proffered by our opponents. To guard the women of Israel from such insidious danger, we are tempted to wander from our main subject, whenever the opportunity offers, to give them refuge and strength by the conviction that for *them*, at least, the Word of the Most High is all-sufficient, containing, as it does, in the historical books, the *practical illustration*, and in the prophets the *spiritual explanation*, of the whole Mosaic system, whether imparted by word of mouth or dash of pen. Of the delivery or non-delivery by the Eternal of an oral law, we write not at all, as it is a subject much too learned and too weighty for a woman; and we are ready and willing to submit our opinions on all points to the wisdom and piety of our venerable sages. We only affirm, what we think no Hebrew will contradict, that as the God of Israel is a God of changeless truth and wisdom, He would not have desired Moses to *write* that which *speech* was to deny; in other words, that each law must be so perfect and so exact a counterpart of the other, that in our present captive state, the Bible provided through the eternal mercy for this very emergency, must be the key to both laws, and so perfect in itself.

Though the evil conduct of the sons of Eli was well known, Hannah does not appear to have entertained a fear as to the effect of their example upon the tender years of her child. It was not likely that she who, in all her individual joys and sorrows, came to her God in prayer, should neglect that holy duty for the welfare of her boy. She had experienced too consolingly the effect of faith and prayer, to doubt them now; and as a mother, a Hebrew mother—one whose whole heart was love and praise to God, we may quite believe that, day and night, her meek and humble orisons arose for her boy, that he might become all that would make him indeed a faithful servant of his God; for in being such, he would be all her heart could wish. Some mothers, indeed, there may be, who, when they send their children from them, and provide them with all things needful for temporal welfare, think they have done sufficient, and only remember them with mere human, and consequently perishable, affections; rejoicing in their prosperity, anxious when ill, desirous for them to "get on,"—an emphatic though not elegant phrase for the world's success. And if they do all they can to forward this "getting-on," in the way of education and lavish expenditure, what more could be required of them? Some will answer, "Nothing." Others may feel, as Hannah *must have* felt, that though their children may no longer be beneath their roof—though all of human means is done, to further their advancement, what will it all avail without the blessing of the Lord? And how may such blessing be attained, save with faithful and unceasing PRAYER? Prayer, that unites us in spirit alike with our beloved ones, and our God. Oh, is there one who really *loves*, be it as a parent, wife, child, betrothed, or friend, and can yet rest secure and happy without prayer? If we have never prayed before, we *must* when we feel love. Can we love in any single relation of life, and yet not feel the craving, the desire, the absolute necessity to pour out our hearts to our God for our beloved ones, and *in them* for ourselves!

Can we rest quiet, incapacitated, perhaps, from active *service* by circumstances, and not at least seek to serve by fervent prayer? And if in every relation of life this must be the effect of love, oh! more than in any other must we find it in a mother for a child! What love can be like hers, so watchful, so changeless, so unwearied? And how may she still the anxious throbbings of her heart, when divided from its earthly treasures, save by simple trust and fervid prayer?

And when we look back on the character of Hannah, as it has already been displayed, can we doubt that such were her feelings, that she could have supposed merely to leave her child with the high priest was sufficient—that nothing more depended on herself? She who in all things had prayed? No, prayer must have sanctified her offering, not only when offered, but when apart from him. She had naught but prayer for him on which to rest. And might it not have been, nay, was it not, that mother's prayer, which retained her boy in such pure and lowly piety, in such singleness of purpose and faithfulness of heart, in the very midst of the licentiousness reigning around? Long before Samuel could have prayed for himself, must Hannah's prayers have ascended for him, and in his favor, both with the Lord and with men—she had her answer.

Every time of her visit to Shiloh, we find Hannah bringing a little coat, or robe, for her child, the work of her own hands, which had fondly lingered on the task from month to month, in the periods of absence; and Eli blessed Elkanah and his wife, and said, "the Lord give thee seed of this woman, for the loan which is lent to the Lord." Now, though not till several verses after the narration of Hannah's address to the high priest, when leaving Samuel with him, these words were most probably spoken when he first accepted the offering of the child; and the Lord did visit Hannah, and granted her three more sons, and two daughters, thus powerfully proving, that the Eternal ever returns double, and more than double, that which we devote to Him; be it the affections, the intellect, the will; or that more active service, charity and good works. Hannah devoted to Him her all, her only one, caring not for the conquest of self which this resignation of her treasure must have demanded; and the Eternal, in His infinite mercy, granted her five in the place of one. And what was it which had originally turned aside her reproach, and inclined the Lord towards her?

No great work—no mighty sacrifice—no wealthy offering; it was none of these, but simple faith and heartfelt prayer.

With the information that she became the mother of five children, Holy Writ concludes the history of Hannah; but knowing the longevity of Scriptural characters, we are justified in inferring that she was spared to feel to the full, all the happiness which her first-born's matured character must have excited.

We hear of not one failing from his earliest childhood. We read of his unvarying integrity and single-minded obedience to the word of his God, from his first repetition to Eli of the Eternal's awful sentence, to the conclusion of his career; interfering as that obedience so repeatedly did, with his own private feelings, alike towards Eli, in the selection of a king, and in all his conduct towards Saul. If Hannah lived until the monarchy, she must indeed have been blessed in the innate goodness and love, and in the popularity of her child, and have felt that in nursing him for the Lord, she had indeed received "her wages."

The history we have been regarding, though brief in itself, is yet so fraught with importance to us as women of Israel, and as women in general, that we trust we shall be pardoned for dwelling upon it in all its bearings at some length. Forcibly as the stories of Naomi and Deborah marked the real position of the Israelitish women, and proved their powers alike of intellect, judgment, and spirituality, as well as the deferential light in which they were regarded by their countrymen, the history of Hannah brings their perfect freedom and equality, even in the marriage state, yet more distinctly forward. Deborah was inspired to do the will of the Lord; gifted, extraordinarily and expressly, to judge and deliver her countrymen. Naomi was a widow, unshackled by either conjugal or household duties, and with no relation whatever to interfere with her proceedings. Hannah was one of two wives, her husband living, and the head of a wealthy household; consequently, she must have had all her part of the domestic economy to look after and perform; yet there could not have been the very smallest restraint upon either her temporal proceedings or spiritual feelings. She does not even ask her husband's acquiescence, much less depend upon his consent to seek the house of God. Her very going to pray must have excited remark, and even scandal, if such had not been the common custom of the nation. And if women were not permitted to pray for themselves, Eli would have rebuked her presumption, and desired her to send her husband, as the only chance of her wishes being granted; instead of which, when once convinced she was praying with earnestness and in sorrow, he bids her "go in peace," for God would hearken to her.

Again, had she not possessed perfect freedom of will and action, she could not have vowed her child to God. Unless she had been perfectly sure that her husband reposed sufficient confidence in her, to abide by her decision, she could not have so devoted him, without, as it were, mocking the majesty of the Lord, by making a promise which she had not the power to perform.

That her vow was subject to the approbation of her husband, we believe, because such deference was commanded in our law But Elkanah's full acquiescence throughout, clearly proves the high esteem in which he held her. She does not ask even *his permission* to remain at home, till her child were old enough to be left with the priest.

In all relating to Samuel, Elkanah was completely secondary. Even in the bullocks, flowers, and wine, provided for the offering, it was Hannah who brought and offered them; Hannah, who addressed Eli; Hannah, who chanted the song of thanksgiving to her God; and Hannah, who devoted her child. The husband and father had no more to do with it, than the simple acts of acquiescence and approval, which he would not have so unhesitatingly bestowed, had he not possessed the most perfect confidence in the judgment and actions of his wife.

That no severe restrictions as to the time, form, or words of prayer, existed in the time of Hannah, is proved by her seeking the Temple to pray when it was *not* the appointed time of service, when there was no one there but the high priest and herself; by her *speaking in her heart* the words which sorrow and entreaty dictated, without any regard whatever to instituted forms, which, though *indispensable* for public service and national interests, will not give all that is needed to individuals. Eli marked the lips of Hannah move, but he heard no voice, for she *spake in her heart, and as her heart dictated.* And in her song of thanksgiving, though she prayed aloud, still it was from the heart alone.

That forms of prayer were not needed in the time of Hannah, as they are now, we acknowledge; and also with all our heart and soul do we reverence their institution, and acknowledge their full value, both nationally and individually. Many and many a one, from incapacity to frame words of prayer, would be fearfully and painfully bereft, did they not possess the invaluable treasure of words of prayer, framed by good and learned men expressly for their use, and hallowed by long years. We are no advocate for the abolishment of established forms; for fully and heartfully we feel their sanctity and value. We would only beseech our young sisters to accustom themselves sometimes in their private hours, to pray and to praise from the *heart*, not always to depend on printed words; not, indeed, to neglect the latter, but to hallow and add to them, by individual petitions from individual hearts. Self-knowledge must be their first step to such secret prayers; for by self-knowledge alone can they discover their natural sins, their greatest temptations, their most secret weaknesses, their favorite faults. Self-knowledge alone can teach them where they are most likely to fail, and where to be unduly elevated; and display broadly and unsoftened, the *true motives* of their every action. Self-knowledge alone can teach them their true position with regard to eternity and God, and for all these things it is, that every individual needs individual prayer, wholly and utterly distinct from established forms; not, as we said above, to take the latter's place, but so to be added to them, as to give them life and breath.

The history of Hannah is all-sufficient for us to be convinced, that such individual and heartfelt prayers are not only *legal*, according to the laws, but *acceptable* to the Lord. No restrictions of man can alter or interfere with that which is *divine;* and, therefore, nothing which may be told concerning the inefficacy of individual prayer, unless guided by certain rules, forms, and words, can do away with the consolation and example afforded us by the history of our sweet and gentle ancestress, alike in the manner of her prayer and its reply, and in her unhesitating, unquestioning, and all-confiding FAITH.

We are thus particular, because we would at once remove the foul stigma flung by scoffers on our blessed faith, that her female children have no power to pray, and are, consequently, soulless nonentities before their God; and bring forward, from the word of God itself, the unanswerable assurance, that woman's prayers *are* heard, and *are* acceptable to Him, needing nothing more than childlike faith in His power to hear and answer, and a loving heart to dictate the imploring words. It is idle for us to say that we cannot pray, for we know not how appropriately to address the Supreme; His awful attributes appal us, and prevent all connected words. Such may be the sentiments of those who keep the Eternal far from them; but not of Israel, His first-born, first-beloved, whose very sins have no power to separate him from His God, if he will but repent and believe. "What nation hath God so near them as Israel, in all we call upon Him for? were the precious words of Moses, confirmed by the whole after-records of the Bible.—Hagiography, Psalms, Proverbs, Prophets, all and every one teem with the same consoling truth, proclaim our God as LOVE, the hearer and answerer of prayer, its gracious receiver, whenever it comes from the *heart*, and is offered up in *faith*. "Call upon me, and I will deliver thee," is the blessed assurance repeated again and again, in different modes of expression, in every part of the Bible. It is folly, it is guilt to keep away from prayer, under the misleading plea that God is a being too pre-eminently holy to be approached. Did we but really love Him as He commands, with heart, and soul, and might; did we but trust in Him, as Abraham did, when "his faith was accounted righteousness;" we should find words enough wherewith to pray and praise. Love would bring us to Him, believing and rejoicing in that inexhaustible love which would in such infinite mercy bend down its reviving rays on us, and lift up the wearied spirit, till it found rest on the healing sympathy of its all-compassionating God.

It was thus that Hannah came to Him, loving Him, trusting Him, yet more than she loved and confided in her husband, the nearest and dearest tie on earth. She did not think herself too unworthy to approach and beseech Him, because she knew that the Law which she obeyed, and the whole history of her people, teemed with His invitations so to do, and His promises to answer. She came to Him, because she knew he loved her, and would have compassion; and because she so loved Him, that it was far easier to pour into His gracious ears her silent sorrows than breathe them unto man. She came to Him, because she not only *loved*, but *believed* with such a pure and child-like faith, that when the high priest bade her "Go in peace, and God grant thee thy petition," she returned to her own home so calmly, so trustingly, that she "did eat, and her countenance was no more sad:"—words that convince us how fully she must have *believed* when she prayed, and not only then, but through her lifetime, for faith is of no instantaneous growth. It is a plant so foreign to this cold, sceptical, questioning world, that it must be nursed and tended into life; it must be a *habit*, not a *feeling;* it must attend our every prayer, our every spiritual aspiration, or when most needed, it will fail us, and plunge us into gloom.

But it may be asked in what need we have such perfect and constant faith. Hannah's position will not bear upon us now, as we have neither high priest nor Temple, nor any visible manifestations of the Eternal's interference in human affairs. We have not, indeed; but we have still His Word, the Bible, wherein so to learn His attributes, His promises, that during our captivity we need no more; for if we disbelieve that Word, no priest, no temple, no apparently visible reply, would give us the faith *we* need, and which Hannah *proved.*

We need faith to believe that God is love, and our souls immortal; that every precious promise in His word is addressed as emphatically to us *individually* as to us *nationally;* to feel that there is another and a brighter World, where "eye hath not seen, neither hath ear heard, what He hath prepared for those that love Him." Faith to know that we are individually objects of His love and care, as surely as that every blade of grass and invisible insect are alike the work of His hand, and the constant renewal of that power which at a word called forth creation. We need faith, to discern the workings of an eternal Love and infinite Goodness in the History of Man, Past and Present; to mark through the evil which is often alone visible, the furtherance of that Divine Will and Perfect Good, which runs as a silver thread through the darkest web, and links this world with heaven—man with God.

It is for all these things we need Faith: that faith which, instead of banishing *Reason*, welcomes and rejoices in her as her companion and handmaid. Faith may exist without reason; but let reason attempt to exclude faith altogether, let the materialist and scoffer laugh and mock at all things which cannot be substantially proved, and on his bed of death what shall support him? Let him explain, if he can, birth and death, the beginning and the end: and then, and not till then, may he contemn and deride those who, contented to be less wise and less inquiring, walk calmly and happily through this dark valley of earth with the angel, Faith, at their side; sending up their lowly petitions on his aspiring wings: and calmly sinking, when the tale of life is done, secure, through faith's simple readings of the word of God, of that everlasting bliss which awaits him in another and purer world.

With the history of Hannah our Third Period concludes; and from the length with which we have treated each separate notice, we have little further to add, save the earnest hope that an *impartial* and unprejudiced study of all that we have brought forward, will convince our readers, that no law for the degradation and heathenizing the Women of Israel could have had existence from the Exodus to the Monarchy; that therefore all statutes to that effect, which may be quoted, must be Human not Divine, and cannot be charged to the Law of God, or regarded as characteristic of the manners and customs of His people.

To us, as women, the whole of the Third Period teems with guidance and consolation, and, as Women of Israel, must satisfy us with the confirmation of our equality and elevation. Shall we, then, feel ashamed of the faith which provides such laws, and the lineage which counts such characters as Deborah, Naomi, and Hannah, amongst our ancestry? Shall we prefer listening to the mistaken zeal which would persuade us that, as Hebrew females, we are lowered and degraded, and can only become spiritually free by deserting the faith of our ancestors, to looking through the Word of God, and, tracing our privileges there, make it our glory to reveal them, through our faith and conduct to the whole Gentile world? Oh! will not every woman nerve heart to prove that her religion comes from that God of Love and Truth, whose words once spoken will last for ever, whose Law once given will know no change; that she has in that faith enough to give her strength to live, and hope to die; aye, and to glory in that blessed Law which cared for woman first, and will care for her for ever?

END OF VOL. I.

THE SEQUEL TO HOME INFLUENCE.

THE MOTHER'S RECOMPENSE.

A SEQUEL TO

"*Home Influence, a Tale for Mothers and Daughters.*"

By GRACE AGUILAR.

1 VOL., 12MO. CLOTH. $1. WITH ILLUSTRATIONS.

"Grace Aguilar belonged to the school of which Maria Edgeworth was the foundress. The design of the book is carried out forcibly and constantly, 'The Home Influence' exercised in earlier years being shown in its active germination."—*Atlas.*

"The writings of Grace Aguilar have a charm inseparable from productions in which feeling is combined with intellect; they go directly to the heart. 'Home Influence,' the deservedly popular story to which this is a sequel, admirably teaches the lesson implied in its name. In the present tale we have the same freshness, earnestness, and zeal—the same spirit of devotion, and love of virtue—the same enthusiasm and sincere religion which characterized that earlier work. We behold the mother now blessed in the love of good and affectionate offspring, who, parents themselves, are, after her example, training *their* children in the way of rectitude and piety."—*Morning Chronicle.*

"This beautiful story was completed when the authoress was little above the age of nineteen, yet it has the sober sense of middle age. There is no age nor sex that will not profit by its perusal, and it will afford as much pleasure as profit to the reader."—*Critic.*

"The same kindly spirit, the same warm charity and fervor of devotion which breathes in every line of that admirable book, 'Home Influence,' will be found adorning and inspiring 'The Mother's Recompense.'"—*Morning Advertiser.*

"The good which she (Grace Aguilar) has effected is acknowledged on all hands, and it cannot be doubted but that the appearance of this volume will increase the usefulness of one who may yet be said to be still speaking to the heart and to the affections of human nature."—*Bell's Messenger.*

"It will be found an interesting supplement, not only to the book to which it specially relates, but to all the writer's other works."—*Gentleman's Magazine.*

"'The Mother's Recompense' forms a fitting close to its predecessor, 'Home Influenee.' The results of maternal care are fully developed, its rich rewards are set forth, and its lesson and its moral are powerfully enforced." —*Morning Post.*

"We heartily commend this volume; a better or more useful present to a youthful friend or a young wife could not well be selected."—*Herts County Press.*

New York: D. APPLETON & CO.

THE DAYS OF BRUCE.

A Story from Scottish History.

BY GRACE AGUILAR.

With Illustrations. 2 vols., 12mo. Cloth, $2.00.

"We have had an opportunity of observing the interest it awakens in different classes of readers, and in no instance has it failed to rivet attention, and to induce a high estimate of the author's powers. Miss Aguilar was evidently well read in the times of Bruce. It is long since we met with a work which combines so happily the best qualities of historical fiction."—*Eclectic Review.*

"The life of the hero of Bannockburn has furnished matter for innumerable tales in prose and verse, but we have met with no records of that famous era so instructive as 'The Days of Bruce.'"—*Britannia.*

"'The Days of Bruce' was written when, in the vigor of intellectual strength, Grace Aguilar was planning many things, and all for good; it was, we know, her especial favorite; it is full of deep interest."—*Mrs. S. C. Hall, in Sharpe's Magazine.*

"It is a volume which may be considered as solid history, but is nevertheless entertaining as the most charming novel ever produced by genius. Sir Walter Scott's name as an author would not have been disgraced by it had it appeared on the title-page instead of Grace Aguilar."—*Bucks Chronicle.*

"This deeply-interesting romance—a composition of great eloquence, written with practised polish and enthusiastic energy. We are not surprised at the eloquence, the warmth, and the pathos with which Grace Aguilar paints love-passages; but we are astonished at the fire and accuracy with which she depicts scenes of daring and of death."—*Observer.*

"The tale is well told, the interest warmly sustained throughout, and the delineation of female character is marked by a delicate sense of moral beauty. It is a work that may be confided to the hands of a daughter by her parent."—*Court Journal.*

"Every one who knows the works of this lamented author, must observe that she rises with her subjects. In 'The Days of Bruce' she has thrown herself into the rugged life of the fourteenth century, and has depicted the semi-civilization of the period in a manner that is quite marvellous in a young woman. Grace Aguilar always excelled in her delineations of female character, while the skill she evinces in the illustration of the historical personages, and her individualization of the imaginary ones, might at once entitle her to a birthplace among historical novelists."—*Ladies' Companion.*

"Her pen was ever devoted to the cause of virtue; and her various publications, exhibiting the beauties and enforcing the practice of the 'tender charities' of domestic life, have, we doubt not, recommended themselves to the hearts of numbers of her countrywomen. The work before us differs from the former publications of its author, inasmuch as it is in fact an historical romance, for this species of writing the high feeling of Grace Aguilar peculiarly fitted her; many of the scenes are very highly wrought; and while it will fix in the reader's mind a truthful idea of the history and style of manners of 'The Days of Bruce,' it will also impress upon him a strong sense of the ability and noble cast of thought which distinguished its lamented author."—*Englishwoman's Magazine.*

New York: D. APPLETON & CO.

"We look upon 'The Days of Bruce' as an elegantly-written and interesting romance, and place it by the side of Miss Porter's 'Scottish Chiefs.'"—*Gentleman's Magazine.*

"A very pleasing and successful attempt to combine ideal delineation of character with the records of history. Very beautiful and very true are the portraits of the female mind and heart which Grace Aguilar knew how to draw. This is the chief charm of all her writings, and in 'The Days of Bruce' the reader will have the pleasure of viewing this skilful portraiture in the characters of Isoline and Agnes, and Isabella of Buchan."—*Literary Gazette.*

"What a fertile mind was that of Grace Aguilar! What an early development of reflection, of feeling, of taste, of power of invention, of true and earnest eloquence! 'The Days of Bruce' is a composition of her early youth, but full of beauty. Grace Aguilar knew the female heart better than any writer of our day, and in every fiction from her pen we trace the same masterly analysis and development of the motives and feelings of woman's nature. 'The Days of Bruce' possesses also the attractions of an extremely interesting story, that absorbs the attention, and never suffers it to flag till the last page is closed, and then the reader will lay down the volume with regret."—*Critic.*

HOME SCENES AND HEART STUDIES.

By GRACE AGUILAR.

WITH ILLUSTRATIONS.

One volume, 12mo. Cloth. Price, $1.00.

The Perez Family.
The Stone-Cutter's Boy of Possagno.
Amete and Yafeh.
The Fugitive.
The Edict; a Tale of 1492.
The Escape; a Tale of 1755.
Red Rose Villa.
Gonzalvo's Daughter.
The Authoress.
Helon.
Lucy.
The Spirit's Entreaty.
Idalie.
Lady Gresham's Fete.
The Group of Sculpture.
The Spirit of Night.
Recollections of a Rambler.
Cast thy Bread upon the Waters.
The Triumph of Love.

New York: D. APPLETON & CO.

WOMAN'S FRIENDSHIP.

A STORY OF DOMESTIC LIFE.

By GRACE AGUILAR.

With Illustrations. One volume, 12mo. Cloth. Price, $1.00.

"To show us how divine a thing
A woman may be made."—WORDSWORTH.

"This story illustrates, with feeling and power, that beneficial influence which women exercise, in their own quiet way, over characters and events in our every-day life."—*Britannia.*

"The book is one of more than ordinary interest in various ways, and presents an admirable conception of the depths and sincerity of female friendship, as exhibited in England by Englishwomen."—*Weekly Chronicle.*

"We began to read the volume late in the evening; and, although it consists of about 400 pages, our eyes could not close in sleep until we had read the whole. This excellent book should find a place on every drawing-room table—nay, in every library in the kingdom."—*Bucks Chronicle.*

"We congratulate Miss Aguilar on the spirit, motive, and composition of this story. Her aims are eminently moral, and her cause comes recommended by the most beautiful associations. These, connected with the skill here evinced in their development, insure the success of her labors."—*Illustrated News.*

"As a writer of remarkable grace and delicacy, she devoted herself to the inculcation of the virtues, more especially those which are the peculiar charm of women."—*Critic.*

"It is a book for all classes of readers; and we have no hesitation in saying, that it only requires to be generally known to become exceedingly popular. In our estimation it has far more attractions than Miss Burney's celebrated, but overestimated, novel of 'Cecilia.'"—*Herts County Press.*

"This very interesting and agreeable tale has remained longer without notice on our part than we could have desired; but we would now endeavor to make amends for the delay, by assuring our readers that it is a most ably-written publication, full of the nicest points of information and utility that could have been by any possibility constructed; and, as a proof of its value, it may suffice to say, that it has been taken from our table again and again by several individuals, from the recommendation of those who had already perused it, and so prevented our giving an earlier attention to its manifold claims for the favorable criticism. It is peculiarly adapted for the young, and wherever it goes will be received with gratification, and command very extensive approbation."—*Bell's Weekly Messenger.*

"This is a handsome volume: just such a book as we would expect to find among the volumes composing a lady's library. Its interior corresponds with its exterior; it is a most fascinating tale, full of noble and just sentiments."—*Palladium.*

New York: D. APPLETON & CO.

THE VALE OF CEDARS;

OR,

THE MARTYR.

A STORY OF SPAIN IN THE FIFTEENTH CENTURY.

By GRACE AGUILAR.

With Illustrations. 1 vol., 12mo. Cloth, $1.00.

"The authoress of this most fascinating volume has selected for her field one of the most remarkable eras in modern history—the reigns of Ferdinand and Isabella. The tale turns on the extraordinary extent to which concealed Judaism had gained footing at that period in Spain. It is marked by much power of description, and by a woman's delicacy of touch, and it will add to its writer's well-earned reputation."—*Eclectic Review.*

"The scene of this interesting tale is laid during the reign of Ferdinand and Isabella. The Vale of Cedars is the retreat of a Jewish family, compelled by persecution to perform their religious rites with the utmost secrecy. On the singular position of this fated race in the most Catholic land of Europe, the interest of the tale mainly depends; whilst a few glimpses of the horrors of the terrible Inquisition are afforded the reader, and heighten the interest of the narrative."—*Sharpe's Magazine.*

"Any thing which proceeds from the pen of the authoress of this volume is sure to command attention and appreciation. There is so much of delicacy and refinement about her style, and such a faithful delineation of nature in all she attempts, that she has taken her place amongst the highest class of modern writers of fiction. We consider this to be one of Miss Aguilar's best efforts."—*Bell's Weekly Messenger.*

"We heartily commend the work to our readers as one exhibiting, not merely talent, but genius, and a degree of earnestness, fidelity to Nature, and artistic grace, rarely found."—*Herts County Press.*

"The 'Vale of Cedars' is indeed one of the most touching and interesting stories that have ever issued from the press. There is a life-like reality about it which is not often observed in works of this nature; while we read it we felt as if we were witnesses of the various scenes it depicts."—*Bucks Chronicle.*

"It is a tale of deep and pure devotion, very touchingly narrated."—*Atlas.*

"The authoress has already received our commendation; her present work is calculated to sustain her reputation."—*Illustrated News.*

"It is indeed a historical romance of a high class. Seeing how steady and yet rapid was her improvement—how rich the promise of her genius—it is impossible to close this notice of her last and best work, without lamenting that the authoress was so untimely snatched from a world she appeared destined, as certainly she was singularly qualified, to adorn and to improve."—*Critic.*

New York: D. APPLETON & CO.

www.ingramcontent.com/pod-product-compliance
Lightning Source LLC
LaVergne TN
LVHW010233110826
845151LV00004B/1281